BLACK NATIONALISM AND THE REVOLUTION IN MUSIC

TO THE MEMORY OF JOHN COLTRANE AND MALCOLM X

BLACK NATIONALISM AND THE REVOLUTION IN MUSIC

by Frank Kofsky

PATHFINDER PRESS, INC.

The photo of Malcolm X on page 248 is by Eli Finer; the photo of McCoy Tyner on page 220 courtesy Liberty/UA Records; other photos in this book by Frank Kofsky.

First Edition, 1970
Second Printing, 1972

PATHFINDER PRESS
410 West Street
New York, N. Y. 10014

PREFACE

In a book by an academic (assuming that I manage to remain one in these perilous times until the moment of publication), it is customary to pay tribute to all of one's learned fellows who have offered their assistance. I would like to abide by the convention, but the fact is that not three (white) academics out of a hundred of my acquaintance believe that jazz music is of sufficient moment to merit a "serious" study (i. e., one with a lot of footnotes). That, indeed, is one of the inequities to which this volume is addressed.

On the other hand, if I am unable in sincerity to render thanks to my colleagues, I certainly must confess my indebtedness to the black people of this country. Without their invaluable, if unintended, assistance — in the streets of Watts, Detroit, Newark; at San Francisco State, Cornell, Howard — the years spent searching for a willing publisher would undoubtedly have lengthened into decades. I entertain no illusions on *that* score.

In addition, I do have a number of obligations which it is truly a delight to be able to discharge. In mentioning those whose views have helped me form my own, incidentally, I hope the reader will be of charitable enough disposition not to visit wrath meant for the author upon anyone else; the shortcomings of this work, alas, are mine alone to claim.

In any event, I am grateful to Ralph Gleason for first acquainting me with what I should now call a materialist understanding of the political economy of jazz (though I have my doubts that he would agree with all the conclusions that I have drawn from his teachings). Cliff and Julia Houdek were endlessly helpful, in more ways than one, in leading me — or forcing me — to clarify my thoughts on the nature of the connection between black nationalism and black music (jazz). Tom McCormick, of the History Department of the University of Pittsburgh, is one of those three in a hundred academics who perceive the aesthetic worth of jazz; he and his wife Jeri encountered considerable peer-group scorn, in the course of conducting our extended early-morning listening and talking sessions, for being so lacking in manners as actually to consort with a lowly graduate student. I received further encouragement to continue with my writing, at various times when

5

6

my confidence in the soundness of my views was at a low ebb, from Pauline Rivelli, editor of *Jazz & Pop*, Bob Thiele, George Breitman, and George Novack.

Assistance of a different nature came from three other sources. The Louis A. Rabinowitz Foundation of New York kindly provided me with a research fellowship that enabled me to visit New York and interview approximately two dozen of the younger black musicians during 1966 and 1967; I am overjoyed that at last I have the opportunity publicly to acknowledge the Foundation's support at a crucial moment. Mrs. Sandy Lujan rescued me at another critical point, by generously volunteering her own scarce time to type portions of the manuscript. It is of course to the musicians themselves, through their incredibly good-natured willingness to cooperate, with only a handful of exceptions, that I owe the completion of this work. I do not know how many, if any, share my views; but I do know that my informal conversations and tape-recorded interviews with them provided me with a wealth of information. Their graciousness in submitting to my prying has been a continuing source of gratification to me; I regret that I lack space to list them all individually. There are others as well whom I should have wished to mention by name, but they will, I fear, be forced to take it on faith that I am both aware and appreciative of their many contributions to both author and book.

I would also like to think that this volume has benefited from my reading in the works of A. B. Spellman, Thomas Kuhn, Karl Marx, Frederick Engels, George Plekhanov, V. I. Lenin, Leon Trotsky, Malcolm X, Francis Newton (E. J. Hobsbawm), LeRoi Jones, Sidney Finkelstein, George Breitman, Robert Levin, Ralph Gleason, George Novack, and others doubtless overlooked; but the verdict on this question can safely be left to the reader.

Gratitude is almost always difficult to express, but in some cases near-impossible. My wife, Jeanne Shepherd Rohmann Kofsky, not only came to my aid in more instances than I can recount as the book was nearing completion, but from somewhere she also found the strength to bear my idiosyncrasies with good cheer during those most trying days. There are not words known to me that would convey my feelings about that.

Frank Kofsky
Sacramento, California
September, 1969

CONTENTS

INTRODUCTION

The Negro musician is a reflection of the Negro people as a social phenomenon. His purpose ought to be to liberate America aesthetically and socially from its inhumanity. The inhumanity of the white American to the black American, as well as the inhumanity of the white American to the white American, is not basic to America and can be exorcised. I think the Negro people through the force of their struggles are the only hope of saving America, the political or cultural America.

Culturally, America is a backward country; Americans are backward. But jazz is American reality — total reality. . . . Some whites seem to think they have a right to jazz. Perhaps that's true, but they should feel thankful for jazz. It has been a gift that the Negro has given, but [whites] can't accept that — there are too many problems involved with the social and historical relationship of the two peoples. It makes it difficult for them to accept jazz and the Negro as its true innovator.

Archie Shepp

There is a curious dichotomy that reigns among white Americans. If they are in the jazz world proper, then they will tend to deny that, whatever else jazz *may* be, it is first and foremost a black art — an art created and nurtured by black people in this country out of the wealth of their historical experience.

On the other hand, if they are not part of the jazz milieu, white Americans will automatically and virtually without exception assume that jazz is black—though not an art—and therefore, though this may go unstated, worthy of no serious treatment or respect. Thus it is that the most celebrated elder statesman of the music, Mr. Duke Ellington, could be denied a Pulitzer Prize for music in 1966, at the very same time as his "triumphs" over Soviet poet Yevgeni Yevtushenko at the First World Festival of Negro Arts were being celebrated by Lloyd Garrison in *The New York Times.* *

In his *Crisis of the Negro Intellectual,* Harold Cruse examines Ellington's rejection for the Pulitzer Prize, and concludes, in rather restrained tones, that "Here was an affront to the entire musical and cultural heritage of every Negro in America." Affront though it may have been, it surely was not unique. Even now, in 1969, for all of the supposedly greater acceptance of black art and culture this country is said to have achieved, only a single black musician, Ornette Coleman, has ever been the recipient of a Guggenheim Foundation award for his work in jazz. So far as the white-Anglo-Saxon-Protestant-dominated ruling-class Establishment is concerned, serious black art is beneath consideration. **

Though the refusal of the Establishment to subsidize jazz on anything approaching the same level that it subsidizes, say, light opera, is indicative of its inherent cultural provin-

---

* Garrison's story, headlined "SOVIET POETS FAIL TO CAPTURE DAKAR" and subtitled "Duke Ellington the Winner in Propaganda Skirmish," appeared in *The New York Times* on April 30, 1966. Garrison told his readers specifically that Yevtushenko was in Dakar "not just to project the Soviet Union's poetic image. He had been urgently summoned from Moscow to do for Soviet propaganda what Duke Ellington had done for the Americans when he played before packed and cheering audiences during Dakar's first World Festival of the Negro Arts."

** As E. Digby Baltzell demonstrates in *The Protestant Establishment,* Jews are hardly more welcome than blacks within the private reaches of the upper class. It should be added that in those cities, such as Los Angeles, that saw a vast outpouring of upper-class conscience money following a black insurrection in the late sixties, little or none of these funds have been channeled into black *music* —i.e., jazz. While artists' and writers' workshops are within the bounds of genteel acceptability, forms like jazz that present a black sensibility operating on its own terms and within its own self-generated limits clearly are not so blessed.

cialism and narrowness, at least it has the virtue of honesty.
After all, the Establishment seems to be saying, jazz, when
you come right down to it, is the music of blacks and belongs
in whorehouses, bars, dives, and other appropriately sleazy
surroundings. What would *we* want to have to do with a music
like *that*? If the class bias of such an attitude is reprehensible,
the willingness to concede the black origins of the music called
jazz is a distinct improvement over the position taken by the
bulk of the white semiliterati of the jazz world.

In the main, these latter worthies have expended reservoirs
of ink in striving to convince their readers that jazz is "American" rather than black. Of course, the American experience
is undeniably a major component of the music; but it is an
experience as perceived by blacks from a vantage point unique
to them. To anyone not involved in grinding ideological axes,
the point is probably obvious and needs little emphasis. That
is just it: an enormous amount of what passes for writing
on jazz stems from an ideological position, the result of an
externally imposed or self-assumed false consciousness. The
thrust of such writing is systematically to obscure, if not deny,
the black roots of the music. As the versatile Archie Shepp
observes above, whites "can't accept" the fact that jazz "has
been a gift that the Negro has given," because, "there are too
many problems involved with the social and historical relationship of the two peoples. It makes it difficult for them to accept jazz and the Negro as its true innovator."

The source of such difficulties is twofold. First, whites are
generally unable to believe that blacks, as a people (as
opposed to a handful of individual "geniuses," whose gifts
are manifested primarily by their good taste in imitating
whites), are capable of creating anything that is of durable
value. Hence even where black achievements are acknowledged
with one hand, as in the field of popular music, the concession is snatched back with the other by consigning these areas
of achievement to the realm of the trivial and ephemeral. In
this way, blacks can be recognized as creators while the significance of their creations can be simultaneously denied. Secondly, because of the socioeconomic structure of the jazz milieu,
most whites who are involved in the music are extremely loath
to describe matters as they actually stand. One of the earliest
descriptive explanations of the causes of such ideological thinking, that by Marx and Engels in *The German Ideology*, besides remaining unsurpassed to this day, is most germane:
"If in all ideology men and their circumstances appear up-

side down as in a *camera obscura,* this phenomenon arises just as much from their historical life process as the inversion of objects on the retina does from their physical life process." [1] The "circumstances" in jazz are quite elementary. To quote Archie Shepp once more: "You own the music and we make it." Presumably it is unnecessary to specify to whom the *you* and *we* refer.

With very minor exceptions, it is whites who do own the major economic institutions of the jazz world — the booking agencies, recording companies, nightclubs, festivals, magazines, radio stations, etc. Blacks own nothing but their own talent. While this in some cases suffices to ensure an adequate livelihood — that is, one comparable to that enjoyed by those whites who practice in the European arts — for the most part it does not. Here an analogy may be useful. In its relation with an underdeveloped country (colony), a more advanced industrial economy (metropolis, "mother country") will use its superior technology to ensure that commodity exchange between the two redounds to the benefit of the latter at the expense (in the form of increasing impoverishment) of the former. The metropolis employs its ownership of capital to generate more capital — i. e., profits. The colony, possessing nothing to exchange save the labor power of its citizens and its natural resources, will have its capital slowly drained away to the metropolis. Just so does the situation stand in jazz. Black musicians, occasionally augmented by a few whites, labor not primarily for themselves, but to enrich those who own the "means of production" enumerated above.

Is it any wonder that this state of affairs goes unrecognized in the literature of jazz? To ask for matters to be otherwise would be equivalent to asking North American economists to conclude that the pattern of U. S. capital investment in Latin America, for instance, functions to retard rather than stimulate economic development ("growth") there. It is very difficult for those who live off the labor power of others to perceive the exploitation inherent in such a situation. It is even more difficult, apparently, for those who function as ideologues and publicists for the owners of capital to arrive at this perception. Hence, if we are to believe their spokesmen, investments by the Rockefellers and Mellons in Latin American petroleum resources are actually philanthropic endeavors undertaken for the betterment of the indigenous population. By the same line of reasoning, it follows that the activity of white-owned businesses in an art created by blacks is least of all for the sake of the profit that just happens to accrue, but is, as everyone ought to know, a form of charity motivated by disinterested love of the arts and the spirit of *noblesse oblige.*

Or so things appear, to invoke the metaphor of Marx and Engels, "upside down as in a *camera obscura,*" in the ideological picture of jazz drawn for readers of its periodical press. The reality is nowhere near that pretty, of course. Here and there an occasional black musician will be able to transcend the handicaps institutionalized in the jazz world and attract a sufficiently large following to enable him to more or less stipulate his own conditions of employment.

Such men, however, are the rule-proving exceptions. On the whole, the vocation of jazz musician is a doubly perilous one and its practitioner is multiply disadvantaged, because he is an artist in a country with only the shallowest traditions of supporting its own artists; and because he is black.

But very little of this manages to trickle its way into the jazz press, and the reasons are scarcely esoteric. Basically, they result from the situation summarized by Archie Shepp: "You own the music and we make it." Part of the ownership Shepp refers to includes ownership of the means of mental production, as these pertain to jazz. To turn again to *The German Ideology* will be instructive. Marx and Engels write that:

> The ideas of the ruling class are in every epoch the ruling ideas; . . . the class which has the means of material production at its disposal, has control at the same time over the means of mental production, so that thereby, generally speaking, the ideas of those who lack the means of mental production are subject to it. The ruling ideas are nothing more than the ideal expression of the dominant material relationships. . . . The division of labor, . . . one of the chief forces of history up till now, manifests itself also in the ruling class as the division of mental and material labor, so that inside this class one part appears as the thinkers of the class (its active, conceptive ideologists, who make the perfecting of the illusion of the class about itself their chief source of livelihood). . . .[2]

To avoid misrepresentation, it is mandatory to insist, together with Marx and Engels, that we have been speaking in general terms; and that all generalities about the material universe admit of certain isolated exceptions. That qualification noted we can proceed with an examination of why the actual relationships governing the production of jazz music so rarely manage to creep into print. As Marx and Engels noted, within the ruling class — i.e., the class of *owners* — there is a division of labor, so that some of the members are cast in the role of "active ideologists," while the others, the "active members," are practical men of affairs. Inside jazz, the first group goes by the name of *jazz critics.*

Since a number of the essays that follow this introduction attempt to deal in some depth with the *modus operandi* of the jazz critic, only the most summary description is required at this point. Let it suffice that until very recently almost all of the best-known American critics have been antiradical whites who supported the main contours of the social status quo, and have made "the perfecting of the illusion . . . their chief source of livelihood." That is to say, linked to the white ownership of the jazz business by ties of economics, race, and social outlook — in short, by material conditions — the jazz critic has had as a major, if not *the* major task, the obscuring of the actual social relations that prevail within jazz society. Since the most glaring reality of jazz society is that of black creation versus white control, it is that reality which most urgently cries out for its nakedness to be shielded behind ideological figleaves.

To illustrate why this should be a matter of such high priority, we need only to consider the greater but analogous repercussions of an open admission by North American corporations that the effect of their overseas economic activity is, deliberately or otherwise, to promote stagnation and resource-depletion rather than development in colonial and semicolonial countries. Clearly, such an admission would be little short of an across-the-board invitation for the expropriation of U.S. firms in every foreign land where their investments were to be found.

Though the sums of money involved in the jazz business are insignificant by comparison, the logic of the situation is similar. While it is undeniable that a relatively small handful of black individuals do benefit from white business investments in the colonial economy of jazz, it is hardly open to question that the black community would be far better off were it in a position to control one of its leading resources, the talents of its people. Under the existing circumstances, however, this is an impossibility. Like Peruvian copper or Chilean nitrates, the "raw material" of jazz — artistry — is dumped on a glutted market where the price it can command is relatively low; whereas those who dispose of the "finished product"

— recording companies, festival promoters, bookers and agencies, nightclub owners — are, by their superior position, enabled to take the lion's share of the profits.

Norman Granz, to cite a not unusual case, was able to amass a world-renowned collection of paintings, largely from promoting concerts and producing recordings of saxophonist Charlie Parker; "critic" Leonard Feather established himself as an Authority on the music of Parker and his contemporaries by being among the first writers to recognize its brilliance, and parlayed this achievement into a position of syndicated preeminence in the field of jazz journalism. Parker himself died the death of a penniless drug addict. His career was extraordinary for incredible bursts of creativity; its ending was all too commonplace. Those who find nothing upsetting in the juxtaposition of the circumstances of Parker's demise and the enrichment of those white business figures whose paths intersected his are no doubt among those who will be wholly surprised when one fine day the continent of Latin America follows the example of Southeast Asia and erupts into revolutionary flames. Their astonishment may be genuine, but their sense of social justice (if that is not an outmoded concept) could do with some sharpening.

In any case, to return to our white jazz ideologue, one of his principal assignments, particularly in recent years, is to disguise in one manner or another the nature of the social relationships that determine the distribution of rewards reaped from jazz. Much of the time, of course, he will be dealing with aesthetic judgments — in which he will almost invariably exhibit European rather than Afro-American preferences — and not with social issues. Yet as the tide of black nationalist sentiment has continued to swell in the nation's ghettos, the attack against "outside" ownership and control of jazz production and distribution has steadily mounted in synchrony. In consequence, jazz ideologues have to some degree been forced onto the defensive and compelled to offer explanations purporting to demonstrate that the prevalent relationships in jazz are anything but exploitative. Their arguments, though they may differ in detail, fall into three main categories:

1. Jazz is not primarily a black or Afro-American art, since "anyone" can learn to play it.

2. Blacks themselves do not support jazz, or at least certain kinds of jazz — a contention often advanced when the writer wishes to discredit certain styles, schools, etc.

3. Jazz has no particular social content; specifically, it in no way pertains more closely to black experiences, perceptive

modes, sensibilities, and so on, than it does to white. At its most vulgar, this argument is condensed into the assertion that jazz is not "protest music," that black jazz musicians are either unwilling or incapable of concerning themselves with social issues, unless manipulated into doing so by some diabolical white puppetmaster behind the scenes (the "Hayakawa thesis"). The racism implicit in such an approach ought to be so palpable to everyone save its formulators as not to require further comment.

All of these arguments find ample illustration (and, I hope, rebuttal) in the chapter dealing with the critics. There are, however, some points of sufficent importance to merit consideration in a very summary fashion here.

I

"Anyone" can learn to play jazz. There is probably a certain amount of truth in this — about as much truth as there is in the assertion that "anyone" can *davin* in Yiddish as a cantor, can teach himself to become a flamenco singer in the style of *cante hondo*, can learn Indian ceremonial dances or Irish sea chanties or Japanese *Koto* music, etc. To be sure, one need not be born Jewish and be raised in an Orthodox home to be a good cantor; but it is a striking fact that there aren't very many Gentile *daviners* of distinction. The same consideration applies to jazz playing, which involves more than merely mastering a given instrument from a technical standpoint. To become even a competent jazz musician, besides gaining control over one's instrument it is also necessary to have learned to hear and think in the jazz idiom and to have assimilated a good deal of the entire previous corpus of jazz improvisation. At bottom, then, learning to express oneself in jazz is not so different from learning to express oneself in a foreign tongue. And while it always is a theoretical possibility that an author can develop as a major voice in a language originally not his own, nonetheless the fact remains that very few in the history of literature have been able to accomplish this feat.

These same considerations serve as the most obvious explanation for the continued domination of all the various readers' polls, critics' polls and musicians' polls by black artists. Because black youth do, after all, grow up in an environment in which Afro-American music of all sizes and shapes (blues, gospel, jazz, Motown) is ubiquitous, such a youngster has an inestimable cultural advantage over the white youth who is not continuously exposed to the same musical fare. Some of this may change with the next generation of white jazz musicians, whose listening habits are, by virtue of the cheap transistor radio and phonograph record, probably becoming more catholic and closer to that of their black peers than was the case for present and previous whites in jazz.

Be that as it may, so far as we may safely generalize about the history of jazz to date, the music must be viewed above all as a product of black artistic consciousness. Whites can learn to play jazz, just as Gentiles can learn to *davin*; but for most whites, as for most Gentiles, this new accomplishment will ordinarily come later in life than if they had been raised in the traditions of the ethnic group that they now seek to emulate; and in most cases the "second language" thus acquired will always be a touch more stiff and stilted for the "outsider" than for the "insider." To say this—a cautionary note included here for the benefit of white critics who are not above willful distortion—does not at all mean that one in any way subscribes to the quaint notion that blacks are "born with a natural sense of rhythm." The truth of the matter is that most outstanding figures in jazz have been black, and that a black boy is therefore far more likely to be motivated at an early age toward choosing a jazzman for his culture hero ("role model" in the jargon of social science), and jazz for his career, than is a white. Conversely, and for identical reasons, a white boy is more apt to relate positively to the image of a corporation president than a black. To deny this amounts to a total disregard for the influence of social environment in molding personality, and consequently really *is* at base a racist approach.

The quintessential black nature of jazz, moreover, can be thrown into even sharper relief by pushing a step further the analogy between assimilating the jazz tradition and mastering a second language. To learn to speak and perhaps write in a second language with reasonable facility is difficult but by no means impossible. To become a genuinely creative and original stylist in the acquired tongue, however, is an accomplishment of an entirely different order; and the number of writers who have been able to pull off the feat is, as noted, minute. It must be kept in mind that when we speak of English literature or French literature it is the most creative figures, the seminal innovators, whom we ordinarily have in mind. Competence, however praiseworthy in itself, cannot be used to define a viable

standard of excellence. The same consideration is directly applicable to jazz. There are (and have been) innumerable improvisers in jazz whose competence is beyond question; without
such artists to perpetuate it, it is highly doubtful if anything
resembling the existing jazz tradition could have survived.
Yet for all their importance, their contribution has been different
in kind from that of the men whose names immediately come
to the fore when we begin to think of the music's outstanding
stylists over the years: Louis Armstrong, Duke Ellington, Coleman Hawkins, Charlie Parker, Dizzy Gillespie, Miles Davis,
Thelonious Monk, John Coltrane, Ornette Coleman, Cecil Taylor. The difference lies in this, that the latter artists are the
ones whose works *define* the basic contours that the music
will follow in its evolution, while the former are those who
will not so much innovate as elaborate on the innovations of
others. In short, jazz, like any field of human endeavor, has
its footsoldiers as well as its generals. Both, needless to say,
are necessary if the continuity of the music is to be insured.

For all of that, it cannot be denied that the innovators, by
definition, are the artists who give the music its direction, carrying it forward by inventing new styles when existing ones
have become threadbare through overuse. It does *not* follow
from this that the rank and file are entirely passive and play
no role in the evolution of jazz styles. On the contrary, it is
this rank and file who, collectively, exert what amounts to a
veto power over the innovators. Those innovations that are
adopted by large numbers of the rank and file and incorporated into their playing are the ones that will survive; those
that are persistently rejected by the community of performing jazz musicians will ultimately end on the discard pile.

Hence to earn a niche as an artist of lasting significance
requires more than simple "originality"; it requires as well
that, in the long run (which may sometimes be very long
indeed), the artist's original ideas meet with a favorable response from the fraternity of jazz musicians as a whole, so
that they may be added to the already existing (and legit-
imated) modes of improvising. Dave Brubeck, to introduce
one example, is certainly unique in his approach to the piano;
but unlike the equally unique Thelonious Monk, his style has
never been sufficiently compelling to produce a "school" of
musicians whose playing can be unequivocally traced back
to him. As a result, one can assert with some confidence after
fifteen years that Brubeck is an occasionally interesting but
essentially minor episode in the development of jazz piano.

His style will go with him to the grave, and the histories of
jazz — should we survive as a race long enough to write and
read them — will relegate his name to the footnotes.

How does the foregoing bear on the question of the black
origins and nature of jazz? The answer is that if we were to
compile the names of the ten or twenty-five or fifty most significant jazz artists, those whose ideas have had the greatest
influence on contemporary and subsequent generations, the
color of such a list would be overwhelmingly black. The number of white musicians who have made a permanent contribution to the tradition of jazz — as opposed to exploring what
turns out to be a musical blind alley, in the fashion of Dave
Brubeck — the number of such musicians is astonishingly small.
More than likely, one could count them on one's fingers. Of
unquestioned importance are pianist Bill Evans and bassists
Charlie Haden and the late Scott LaFaro. Depending on how
tightly one wishes to draw the line, a moderately good case
could be made for the inclusion of such popular but basically uninfluential performers as Jack Teagarden, Stan Getz, Bix
Beiderbecke and Benny Goodman, none of whom have inspired numerous disciples; and, if one wants to be extremely
generous, Artie Shaw, Woody Herman, Pee Wee Russell and
Stan Kenton. In sum, a dozen — not exactly an impressive
host. And even if we double the number, on the assumption
that some noteworthy musicians may have been overlooked,
the figure is still comparatively minute. It is probably safe
to state that there have been more black innovators of consequence on any *two* instruments we might choose at random
— trumpet and trombone, say — than there have been whites
on all instruments put together.

The overwhelming prevalence of black innovators in jazz
can easily be related to our earlier "second language" analogy. Just as it is far more likely that a French rather than
an English novelist will be the originator of some potent new
stylistic departure in French letters, so it is to be expected
that the major revolutionary developments in jazz — the abrupt
discontinuities in modes of improvisation — flow from the hands
and instruments of blacks. Ghetto blacks, if you will, "speak
jazz" (or blues or gospel) as their "native tongue" as Italians
"speak opera"; whereas for most whites it is a "language" that
must be acquired, sometimes not without a great deal of painful effort and highly disciplined study. Hence consider the
difference in situation of two youths, one black, one white,
in their early twenties. The black youth, having unconsciously

assimilated much of the jazz tradition as part of his culture, can take this tradition more or less for granted when he begins his career in music. As a result, all of his energies and talents can be given over to the elaboration of a personal style of his own — one that may be revolutionary in its impact on his peers. The white youth, on the other hand, must devote his efforts not so much to becoming a unique voice, but to the necessarily prior problems of simply mastering the jazz vernacular, *acquiring* the tradition. The first youth, therefore, finds the way open to becoming a creator; the second is satisfied if he can achieve something better than run-of-the-mill competence.

It is essentially for this reason that most whites who enter the jazz world do so as imitators of black innovators. Unable to aspire to innovation themselves, they are content if they can produce reasonable facsimiles of their artistic mentors. Conceivably the clearest illustration of this phenomenon came in the forties and fifties in the form of a "school" of white saxophonists who drew their inspiration from Lester Young. Their number was formidable, including Stan Getz, Jimmy Giuffre, Allan Eager, Herbie Steward, Brew Moore, Zoot Sims, Al Cohn, Serge Chaloff (who played baritone, but was nonetheless heavily indebted to Young for his approach), and probably others whose names escape me. Aside from Getz and perhaps Chaloff, none of these players could be said to be original or innovative in any meaningful sense of those words. Their major achievement was that of carrying on the style of Young after its creator himself passed from the scene.

Apparently, the immense effort required to master the intricacies of a single jazz style — or, to broaden the perspective, a single artistic style — is so great as to force a kind of commitment-for-life from the artist. It is as if he had said, "Having invested all my psychological resources in learning this particular style, I have exhausted my artistic capital and cannot push myself beyond my present limitations." At any rate, such an hypothesis accounts for the fact that, once having become fluent in the jazz idiom, most white musicians do not forge ahead to become original stylists but continue with their first style for the remainder of their careers.

For that matter, black jazzmen who are innovators seldom make more than a single great contribution in their lifetimes. Their single innovation usually comes early in their careers — typically, during the twenties — and after that they persist in following the same lines. Again, it seems as if the psychic energy required to produce the innovation acts to weld the loyalty of the artist to his style and prevent him from moving forward from that point of stasis. Thus, though the black musician in jazz may indeed be more innovative than the white, there is a fundamental similarity between the two, in that once a style, whether original or copied, has been arrived at, it is in the majority of cases impossible to set it aside for a newer, more revolutionary one.

The number of musicians of either color who have been able to generate more than a single innovation, or even modify their mature style, is, as we would anticipate, truly insignificant: Miles Davis, the late John Coltrane and perhaps Coleman Hawkins, Sonny Rollins and Pee Wee Russell are the only ones whose names come to mind. In contrast, the number of innovators whose names are identified with a single stylistic innovation is much longer: Louis Armstrong, Lester Young, Dizzy Gillespie, Charlie Parker (up to his premature death at thirty-five in 1955), Thelonious Monk, Jay Jay Johnson, Roy Eldridge, Cootie Williams, Bubber Miley, Jelly Roll Morton, Kenny Clarke, Juan Tizol, Tricky Sam Nanton, and so on— another twenty or thirty names could be added with no trouble whatsoever, but I believe the point is already firmly enough established.

It will be useful at this juncture to have recourse to a totally unrelated field to provide what may be the final word in the foregoing argument. Thomas S. Kuhn, in his examination of epoch-making innovations in science,[3] calls attention to two characteristic facts about the originators of such innovations: (1) generally, they are young at the time that they produce their greatest work; (2) only rarely are they ever able to generate a second, equally revolutionary contribution to their particular field. Kuhn explains the latter finding by hypothesizing that once a new scientific "system" has been devised and accepted— for example, the Newtonian system of the eighteenth century— the scientists who have been won over from its predecessor transfer all their loyalty to the newly accepted orthodoxy. It then becomes, in the most literal fashion, unthinkable for the scientists to question this orthodoxy, inasmuch as they have by then made a tremendous psychological commitment to its being correct.

Yet the *next* generation of scientists will have made no such commitment; they will have been educated (perhaps *indoctrinated* is a more accurate term) in the new orthodoxy, which, because of the nature of science teaching in the West, they will accept as "natural" and "self-evident," if, indeed, they do not conceive of this orthodoxy as the only *possible* way of viewing the natural universe — notwithstanding the fact that their predecessors had to conduct a prolonged mental struggle before they could bring themselves to accept it. Having no particular stake in the prevailing orthodoxy, the new generation of scientists will be less emotionally tied to it and consequently more likely to see its shortcomings — especially while they are still young, with no established careers to risk but only those to be gained (thus Kuhn's first result, the youthfulness of scientific innovators). Hence it will fall to this generation or one of its successors ultimately to demolish the new orthodoxy and replace it with yet a newer one, which in turn, of course, will undergo a similar destruction.

The men who undermined Newtonian physics — Planck, Bohr, Einstein — were all trained in that system of thought and, at least at the outset of their careers, considered themselves stalwart adherents. Similarly, the men who overthrew Bohr's model of subatomic physics were men who had been raised on it as undergraduates, and so on, to the present day of "strange" particles, unified field theories, and the like. The same could be demonstrated of other sciences equally well, as, for example, in chemistry, where the phlogiston explanation of chemical reactions was done in by investigators originally schooled in its soundness.

The parallel with jazz — or, as I have tried to imply throughout, any art — should not be difficult to discern. A young black born around 1940 in a metropolitan ghetto in the North, for example, will imbibe jazz of the bebop period as effortlessly as he does the proverbial mother's milk; it will be for him what Newtonian mechanics was for an eighteenth-century astronomer. If he decides to become a jazz musician and sets for himself the problem of working out an original style, bebop will of necessity be the music which he must progress beyond. It will be too commonplace, too tame, too devoid of excitement, too lacking in the unexpected, too uninspiring — it will be what "everyone is playing." Only a very unambitious youth would be satisfied at setting his sights so low as to recapitulate bebop without seeking to extend it, develop it and, in the end, subvert it. For the white youth of the same age, however, the situation will be entirely different. Where bebop for the black was banal and a bit of a bore, in the case of the white it will come as a tremendous awakening, exotic, novel, unprecedented. His whole being will be thrown into trying to cope with its strange cadences and phrases, originally so outlandish. Is it any wonder,

then, that the black musician will not rest until he can expunge
the sound of Charlie Parker's virtuosity from his mind's ear,
while the white will be happy only when his sound is virtually
a duplicate of that of Parker, who has posed the most absorb-
ing and demanding artistic challenge of the lad's entire career
up to that time?

In the previous paragraphs I have sought to argue for the
view that jazz not only sprang originally from black roots,
but that because of the segregated nature of this society, in
which white and black youth develop largely along separate
cultural-psychological lines, it has to this moment remained
tied to these roots and gives no evidence of being about to
change. For only if the black origins of the music are understood does it become possible to make any sense out of the
post-war evolution of jazz or to account for the early eruption
of black nationalism in all its myriad forms within the world
of jazz players and listeners.

II

It is not the consciousness of men that determines their
existence, but, on the contrary, their social existence
determines their consciousness. At a certain stage of
their development, the material forces of production
in society come into conflict with the existing relations
of production, or — what is but a legal expression for
the same thing — with the property relations within which
they had been at work before. From forms of development of the forces of production these relations turn
into their fetters. Then comes the period of social revolution. With the change of the economic foundation
the entire immense superstructure is more or less rapidly transformed. In considering such transformations,
the distinction should always be made between the material transformation of the economic conditions of production which can be determined with the precision of
natural science, and the legal, political, religious, aesthetic, or philosophic — in short ideological forms in
which men become conscious of this conflict and fight
it out. [4]

Blacks themselves do not support jazz. This thesis represents,
it will be recalled, the second argument of the dominant ortho-

doxy, the Revealed Wisdom, of the bulk of the ideologically oriented white jazz critics. To attempt to refute it with numbers would be a tedious and probably ultimately hopeless task. To begin with, no reliable statistics — on record sales, club patronage, concert/festival attendance, and the like — that I know of are to be found. And even if there were such figures in existence, what indeed would they prove? If, for example, the amount of money spent on jazz recordings were higher for whites on a per capita basis than for blacks, would this indicate that whites are more likely than blacks to purchase (and enjoy) jazz albums? Or that pernicious racial differentials in income prevent blacks from indulging their aesthetic tastes as freely as whites? If *Shelly's Manne-Hole*, in the midst of white Hollywood, draws a higher proportion of white customers than black, are we to conclude that jazz must therefore be more popular with whites? Or could it be that the combination of an alien location and exorbitant admission and other mandatory charges conspire to keep away not only the black but the young of *all* colors?

We will therefore leave vulgar empiricism to the vulgar empiricists and the behavioristically oriented in general, who will surely be happy with the gift, and approach the issue from an entirely different perspective. Prior to embarking on that analysis, however, it may be remarked parenthetically that anyone on a college campus with a sizable black student population will not need elaborate calculations to be convinced that jazz does without doubt have the emotional support of the young black generation. Wherever Black Studies courses are being undertaken, jazz — at long last! — is being readily incorporated into the college and university curriculum. Our jazz critics may remain obdurate, but the history of the next few decades ought to settle the question of the relationship between the black community and jazz once for all.

Instead of straining futilely to obtain a head-count of such items as jazz-record purchases and club attendance, it is my purpose to investigate the relationship between blacks and jazz by a brief and very schematic consideration of some turning points in the social history of the music since World War II. This will show, I believe, that the only way in which its development can be comprehended is on the assumption of an intimate and persistent symbiosis between the music and the community out of which it is continuously being gestated. Such a consideration will in no sense be "a history of jazz"; both the space and the will for a project of that magnitude are lacking here. What I rather wish to call attention to is the way in which jazz has evolved roughly in phase with the most important events to take place in the ghetto.

There is in international jurisprudence the concept of dual citizenship, whereby a child born to parents not living in their native land has the citizenship both of the parents and of the country of his own birth. In a certain sense black Americans can lay claim to a kind of dual citizenship of their own: they are in the country, but not always of it. They are, more than any other ethnic group save perhaps the Spanish-speaking and the Asian-American, heir to a culture that is uniquely their own and thus at least partially hidden from whites. (Of course each distinct ethnic-religious group will have retained certain fragments of a culture, but the culture of blacks is much more intact — a difference in kind rather than degree — than that of all but the most recent immigrants.) By virtue of this "dual citizenship," black people often respond not only to events that shake and move the rest of the country, but also to those that barely even register with the white population. Among the most obvious recent examples has been the gaining of independence during the 1960s by the former colonial states of Africa — a series of events that, as Harold R. Isaacs has shown, [5] had profound psychological and political consequences in the ghetto, though white America was only subliminally aware of African developments. The assassination of Medgar Evers, Malcolm X, and Martin Luther King, Jr., undoubtedly had immensely greater effect among blacks than whites; and it is probable that although the assassination of the two Kennedy brothers was perceived as a tragedy by whites, it was seen as a tragedy *and* a direct blow at blacks by the latter.

If the position of black people in this society is anomalous — they are at once both in and not in the white socioculture — that of the black jazz musician is multiply so. Conceivably the single most acutely experienced contradiction of the jazz musician's role is that of being simultaneously the object of adulation by his public — including a sizable number of white devotees* — and the object of something that, at its extreme,

---

* For example, whenever a certain famous black trumpeter plays the Village Vanguard in New York, the narrow corridor between the kitchen, where the musicians ordinarily spend their breaks, and the main room is lined with attractive young white women. As he returns from the kitchen to resume playing, he makes it a point to bestow a lingering caress on the behind of each of the females waiting in attendance. The latter can then return to their tables to brag of their exploits to their less adventurous sisters.

approaches contempt by those businessmen who control his economic opportunities. It is not unusual for a jazzman to return home after an evening of applause to, say, a rat-infested hovel in New York's Harlem or East Village. The abrupt transition from being a celebrated artist to being a penniless and persistently exploited commodity is, of course, at the root of Archie Shepp's observation that "You own the music and we make it." That indignity, however, is not the sole one to which the black musician is exposed. He must also watch as less talented but more palatable white imitators and popularizers reap the financial benefits of black innovations (Paul Whiteman, Benny Goodman, Frankie Laine, Al Jolson, etc.). Finally, like all artists (as differentiated from entertainers), the jazzman on occasion does "get ahead of" his public. This means that even though the black community can in the long run be expected to provide sustenance for jazz, the long run may prove in certain cases to be the artist's most creative years. All of these processes interact in such a way to expose the black musician to a maximum of insecurity and isolation; and they naturally cause his alienation to run continuously at a very high pitch. For he must cope not merely with being black, or being an artist, or even being an artist who happens to be black — any one of which alone would stagger the ordinary mortal — but with the almost insuperable obstacle of attempting to define himself as a black artist, practicing a black-based art in a country that is deathly afraid of both its artists and its blacks. That jazzmen, confronted with this hostile situation, have sometimes sought refuge in various narcotics is not to be wondered at; the marvel is that there are any who have not wholly succumbed to this form of escapism. Nonetheless, a destructive and inhumane environment will eventually take its toll in one form or another. The two most influential figures of the last thirty years, Charlie Parker and John Coltrane, were both dead before their forty-first birthday.

It could well be that the best vaccine against early death from the cumulative effects of existing in a dehumanizing, racist environment is political consciousness and action aimed at undermining the status quo. Such, at any rate, is suggested by authors as different as the pacifist Albert Camus (in *The Rebel*) and the revolutionary Frantz Fanon (in *A Dying Colonialism*). Be that as it may, it should be readily apparent to any honest and reasonably sensitive observer-participant that a substratum of black resentment has, as I hope to demonstrate, been almost from the very first an integral aspect of the jazz world. The reasons for this are anything but complex or obscure, and ultimately they all pivot about the central dichotomy of black creation versus white control. The fact that black musicians can at one and the same time be lionized and callously used serves to make the jazz milieu a most explosive one, and the black artist himself a likely candidate for conversion to some form of black nationalism.

This is not meant to assert that all jazz musicians, now or at any time in the past, have been explicitly militant black nationalists. To advance such a proposition would be historically wrong on two counts: first, it would ignore the manner in which nationalism in the ghetto waxes and wanes in response to developments in the political economy of the United States and the world; secondly, it would neglect the very serious economic reprisals to which all but a sprinkling of jazz musicians would leave themselves open were they to declare themselves unequivocally in favor of black nationalism or separatism. What is being maintained, on the contrary, are two other theses: (1) that a certain residue of protonationalist thinking, sometimes very inchoate and scarcely articulated as such, has always been present in jazz, even to the point of influencing the timing and the direction of stylistic innovations; and (2) that in recent times it has been the jazz musicians who, of any identifiable group of blacks, have been the first to be converted and to espouse the tenets of black nationalism.

The last point needs particular emphasis. In 1969, we have already seen nationalist-minded protests by black entertainers, amateur and professional athletes, students, and even that most conservative, apathetic and essentially apolitical, group, academics. That and the prevalence of certain nationalist-derived life-styles ("natural" hairdos for both sexes, African *dashikis*), especially among the young, has led whites to take nationalism — or at least its trappings — for granted among blacks, and to assume that beneath every natural head of hair there lurks a cortex brimful of nationalist ideology. Besides not being true, these assumptions mask the fact (which must here be again insisted upon) that nationalist ideas first gained wide currency within the jazz milieu. There should be nothing surprising in this, for in no other sphere is the disparity between the level of black achievement and the lack of appropriate white recognition (in socioeconomic terms) as gross as in jazz; nowhere else, that is, is a black man venerated as an artist of the greatest creative potential at precisely the same moment as he is being pushed into the gutter as a nigger.*

So jazz musicians have ample cause for being particularly susceptible to the siren strains of black nationalism. To say that much, however, still leaves unanswered the question of why black nationalism has not been uniformly rampant during every phase of jazz's history, but has instead shown rather sharp fluctuations. To attempt to provide that answer will require that we go beyond the confines of the jazz world itself to consider its relationship with ghetto society.

As I have been at pains to underline, the history of jazz cannot be written (other than very superficially) as aesthetic history alone; instead, we are compelled to regard the music as one aspect of the social history of black people in this country. Doing so immediately disposes of such notions as "black people themselves do not support jazz" — dilapidated, impoverished theses whose effect at best would be to deny credit to a people for their achievement in the face of Herculean obstacles.

Ideas, Marx and Engels observe, have no independent history of their own; only *men* have history. The same applies to jazz, music in general, or any art: there is no history of art apart from that of the men and women who created it. An elementary point, the reader may demur; but if so, one that appears to have escaped the field of view of the white jazz critic. For that reason, at the risk of being redundant, the point is advanced yet once more. We cannot permit ourselves the luxury of speaking of the history of jazz while at the same time divorcing it from the social biographies of those who made the music and those who, at each phase in its evolution, responded to it.

To illustrate this it will be well to consider how the fate of jazz is inextricably bound up with that of the black ghetto that nurtures it, using the last quarter-century as our "laboratory."

---

* Literally, and not merely in metaphor. A few years ago, Miles Davis, the trumpeter, was spending an intermission walking outside the New York nightclub where he was in the midst of an engagement when, without provocation, a white policeman began beating him over the head with his club. Similarly, the brilliant composer-pianist Cecil Taylor was on his way home from a concert when he was set upon by a gang of young white toughs, and his hands so injured that he could not play for some time. What would have been the reaction had these brutalities been inflicted on, for instance, Leonard Bernstein or, for that matter, Lawrence Welk? Beside the pain and injury of the beating itself, there is the further humiliation in the white public's relative indifference to the event — after all, it wasn't as if a white man had been attacked, was it?

Just as the Second World War was about to break out, a new generation of young black innovators was assembling in New York to perfect their then novel approach to improvisation. The names of these men are by now familiar to anyone with more than a passing acquaintance with the music: Charlie Parker (saxophone), Dizzy Gillespie (trumpet), Thelonious Monk and Bud Powell (piano), Max Roach and Kenny Clarke (drums). Before much time had elapsed, there was also a second line of bebop (as the new music came to be called) players — Miles Davis and Fats Navarro (trumpet), Dexter Gordon and Wardell Gray (saxophone), and others. Meanwhile, the war had indeed begun, with a variety of consequences for jazz. On the one hand, the war was able to accomplish something that Franklin Roosevelt's New Deal, bound as it was by the "rules of the game" of private-ownership capitalism, could not: the pall of a more than decade-long depression was finally lifted. For blacks, this meant an acceleration of the trend propelling them out of the South, into the cities and, temporarily at least, into the ranks of the industrial work force. The orders for war production that got the wheels of industry turning and, thanks to a shortage of labor, brought blacks into the factories, also put money into their pockets.

Undoubtedly, some of this money was spent on music and other arts, but outside of New York the new bebop style was delayed in its dissemination. For the wartime shortage of shellac (reinforced by a year-and-a-half strike by the American Federation of Musicians) led to a concentration of what phonograph record production there was on juke-box hits and a drastic cutback on recordings of black music (i.e., jazz and rhythm and blues). The result was that for four or five years jazz artists were at work on perfecting the new style, all the while denied access to their usual audience via the usual channels of record sales. It is not very surprising, therefore, that by the time the war had come to an end, a gap had begun to open between the radically new bebop players, most notably Parker and Gillespie, and the lay jazz audience. For that matter, even some young black musicians who had spent the war years in uniform later confessed to being taken aback the first few times they were confronted with the seemingly "crazy" procedures (musical and otherwise) of the bebop musicians.

However serious and deep this split between artist and community, it was on the way to being healed when the inevitable postwar economic downturn overtook the country as a whole. (At that time, recall, the Cold War had not yet been fully insti-

tutionalized as a means of subsidizing giant corporations and
thus preserving capitalism.) Ultimately, the handy "coincidence"
of a colonial war in Korea was to provide the traditional
means of staving off economic stagnation and rescuing capitalism once again. [6] But before that could happen, the slump
had made grave inroads into the support that the black community was able to provide jazz. Traditionally last hired and first
fired, when the economic stagnation began to hit — and in not
a few cases, even before — blacks were driven out of many of
the positions they had been able to find in industry during the
war; these losses were for the most part never reversed, even
after the economy began to recuperate in the wake of Korea.
In this way bebop was deprived of the traditional public for
jazz at what was clearly a crucial moment; thus undermined,
the music itself was forced underground. (A summary reading
of the jazz press from the late forties bears eloquent witness
to the sudden demise of bebop in the number of dance halls
abruptly forced to close their doors.) Bebop never got beyond
the status of a nascent movement. A few more years of pros-
perity would in all probability have been decisive for its survival. Without those years, it was reduced to the level of a
cult, and many of its most famous practitioners vanished into
obscurity (as was true, for example, of Thelonious Monk and
trombonist Jay Jay Johnson; the latter went to work in the
Post Office).
    When the economic revival finally commenced, moreover,
the country was in a far different state of mind than it had
been in the late forties. It is only with the greatest trepidation
that the historian may venture to generalize about such neb-
ulous entities as "the national mood." Nonetheless, it should
be quite evident that the fearful, even paranoid days of the
early Cold War period (roughly, from Korea to the end of
Eisenhower's first term) were not such as to provide a very
hospitable environment for the unabashedly emotional music
that was bebop. Though highly sophisticated, bop was nevertheless an art of raw electric energy; to flourish, it required
a public that could appreciate its naked passions and unin-
hibited romanticism. Such a public, however, was not to be
found in jazz any more than it was in literature or painting
during this period. It was as if, to speak metaphorically, the
national obsession with "the Communist menace" monopolized
all of the country's creative wellsprings, in the process shifting
attention away from any serious concern with the arts, politics,
and meaningful intellectual or spiritual endeavors in general.

To document this contention would be, if not impossible, extremely difficult; but that is a task that may safely be left for the empiricists. To anyone who has lived through, or even read the newspapers of, that era — whose best remembered public figures arc, variously, J. F. Dulles, Eisenhower, Joseph McCarthy and Norman Vincent Peale — the contention will not demand additional evidence.

The jazz style that began to emerge as bebop went under was entirely in keeping with the character of the early Cold War period. Even the name of the style itself — *cool* — reflected the change. It would never have occurred to anyone who knew the music to refer to bebop as "cool," for bebop was above all a music of engagement, with the feelings of the players, especially its symbolic leader, Charlie Parker, out in the open for all to see. As a style, cool was anything but that; it was the quintessence of individual *dis*-engagement. If you want to hear the difference, compare a solo by the father of bebop trumpet, Dizzy Gillespie, to one from the cool period by the then-idolized but now almost forgotten trumpeter Chet Baker. Where Gillespie ranges over the entire horn, plays at the top and bottom of its range, is not afraid to be triple fortissimo as the passage demands, packs his solos full of flurries of rapidly cascading short notes, and is generally expressive in a florid, full-blooded manner, Baker's approach is smooth to the point of blandness and almost completely devoid of excitement. He eschews both loud notes and high ones, his phrasing is mostly legato with relatively few short notes and many long ones, so that the overall effect is one of "pretty" but rather vapid music. By virtue of what he has excluded from his playing — high notes, loud notes, staccato attacks, etc. — Baker is compelled to express himself within a very limited, even constricted emotional range. It is theatre with all the passions politely expunged, painting with all the vivid tones prohibited. Naturally, it has no lasting appeal. There are still plenty of collectors who will play Louis Armstrong's Hot Five records from the twenties, but no one, to my knowledge, who has continued listening to cool jazz.

The cool style in music was almost wholly a development due to whites. The only prominent black player to be involved was Miles Davis; and Davis himself repudiated cool when, in the mid-fifties, he began to evolve in the direction of more loose, emotional, blues-rooted music that paid explicit deference to the black base of jazz. With the single exception of Davis, the figures who led the cool movement were white and, save

in one or two instances, are now in complete obscurity so far
as jazz is concerned. In its own way, by the force of negative
example, the cool period can tell us something about the nature
of jazz: first, that jazz cannot remove itself too far from the
experience of the ghetto and still retain its vitality; second,
that whites in the main cannot bring to bear the requisite background, either musically or socially, to furnish the major force
in sustaining the music and perfecting new innovations.

In one way, it is useful to look at cool jazz as a musical
counterpart to the Beat literary movement. Both celebrated the
virtues of passivity and withdrawal—we should today call it
dropping out—over those of active engagement. To display
emotion within either the cool or beat milieus was at once
to brand oneself as hopelessly square. And so it is no accident
that when Beats were gathered in their pads, cool music, rather
than bebop, rhythm and blues, or rock and roll, provided
the musical backdrop. Both Beat literature and cool music
have to be seen as the only form of rebellion—that of disaffiliation, as opposed to direct battle with the status quo—available to young, alienated whites during the first years of the
Cold War. (Alienation, of course, was at high-tide levels for
Beats as well as cool-jazz people, though these circles often
overlapped considerably.) Later, when blacks had begun to
mount a more direct attack on Cold War society, Beats and
cool jazz fell by the wayside. Beats yielded to student radicals,
civil rights workers, black nationalists, hippies, yippies, and
so on; cool, to various forms of black revivalism within music,
to be dealt with presently.

Besides being a musical parallel to Beat literature, however,
cool jazz also represented a more or less conscious attempt
to "whiten" the music, to "bleach out" its Afro-American roots.
As will emerge in the following section, one of the driving
forces behind the search for a new mode of expression that
culminated in bebop was to devise a music that "they" couldn't
play; in this way would the question of white ownership versus
black creation be addressed. The search was largely successful,
for there were, initially at least, very few whites who were
able to cope with the intricacies of bebop. That being the case,
it shouldn't be too surprising that once blacks were forced
underground by economic considerations and the playing as
well as the control of jazz was left in the hands of whites, one
of the first things that was done was to assert the primacy
of white, or Western, values over black, or African, ones. By
this I don't mean that such an aim was ever explicitly pro-

claimed — or even that it was ever consciously formulated. What I do mean was that the cool period saw an attempt by white musicians to divest jazz from its historical black moorings and transform it into a music to which "they," the whites, might more easily relate. Usually, this was done under the shibboleth of making the music more "legitimate," which translated as "respectable to white middle-class audiences," which in turn translated as "more like European concert music" (sometimes mistakenly termed "classical").

The center for such bleaching efforts was California, mostly Los Angeles, to a lesser extent the San Francisco Bay area. In New York, though jazz activity was at a low ebb, record companies such as Prestige, Savoy, Blue Note, and others were still releasing occasional albums by black artists whose point of departure was bebop; and these musicians continued to dominate the "scene," minuscule as it might be. On the West Coast, contrariwise, the field was essentially virginal, the only established jazz activity at that point being devoted to white Dixieland bands. (Contemporary Records, one of the companies formed to record cool jazz in Los Angeles, was in fact an offshoot of a Dixieland recording company, Good Time Jazz.) Hence in California, whites did not have to deal with the problem of dispossessing an entrenched group of black bebop musicians, for the simple reason that such a group did not exist — or, to be more accurate, where such groups did exist, they had slight access to recording companies.

The white musicians involved in California cool jazz — which later came to be called, with more precision but less evocativeness, West Coast jazz — came from a variety of sources. Many of them — Shelly Manne, Shorty Rogers, Art Pepper, Bud Shank, Bill Holman, and others — settled in southern California after a lengthy apprenticeship in one or another of the bands of Stan Kenton, himself devoted to "dignifying" jazz by propelling it in the direction of second-rate contemporary European music. Others — Jimmy Giuffre, Stan Getz, Zoot Sims — came from one of Woody Herman's "Herds." Still others were expatriates from the East Coast — such as Gerry Mulligan — or indigenous musicians without much previous reputation — Chet Baker, Dave Brubeck, Bob Gordon. Today, only a small fraction of these musicians are in any significant way linked to the jazz world. Those who have not been able to find a safe, if uncreative, niche in the Hollywood recording studios have, with only few exceptions (Brubeck, Mulligan, Paul Desmond, Zoot Sims), become, in Orwell's phrase, unpersons so far as the jazz audience is concerned. At the peak of their popularity in the mid-fifties, though, cool and/or West Coast white musicians (there were black musicians, too, in California, but they were almost entirely excluded from the cool movement and therefore "didn't count") bid fair to shape all succeeding jazz in their likeness. Those were the years that Chet Baker, for example, triumphed over Dizzy Gillespie and Miles Davis in the various "critics" polls.

What nearly all the cool musicians had in common, especially in California, was some exposure to European composed ("classical") music, and an intense desire — born equally, one supposes, out of status-striving and the feelings of inadequacy that come with working in an "inferior" (i. e., nonwhite) art — to make jazz more like it. The music of Dave Brubeck, with its literally heavy-handed allusions to Baroque counterpoint, is a particularly good instance in point, because Brubeck has never made any secret of the fact that he wanted to "classicize" jazz. (Ironically, the pianists who have brought off the most skillful wedding of European and Afro-American musics, Cecil Taylor and Bill Evans, have done so without any of the attendant ballyhoo that Brubeck received. Taylor, in fact, continues to lead a borderline existence just this side of total poverty, while Brubeck, naturally, is a man of some wealth. But Taylor is black and his music has some depth, whereas Brubeck . . . . oh, well, does it even have to be said any more?) In the early days of his popularity, much was made of Brubeck's abbreviated study with European composer Darius Milhaud — as if this gave him special qualifications to determine the future of jazz! But Brubeck was not alone. Shorty Rogers and Jimmy Giuffre — every album jacket made it a point to mention this — were "studying" with Dr. Wesley La Violette, whoever he may be; and so it went. No respectable white musician could afford to be caught not "studying" with some European musician, theorist or composer. How much relevance all of this study had for the creation of jazz was, to be generous, dubious; but it was part and parcel of the times, and woe, indeed, to that cool or West Coast musician so indiscreet as to violate the code.

As a result, there was never such a plethora of fugues, concerti, divertimentos, rondos, and the like, at any time in the history of jazz. How they ever sold, if they ever did sell, what public bought them, who ever listened to them — these are riddles of the Sphinx. Fully three-fourths or more of the white cool/West Coast music of that era is unlistenable today; I, for one, have long since disposed of my collection. My guess is that those people who still count themselves among the jazz community have done likewise, for the only conceivable value such works might now possess has less to do with music than with nostalgia (if there be anyone mad enough to yearn for such a cramped and ugly time).

But if nothing else, the history of cool/West Coast jazz demonstrates with surpassing clarity what happens to the music when it becomes the plaything of middle-class whites with huge hungerings after the trappings of peer-group respectability. Never has there been a period when control of the musical end of jazz has been vested so completely in white hands; and never has there been a period of such wholesale aesthetic bankruptcy. It does not require occult powers to detect the relationship between the two. The conclusion is inescapable that whites, as late as the 1950s, did not have the sociocultural resources that would enable them to bring to jazz sufficient vitality to cause the music to survive, much less grow. And by extension, it demonstrates the validity of our earlier thesis, that innovation in jazz is indeed rooted in the black community.

The *sine qua non* for white domination of jazz playing was black nonparticipation. As soon as blacks were, as a consequence of the very uneven post-Korean economic upturn, once more able to enter the jazz marketplace both as creators and consumers, the already shaken white hegemony of the cool/West Coast jazz years was further undermined and ultimately demolished altogether.

The name the jazz journalists gave to the style that first challenged and then replaced cool and West Coast jazz was *hard bop*. While not particularly felicitous, the title was apt, for it highlighted the fact that the new black music of the midfifties was for the most part based on bebop, but that there was a new component as well, whence the adjective *hard*. The sources of the added hardness of hard bop — which later became known as *funky*, and after that, *soul* — were double; investigation of them sheds a great deal of light on the nature of the process by which stylistic change in jazz generally comes about.

Viewed as strictly a *movement among musicians* (which it wasn't), hard bop amounted to a black rebellion against the bleaching tendencies of the cool/West Coast whites. As such, it tended deliberately to lay particular stress on the contemporary fundamentals of urban black music, in the form of blues and gospel. Thus the clarion call of the hard bop

movement, as Ralph Gleason has pointed out in other contexts, was Miles Davis's version of *Walkin'*, recorded April 29,
1954.

Still restricting our perspective to musicians, there are two
features of note about *Walkin'*.

First, it was a twelve-measure blues, one of the simplest
chord structures of jazz, and accordingly among the frame-
works most conducive to emotion-laden improvisation; traditionally, in fact, the index of a jazz musician's prowess has
been his ability to play profoundly (not to be confused with
sentimentally) on the blues "changes" (chord progression). In
choosing a blues as the basis for his manifesto, therefore,
Davis—who was himself, recall, initially a significant figure
in the cool/West Coast movement—implicitly made clear his
rejection of cool procedures and criteria. For the cool musicians, like most white would-be improvers of jazz, were not
particularly fond of the blues. They especially prized complexity of structure over impassioned improvisation, and tended to relegate individual soloing to a very distant second place
after contriving "advanced" harmonies, counterpoint, and melodies for several instruments. *

Secondly, the very title itself, *Walkin'*, was a sharp slap
at the arid, insipid, Europe-oriented cool way of thinking,

---

* As a general rule it can be stated that innovative black jazz
artists, e.g., Charlie Parker and John Coltrane, have been most concerned to find ways of *heightening the emotional intensity* of the
music, especially the ad lib portions, whereas whites who aspire
towards the role of innovation, e.g., Don Ellis, Stan Kenton, lean
toward the notion of enriching jazz by incorporating new *technical
devices* into jazz *as ends in themselves*. This latter tendency was
particularly noticeable during the cool period, not only in the bor-
rowing of forms identified with Western European music, but also
in the use of several instruments—flute, oboe, English horn, French
horn, cello—only rarely associated with jazz but given prominent
place in European music. Of these instruments, the flute alone has
found a permanent niche in the tradition of jazz improvisation. As
for the primacy of written form over improvised content, consider
the composition *Circling the Blues* by saxophonist Lenny Niehaus,
a much more impressive than average West Coast performer. *Circling
the Blues* was written in the standard (for blues) twelve-measure
format, but with one difference: at the end of each twelve-bar segment, the harmony would modulate not back to the tonic chord
(I) as in an ordinary blues, but to the subdominant (IV) or dominant (V)—at the moment, I forget which, and it isn't really important—until the entire cycle of twelve (major) key signatures had

with its welter of too clever fugues, canons, sonatas, and what
have you. The contrast between the unpretentious *Walkin'* and
the straining-to-be-genteel of, say, the *Divertimiento in C Minor
for Three Reeds* can scarcely be exaggerated. Too, it was
Walkin' rather than *Walking* — i. e., the self-conscious use of
ghetto argot as a manifestation of cultural nationalist pride
in one's black roots. So that between the playing — Davis used
as soloists such veteran blues improvisers as Milt Jackson
(vibraharp), Lucky Thompson (tenor saxophone), and the
bebop drummer Kenny Clarke — and the title, the extent of
Davis's breakaway from the sterility of cool/West Coast convention could hardly be exaggerated.

But though hard bop was a revolt of black musicians against

---

been traversed (e.g., F to B-flat to E-flat to A-flat, etc.). Niehaus,
as quoted in the album notes, was inordinately proud of this achievement. That he impeded the fluidity of improvisation by imposing
this artifice on his soloists — some of the sharp keys are quite un-
suitable for blues playing — seemed not to bother him in the least,
if in fact it even crossed his mind. Thus, typically, was expression
of feeling sacrificed on the altar of pseudoserious invention during
the cool era. Nor did that mode of thinking end with the demise
of cool styles. Though currently there is no identifiable "West Coast
school" of jazz musicians extant, the southern California recording
studios are still dominated by white jazz musicians, particularly
in the brass, reed, and percussion instruments.

It is a striking fact that these musicians, whenever they record
albums of their own, continue to be obsessed with techniques at the
expense of expressivity; the main difference is that, with the shift
in fads from the fifties to the sixties, the techniques are now as often drawn from India as from Europe. The result is that while white
West Coast musicians have taught themselves to play in all manner
of unusual time signatures such as 11/17, have built some instruments that play microtones (those notes that would lie "in the cracks"
on the piano) and have incorporated the sitar and tabla in their
music — all devices designed to make jazz resemble Indian raga as
closely as possible — their improvising is still largely weak and un-
persuasive by comparison with what contemporary black musicians —
Cecil Taylor, Pharoah Sanders, Albert Ayler, Ornette Coleman, Don
Cherry, the late John Coltrane — have been producing. On occasion,
I have had the priceless opportunity of observing these white studio
musicians as they watched some of their black avant-garde colleagues.
Their reaction mingled incredulity and essentially quiet but thoroughly racist derision in roughly equal proportion. The notion that jazz
could actually be played *like that* — with so much forcefulness and so
little ersatz refinement — seemingly had never penetrated their skulls.
More's the pity.

the alien sensibility of cool, it was considerably more than just that. In actuality, it seems in retrospect most unlikely that the hard-bop movement could ever have come about without simultaneous developments in the black community — developments that hard bop reflected and gave musical expression to. I am thinking, in the first instance, of the earliest stirrings of the contemporary black liberation movement — the NAACP suit in Brown vs. the Board of Education (decided by the U. S. Supreme Court in 1954), the Montgomery bus boycott and the rise of the late Dr. Martin Luther King, Jr. (1956), the Little Rock, Arkansas, school-integration crisis (1957), and so on. These monumental events helped redefine the concept of self held by black people, helped shatter whatever habits of apathy and accommodation to inferior treatment may have existed previously.[7] Because of all the contradictions of the black jazz musician's position in society, it was all but inevitable that this group would react first and most strongly to the efforts of black people to free themselves from the historic shackles of racist subjugation. Initially, the reaction took the form of a renewed pride in the black roots of jazz, the blues, and the gospel music of the black churches. Later, as the liberation movement grew in size and scope and developed greater consciousness in the course of the struggle, this pride and assertion of black-based values was advanced more overtly, and the symbolism, such as was to be found in Miles Davis's *Walkin'*, became less esoteric to decipher.

The nascent black liberation movement was probably the major social force impinging on the consciousness of black jazz musicians in the mid-fifties, and it is, as I have said, unthinkable that the hard bop repudiation of cool jazz could have taken place in its absence. Still, the liberation movement was not the only social stimulus compelling blacks to restructure their views of reality and act accordingly. For the sake of historical completeness, a stab should be made at identifying some of the other leading components of social change. The parallel movement of the African peoples for the ending of colonialism (even though in most cases this ending left the mechanism of neocolonial exploitation intact) made a profound impact on the way in which American blacks perceived themselves. In jazz, as we shall see, the influence of the liberation of the African states early on played an important role in fueling the hard-bop rejection of European-oriented cool aesthetics; it can be traced, for instance, in the numerous references to Africa that begin to appear in the titles of black musicians' compositions after 1954.

Less dramatic but still of great significance was the ongoing trend for blacks to move from the rural, agrarian South to urban centers in the North, West and, sometimes, within the South itself. Besides the cultural shock involved in such abrupt rural-urban transition, there were for blacks the further frustrations and disappointments when it was realized that the allegedly liberal North and West had methods and means for keeping the black man "in his place." The anguish that such realization engendered showed up in jazz as another force propelling blacks in a nationalist direction.

Related to the latter is the cautionary note of the distinguished Belgian economist Ernest Mandel, that "we must not overlook the objective stimuli which have grown out of the inner development of American capitalism itself" in seeking to understand black nationalism. Mandel, of course, is not concerned specifically with the formation of the new, post-cool aesthetic in jazz; but his words are nonetheless of the greatest relevance. Pointing to the "rapid decline in the number of unskilled jobs in American industry" as the "nexus which binds the growing Negro revolt, especially the revolt of Negro youth, to the general socioeconomic framework of American capitalism," he goes on to observe that

> The long . . . boom [after the Korean War] and the explosive progress in agricultural productivity were the first factors in the massive urbanization and the proletarianization of the Afro-Americans: The Northern ghettos grew by leaps and bounds. Today, the average rate of unemployment among the black population is double what it is among the white population, and the average rate among *youth* is double what it is among adults, so that the average among the black youth is nearly four times the general average in the country. Up to 15 or 20 percent of young black workers are unemployed: This is a percentage analagous to that of the Great Depression. It is sufficient to look at these figures to understand the social and material origin of the black revolt. [8]

When one considers Mandel's remarks in light of the fact that the newest black players are themselves always drawn from the ranks of the young, it seems a reasonable conclusion that the concerns of black youth, including those arising from structural changes within the U. S. political economy, will sooner or later find an outlet in the most recent styles — and especially important, *changes* of style — in jazz.

And so it was, though this was not sufficiently appreciated at the time, during the period of the transition from cool to hard bop and its successors. While the movement away from cool to more affirmatively black styles in jazz was spearheaded at first by Miles Davis, and later, Horace Silver (piano) and Art Blakey (drums), all of whom had attained the status of veterans, in the first ranks of the revolt were also numerous younger men from Northern urban centers: trumpeters Clifford Brown (Wilmington, Delaware, and Philadelphia), Lee Morgan (Philadelphia), and Donald Byrd (Detroit), saxophonists Sonny Rollins (New York) and John Coltrane (Philadelphia), bassists Wilbur Ware (Chicago), Doug Watkins and Paul Chambers (both Detroit), pianists Tommy Flanagan (Detroit), Mal Waldron and Wynton Kelly (both New York). Either born in these Northern ghettos or taken there at a young age, the consciousness of these young men, it is now clear, would be different in kind from that of an earlier wave of black musicians who had emigrated from the South and Southwest. Like the generation of avant-garde musicians who followed them in the 1960s, the young black players of the late 1950s were highly literate, both musically and politically. That they chose to simplify the framework of jazz from the overtly formalized, effete and mannered conventions of the cool/West Coast period was due not to their inability to master these conventions, but from their fundamental refusal to concede that the game was worth the candle. Thus they instead formulated a new set of stylistic guidelines that combined the complexity of bebop with a heightened stress on the black basics, blues and gospel music.

Although it is not my intention to write a history of jazz criticism, something must be said of the critical response to hard bop, for it illustrates the impressive gap that looms between the sensibility of the ghetto and that of the respectability-loving, implacably white middle-class mentality that continues to hold sway in writing about jazz. It could have been anticipated that *any* change from cool would probably have been condemned: jazz critics, no less than others, prefer the reassurance of the familiar to the risk of the untried, stability to change, and the protection of their investment in acquiring expertise against any threat that might undermine their hard-won hegemony. What is particularly interesting in the case of hard bop — and this is, once more, a parallel between the development of hard bop and that of the avant-garde some years later — was the nature of the negative critical response. Without always saying so in so many words — for there are some things better left unsaid — the critics attacked the hard boppers for deviating from white or European standards in the direction of Afro-American ones. *

Inasmuch as saxophone players have been in the vanguard of every major innovation in jazz since the bebop revolution of the early 1940s, it was not surprising that saxophonists, particularly Sonny Rollins and John Coltrane, bore the brunt of the critical attack. Both Rollins and Coltrane (who were often linked, in any case) were continually being brought before the critical tribunals for their alleged "harsh" or "bad" or "honking" tones. Implicit here was the doubly untenable assumption that there is something in jazz than can be specified as a "good" or "pleasant" tone, and that the critics were gifted above ordinary mortals in being privy to the knowledge of what constituted such goodness, pleasantness, etc.

Both assumptions, needless to say, would have been highly suspect — had they ever been articulated. That was just it: they never were. This at least partially because the critics did not have the insight to see that their assumptions were only assumptions; and as such, vulnerable in the extreme. The notion that there is a single standard of goodness in art is hardly likely to find many adherents among those familiar with the checkered evolution of the arts in Europe and the United

---

* As remarked, this same feature was also present in the avant-garde revolution associated with John Coltrane, Ornette Coleman, Cecil Taylor, and others, as several chapters in this volume attempt to bring out. The innovations of Coltrane, Coleman and their followers were widely and repeatedly derogated as "antijazz," out-of-tune and aimless meanderings, deplorable lapses of taste, and the like. In sum, these accusations meant only that European values (e.g., of tone, of adherence to the dodecaphonic scale, of propriety and decorum among the white middle class) were being sacrificed to the development of indigenous Afro-American ones. Such a development, however, inevitably ran afoul of the pro-European biases of the critics, as manifested by their persistent assertion that pianist Thelonious Monk plays "wrong" notes (wrong to *whom,* one wonders?) and their preference for facile but shallow European-oriented players (pianist Oscar Peterson, saxophonist Charles Lloyd) over more profound non-European-oriented improvisers (Monk, John Coltrane).

States since the Renaissance; even fewer still are likely to support the position that momentarily prevailing critical dicta
are to be taken as anything approaching Instant Enlightenment or Revealed Truth. And if this is true of European art,
where major stylistic changes take place perhaps once every
generation, how much more must we insist on a measure of
critical caution in jazz, where a given style may hold sway
for as little as five or ten years before yielding to its successor?* Not that these considerations in the least fazed the critics
of the 1950s, who continued virtually as one to insist on the il-
legitimacy of the playing of Rollins and Coltrane, until a mass
shift in popular tastes literally forced many of them to give
way. (Interestingly enough, a number of critics at that point
dropped into oblivion, along with the cool/West Coast heroes
they had persisted in championing until the very end.)
What in fact was at the base of the critical rejection of hard
bop was, as I have stated, its deviation from white-defined,
Europe-oriented, standards of timbre, inflection, attack, and
so forth as elaborated during the preceding cool period. Some
of the reviews of hard-bop players, saxophonists especially,
made the criteria for criticism almost embarassingly clear.
Thus Nat Hentoff could write as late as 1957 that

> Coltrane's tone is often strident at the edges [implicit
> assumption: stridency is bad] and rarely appears to
> sustain a legato softness [obviously good], as Getz
> can [Stan Getz, a white cool saxophonist].
>
> Coltrane has a feeling for variegated moods, but
> his tone doesn't yet display enough [??] range and
> control of coloration when he expresses gentler, more
> complex feelings [i.e., Coltrane is too bestial].
>
> Another horn—a gentler trumpeter, say—would have
> helped complement the not always attractive [to whom?]
> Coltrane sound. . . .9

To the critical mind, hard bop sinned not only in abandoning
accepted procedures, but in abandoning white ones for black.
   Critics or no, however, the hard-bop revulsion from the
tepidity of cool/West Coast jazz could not be contained. As

---

* Because the technology and mass distribution of the phonograph
record makes for more rapid dissemination of artistic innovations
than was possible, until very recently, in the European arts of painting, sculpture, music, literature, theatre, and the like.

cool grew increasingly inbred and passionless, its inability
to fashion a music of any emotional substance emerged with
greater and greater clarity; especially when juxtaposed against
the infinitely more demonstrative and muscular hard-bop styles.
The result was not long in doubt. Some cool musicians attempted to swim with the new tide; most were unable to retool their
style; and in either event, the massive shift in taste that was
heralded by Miles Davis's *Walkin'* in 1954 soon made it clear
that all but a few cool stylists had fallen permanently from
public favor. A decade and a half later, the only cool figure
of major stature to retain a following of some size is Stan
Getz — and even he has revamped his playing to incorporate
some ideas from black saxophonists John Coltrane and Sonny
Rollins. The other cool players, as remarked above, have
mostly either left music entirely or retreated into the economically secure but musically trite haven of the recording studios.

The subsequent evolution of hard bop is greatly instructive
from the standpoint of our effort to lay bare the nature of the
connection between jazz and the black community. The name
hard bop, to begin with, was probably not that of the black
musicians themselves, but of some reviewer or album-notes
writer faced with the problem of understanding a style new
and strange to him. The artists directly involved, on the other
hand, had a variety of titles for their art, the first of which
was *funky*. Right here we commence to have our noses rubbed
in (if that be what it takes to produce understanding) the black
roots of the anticool revolt. Funky is a piece of Afro-American
argot; at its most literal, it means dirty, smelly, with particular
reference to odors said (by blacks and whites) to be found
especially in the ghetto. But black Americans, as possessors of
a separate culture with the necessity of defending it from the
depredations of hostile surroundings, have long since perfected
the art of remaking the English language into a new tongue
to serve exclusively black needs.

Thus black musicians, for instance, had earlier subverted the
word bad into its dialectical opposite, a term of approbation:
"Man, that cat is *bad!*" In its jazz usage, funky, obviously
enough, represented an extension of this tradition. To describe
a musician as funky — i. e., unwashed, repellent — meant that
he was *worse* (that is, better) than just *bad* — he was . . . *funky*.
But beyond this, funky was a uniquely *black* idiom; like many
"foreign" words and phrases (*chozzerei, schlemiel, mensch,
mazel tov,* and others in Yiddish) it has no precise equivalent
in standard English. Hence to call a composition, a passage,

or a player funky was not only to offer praise in general, but a means of lauding the object of praise for its *specifically black qualities*. A black musician might admire, say, one of Beethoven's symphonies; he might even enthuse over the composer as "a bad cat"; but it is highly doubtful that it would ever occur to him to refer to any of the music as funky. That particular term would in all events be reserved for artists who were expressing their ideas in a particularly Afro-American idiom. The fact that the black artists who comprised the first wave of the anticool revolt choose to call their style of playing funky is therefore of the greatest significance. It immediately proclaimed: "Look! This is *our* music — a product arising from *our* experience, and only our experience." Black audiences did not have to have the new connotation of the word explained to them; they knew, or could feel, readily enough what the musicians were striving to convey. White audiences, by contrast, were another matter entirely, as the profusion of articles in the jazz press devoted to explicating funk — the word and the style — bore eloquent testimony.

Funky, in its turn, was succeeded by *soul* as the name for post-cool black music. In no sense, however, should this process of simple replacement be regarded as a repudiation, as funky had been a repudiation of cool. Rather, two other social forces were at work in bringing about the change. There is, first of all, even under ordinary circumstances, a fairly rapid turnover rate in ghetto argot. The black urban subculture is one that greatly prizes verbal agility and other forms of public display; nothing could be a clearer demonstration of squareness than the use of yesterday's hip term (or dance or clothing style) today. The consequence is the continuous obsolescence of a portion of the spoken idiom of the ghetto, especially that of the jazz musician, who, as one of the acknowledged shapers of ghetto taste, is looked to as a source of new styles, both musical and otherwise. * Besides this built-in search for innovation, words describing styles in jazz — or in any other field of popular culture — are particularly subject to rapid debasement, as first the merchandisers, and then the media, seek out such terms and quickly convert them to catchphrases and then into hideously unbearable cliches. As album after album with "funky" some-

---

* Miles Davis, for instance, has long been a sartorial pacesetter. Fashions that he inaugurates will soon begin to appear on other musicians, even spilling over into the consumption habits of nonblack youths. The revival of the double-breasted suit is a vivid case in point: the first such suit that I saw worn in the 1960s draped the lithe figure of the trumpeter during a San Francisco engagement.

where in the title was released, the more sensitive musicians naturally began to recoil from use of the word, until it died an early — and yet by that time wholly unmourned — death. Such linguistic overkill has not been unique to jazz. More recently, we have seen terms from the vocabulary of rock 'n' roll and youth culture in general undergo an equally accelerated evolution, as witness the rapid demise of "folk-rock" and "psychedelic" (a word that no one I know can use any longer, save in inverted commas, without blushing), to name but two. In any event, faced with the lightning-like preemption of "funky" by the recording companies, black musicians responded by moving to "soul" to describe what was in essence the same style.

There can hardly be any doubt, certainly not in 1969, that *soul* in some loose but inclusive way has reference to the Afro-American experience, and in that sense is virtually identical with "funky" as a descriptive term. After all, has it not been observed that in every urban insurrection of the 1960s, black businessmen have written the words "soul brother" in large letters on the windows of their establishments in order to have them spared by the insurgents? And in the magazines devoted to chronicling the vagaries of the entertainment industry — *Billboard, Variety, Cash Box,* and others — the phrase "soul music" is used as an euphemism for popular music performed by black artists (or their white imitators). * These things (others could be added) make it clear that soul and funky were at root synonymous, the only significant difference being that soul has apparently come into general usage from the Afro-American church (it can be found quite frequently, for example, in the rhetoric of the late Dr. King), and as such was sometimes employed by musicians who wished to make explicit reference to the musical traditions of that church (as when, for instance, bassist Charles Mingus titled a composition intended as an evocation of a prayer meeting in a black working-class church, *Better Git It In Your Soul*). In the main, however, "soul" was invoked to demarcate a music that was black in sensibility and point of origin. Numerous were the interviews during the late fifties that stressed that only those who "had soul" could play in the soul style, and that these were "soul brothers" — a thinly-veiled assertion that the most authentic jazz stylists were Afro-American. (The assertion had to be made in a concealed, Aesopian form, because of the hostility of the white press to any more overt claims.)

It should be kept in mind that the funky-soul trend in jazz

---

* The earlier phrase was the much more blunt "race music."

was occurring in synchrony with the heating up of what was then called the civil-rights movement; and that, in fact, the latter was, as stated at the outset of this section, one of the decisive historical developments in bringing about the funky-soul rebellion from cool playing styles. The easiest way to demonstrate the truth of this proposition, and also at the same time to bring out the continuity that underlay funky and soul jazz, is to consider a representative selection of titles given by black artists to their creations. What we shall see is that, taken en masse, these titles are strong evidence for the growth of (to use today's term) cultural nationalism among blacks. Though not explicitly either nationalist or political in nature, nonetheless, such works testify to the rising pride in blackness of Afro-American jazz artists. For convenience, and not altogether arbitrarily, I have grouped the titles into two classifications.

1. *Afro-American themes:* Included under this rubric are all compositions which deal with anything specifically and uniquely black, whether pertaining to the Afro-American religious experience (examples: *The Sermon, The Preacher, Right Down Front*), manifestos of cultural pride (*Bronze Dance, Black Diamond, Dis Hyeah* ["this here" in the dialect of the streets]), references to black history (*Work Song*, an attempted recreation of the singing of slaves in the antebellum South), panegyrics to leaders in the struggle for black liberation (Max Roach's composition *Garvey's Ghost**), and so on. To be emphasized with particular vigor is that very few if any titles of this nature were to be found prior to 1954 or 1955, and even after that date similar titles were almost never (i.e., in fewer than a dozen instances) either devised or recorded by white musicians. There seemed to be operative, that is, an unspoken consensus that titles with words such as funky, and soul, titles that dealt with the Afro-American church, and titles invoking some particular aspect of the black experience were to be reserved for blacks alone. **

---

* Which earned for its composer the following critical comment: "Roach's search for racial heroes has led him into some strange positions: . . . *Garvey's Ghost* is heroic and grandiose in conception and feeling, giving rise to a picture *oddly at variance with what is known* [to whom?] *of his 'leadership.'*" Emphasis added; *Down Beat's Jazz Record Reviews,* vol. VI, p. 146.) Thus spake white criticism.

** To the degree that the equation between funk, soul and other related themes and the black musician were accepted, to that degree

A partial listing of such titles, obtained from a rapid perusal
of the jazz press for the five years between 1957 and 1961,
is, in addition to the foregoing, as follows: *Moanin'* (the prayer
of a black worshipper); *Justice* (a play on the popular "standard" *Just You, Just Me* – just us = justice; but also an obvious
"protest" theme, as in the Nation of Islam's call for Freedom,
Justice and Equality); *Original Faubus Fables; Filthy McNasty*
(who is clearly very funky); *Doin' the Thing* (argot); *Soultrane*
(dedicated to John Coltrane); *Cookin'* (a black musicians'
term for swinging); *Plenty, Plenty Soul; Sermonette* (black
church); *Barrel of Funk; Ezz-thetic* (written for a black culture-
hero, prizefighter Ezzard Charles); *Talk that Talk* (i.e., speak
in black argot); *Big Hunk of Funk; No Smokin'* (meaning
its opposite, smokin' = cookin' = swinging); *Soulville: Home
Cookin'* (a play on words; see the entry for *Cookin'*, above);
Funk Oats: Dat Dere (= "that there"; see entry for *Dis Hyeah*,
above); *Them Dirty* (= funky) *Blues* (i.e., a particularly black
way of playing the blues); *Waltz de Funk; Head Shakin'*
(what you do when listening to soul jazz); *Funk Mama; Amen*
(church); *Free* (what blacks want most to be); *It's Time* (for
liberation); *Little Brother Soul; In a Funky Groove; Workin'*
(=cookin'); *Down Home* (in the South; also a way of playing
=funky); *Opus de Funk; Soul Junction; Soul Me; The Message*
(analogous to *The Sermon*); *Sister Salvation* (church); *Wednes-
day Night Prayer Meeting; Cryin' Blues; My Jelly Roll Soul;*

---

would the black musician—for once—possess an economic advantage
over his white counterpart. For if funk or soul were indeed to be
considered the essence of jazz, and if only blacks were privy to experiences that allowed the expression of funk/soul, then clearly white
musicians would be rendered superfluous. Such considerations, consciously or otherwise, must surely have played a part in sustaining
the funk-and-soul phenomenon. On the other hand, many white cool
musicians—Stan Getz, Barney Kessel, Bud Shank, Herbie Mann,
Shorty Rogers, Cal Tjader, Laurindo Almieda, Charlie Byrd—excluded by definition from the funk-soul school, attempted to retaliate
with a weapon that whites *could* master, the bossa nova. Though it
did enjoy a brief spurt of popularity simultaneous with the zenith
of soul styles, the bossa nova fad quickly played itself out and made
little lasting impression on the music. Interestingly enough in the
light of the suggested antithesis between Afro-American funk-soul
and white bossa nova, almost no black musicians participated in
the latter craze (the only one who comes to mind is Cannonball
Adderly, who wrote one quasi-bossa nova piece, *Jive Samba*; Cannonball's aesthetic, it should be kept in mind, has always been attuned
largely to satisfying the current demands of the marketplace.)

Blue Soul; Dig Dis (ghetto vernacular); *Soul Station; Big Fat Mama* (a particular type of black woman); *Soul Searchin';
Sister Sadie* (a member of the church, whence springs the custom of addressing women as "sister," men as "brother"); *The Nitty Gritty; Soul Sister* (related to *Sister Sadie*, above); *Soul Brother; Soul Meeting; The Prophet* (the Honorable Elijah Muhammad, head of the Nation of Islam, or "Black Muslims"); *Miss Ann* (wife of Mr. Charlie, as in James Baldwin's play, *Blues for Mr. Charlie*); *Yes, I'll Be Ready* (for freedom; described by the reviewer as "another one of those gospel-inspired numbers"); *Black Groove; Like Church* (music); *Funk Underneath; Sack Full of Soul; Filet of Soul; Hog Callin' Blues; Devil Women* (voodoo survivals); *Eculsiastics* (church); *Hip to It* (black vernacular); *Con Alma* (translation: with soul); *Bowl of Soul* (to be consumed, presumably, with filet of soul); *Ribs an' Chips* (soul food).

2. *African themes:* In addition to giving their pieces names that in some way or other related to Afro-American culture, many black musicians made their consciousness of ethnic heritage explicit by using African-derived titles. In this connection, there are two points to be made. First, the pro-African orientation of the black jazz musicians — beginning in the early 1950s with saxophonist Sonny Rollins's composition *Airegin* (to be read, with typical Rollins unpredictability, backwards) — was visible long before that of the black community as a whole. The same is true of Afro-American cultural consciousness in general. Secondly, since there never evolved an African "school" of playing in the same way that there was a funky/soul school, no particular material rewards could be anticipated by the jazz musician who chose an African title for his composition or album, hence no question of extraneous motivation can possibly be raised in using such titles as an index to the growth of nationalist feelings among black musicians. The first such "African" title that I am aware of is, as mentioned above, Rollins's *Airegin;* note also in this context that Rollins, like John Coltrane, was recorded through the intervention of Miles Davis and was, with Davis and Coltrane, a symbolic leader of the hard bop/funky/soul movement. Other titles from the years 1957-1961 include: *Ritual* (according to the reviewer, "a vividly presented [Art] Blakey composition, based on his knowledge of African tribal music" *); Dakar: Tanganyika Strut: Africa;*

---

* The review continues: "On the track preceding it, Blakey speaks for two minutes on the African origins and inspiration for the composition. Then he digs in."

African Lady; Bantu; Uhuru; Kwanza; Kucheza Blues; African Violets; Katanga; Dahomey Dance; Message from Kenya; Man From South Africa (Nobel Laureate Albert Luthuli); *Effendi; African Waltz.* As with the selections whose titles refer to Afro-American themes, the frequency of African-inspired names roughly increases with time after 1955.

All these selections with Afro-American and African titles bear witness to the growth of what is now conventionally called cultural nationalism among blacks. They demonstrate, that is, the increasing sense of cultural self-awareness and pride in heritage of Afro-Americans in the last decade and a half. As such, however, this new awareness and pride is not inherently political in nature; it need not, for instance, be expressed in formulations calling for a radical restructuring of the society — a separate black state, say, or collective ownership by black people of all the economic resources within their communities. Cultural nationalism of this stripe may indeed go no further than the current "black is beautiful" slogan.

In jazz, it is possible to discern with some precision the cresting of the cultural nationalist wave around 1961-1962, with a pair of compositions: pianist Randy Weston's *Uhuru Afrika* (Freedom Africa, 1961) and saxophonist Oliver Nelson's *Afro-American Sketches* (1962). Both suites were essentially celebratory; the former was described by one white critic as "just a warmly felt tribute to the new African nations by Afro-American musicians," * the latter was a musical version of Afro-American history from the time of slavery and before (titles included: *Message; Jungleaire; Emancipation Blues; There's a Yearnin'; Going Up North; Disillusioned; Freedom Dance*). Beyond this point it was not possible to go — at least not in a purely cultural nationalist vein. Once it has been proclaimed that black is indeed beautiful, the pinnacle of cultural nationalism has been reached; there is nothing more to do save to repeat the message — and no message can bear more than a certain amount of repetition — or to progress to something new. The majority of the musicians who were contemporary with Randy Weston and Oliver Nelson had no other message to offer; and after *Uhuru Afrika* and *Afro-American Sketches*, it started to emerge clearly that the cultural nationalist, black-is-beautiful approach had yielded about all of which it was capable. The result, predictably enough, was an impasse in musical as well as sociopolitical terms (the two ordinarily

---

* White readers were further reassured that "there is no racism [sic] of any kind involved here."

march hand in hand in jazz, as this essay has sought to
illustrate). Soul and funk recordings continued to be issued, but
by 1962 or thereabouts the spontaneity and vitality of funk-
soul had been pretty thoroughly depleted through overexposure.

It remained for a younger group of black jazz artists to
break the impasse by going beyond simple affirmation of black
values to *negation*. Negation, as Herbert Marcuse has shown
in his classic study of Hegel and Marx, [10] is at the root of the
dialectical method; whether or not the young black jazz players
of the 1960s were conscious dialecticians (some were), negation
of the status quo — in music and the social order alike — was
nevertheless their starting point. Inasmuch as a detailed examination of that two-pronged negation forms the body of this
work, there is no need for me to go into it now. In order not
to leave my readers with a mistaken impression, however, it
should be observed that, even as cultural nationalism held
sway, there were attempts by established musicians to get past
its limitations to work out the basis for a new and more viable
musical-political synthesis. These musicians — chiefly, drummer
Max Roach, saxophonist Sonny Rollins, bassist Charles Mingus — are not properly grouped with the present generation of
innovators; they are, rather, among the sources of its spiritual
inspiration. They stand in relation to the Archie Shepps, Albert
Aylers and Pharoah Sanderses of the late 1960s as Babeuf and
the Conspiracy of Equals stood to the Communist movement
of Marx and Engels's day: a foretaste of the *political* radicalism that was to come.

Sonny Rollins first, then. In 1958 he recorded for Riverside an album entitled *The Freedom Suite,* one half of which
was devoted to the *Suite* itself, a musical depiction of the Afro-
American struggle for liberation from oppression. In the notes
to the album (unfortunately, my copy has been lost, so I must
write from memory), Rollins was quoted as saying that despite the fact that Afro-American contributions were at the base
of this country's popular music and humor, black people had
never even begun to receive the appropriate recognition or
rewards for their achievement. Evidently, these remarks (which
were really fairly innocuous) caused such a furor that Riverside pulled *The Freedom Suite* off the market and reissued it
with a new title: *Shadow Waltz,* the name of the second-short-
est piece on the recording. For the reissue, moreover, anno-
tator-producer Orrin Keepnews, half-owner of the Riverside
firm, wrote a new set of notes which went to great lengths
to deny that the *Freedom Suite* had any particular relevance

to black people; instead, according to Keepnews, notwithstanding the saxophonist's own diametrically opposed statements, Rollins had in mind the problem of freedom "in general" when he composed the *Suite*! It probably surprised no one when the *Freedom Suite* turned out to be Sonny Rollins's final recording for the Riverside label.*

There was no single event as dramatic as Sonny Rollins's *Freedom Suite* incident in the career of Charles Mingus, though he was reputed to be hostile to whites — wouldn't you be? — and noted for his outspokenness. (I, along with what I assume to be numerous other white critics, have been the recipient of letters from him filled with scathing denunciations.) One year, in combination with Max Roach, he attempted to set up a counterfestival to protest the blatantly antiartistic circus known as the Newport Jazz Festival. Like that of Roach, Mingus's band was a haven for young iconoclasts — Eric Dolphy, Joe Farrell, Richard Williams, Ted Curson, Roland Kirk, Mal Waldron, Paul Bley, to mention a few — many of whom went on, or would have gone on had they lived (Dolphy died prematurely), to lustrous careers. Finally, to complete the indictment, the bassist began his own recording company, so that he would no longer have to suffer the fate of a pawn in the game of the white-controlled jazz record industry. It may be sheer coincidence, of course, but after all this Mingus has not worked in jazz for several years. Why? Those who know, aren't talking; and the jazz press, as could have been anticipated, has shown not the least glimmer of interest in pursuing the story. In any case, Mingus's later career, like Sonny Rollins's *Freedom Suite*, for many years stood — and was perhaps intended to stand — as an object lesson for any musician rash enough to voice a nationalist ideology that calls into question the reigning deities of the status quo.**

---

* The story has a sequel. Several years later, Riverside went into bankruptcy proceedings and its catalog was ultimately purchased by ABC Records, which then proceeded to reissue selected items from it. One of these was *Freedom Suite/Shadow Waltz*, for which I had the privilege of writing yet the third set of album notes. It gave me immense pleasure to recount in detail therein the cravenness of Riverside's management in exercising political censorship over the work of one of the country's foremost black artists.

** I was able to verify that Charles Mingus himself sees the business structure of the music as responsible for keeping him unemployed, which is at least supportive evidence for the thesis I advance. A rare

The same could be said with equal validity of Max Roach, who, like Mingus, has been missing from the jazz circuit in recent years—with no explanation either sought or offered by the jazz press, let it be once more added. Of all the musicians prior to the present generation, Roach—with Mingus, an original bebop innovator—was the single most unabashedly radical nationalist in jazz. Roach's recording, with his wife, singer Abbey Lincoln, of *We Insist: The Freedom Now Suite,** followed by Miss Lincoln's *Straight Ahead* album, was undoubtedly a turning point in the historical evolution of political black nationalism in jazz, for both, but especially the latter, openly espoused what was then (1961) the dominant strain of political black nationalism, the separatist philosophy of Elijah Muhammad and the Nation of Islam (there were at the time rumors that the drummer and his wife had affiliated with the NOI, but these were never confirmed).

The aftermath was a genuine tempest in a teapot, a "scandal" that rocked the provincial world of jazz—or rather, the provincial world of white jazz critics—from one end to the other. *Down Beat,* the principal jazz magazine of the day, brought virtually all its guns to bear on the Roach-Lincoln duo, and there were more articles, reviews, panel discussions, and whatnot expended on the bogus subjects of "reverse racism," "Crow Jim," and the like, than I ever remember being devoted to such a *genuine* issue as inferior treatment of black artists by white establishments (hotels, nightclubs, etc.) during my entire tenure with that publication.** It goes almost without saying that

---

personal appearance at the *Both/And* club in San Francisco early in October, 1969, gave me the opportunity to raise this point with the bassist. In our conversation, he repeatedly came back to the booking agents as those whose ill will had denied him work. The booking agent functions as a middleman between artist and employer, and is therefore in a position to gratify both his likes and his dislikes. Literally, it does not pay to incur the wrath of too many of their number. And, of course, all the major agents of whom I have heard are white.

* As an instance of how developments in jazz presage those in the black community as a whole, the title of the Roach-Lincoln suite, *Freedom Now,* became the name of a political black nationalist party in 1964. The *Suite* itself was recorded in 1961.

** For instance, Ira Gitler, the critic assigned by *Down Beat* to review Miss Lincoln's *Straight Ahead* album, denounced her as a "professional Negro," adding that he considered her "misguided and naive," since "we don't need the Elijah Muhammad type of think-

virtually all of this vast expanse of print was utter rubbish.
Blacks, musicians or otherwise, had given no indication of
wishing to subjugate or oppress whites because of their color;
and even if they had, they lacked the power to carry out such
designs and were not about to obtain it within the near future.
But to refute the charges brought by *Down Beat* against Roach
and Miss Lincoln is to dignify spurious charges by investing them
with a patina of rationality. In point of fact, what the staff of
Down Beat was concerned with was less the *substance* of the
Roach-Lincoln protest than its simple *existence.* Regardless of
whether what Roach and Miss Lincoln had said was true or false,
racist or nonracist, relevant or irrelevant, the pair themselves
had to be suppressed or, at the very least, discredited — again,
as in the case of Charles Mingus, for the "benefit" of those
black musicians who just might be foolhardy enough to harbor
similar heretical tendencies of their own. In one sense, these
tactics of vilification and harassment "worked": as was earlier remarked, not much has been seen of the Roach-Lincoln
group of late. In another sense, though, the tactics were a
complete failure. The spread of radical political ideas, especially those associated with black nationalism, was not — could
not be — stemmed. Today, I know from my own interviews
with young black musicians, that radical nationalist ideas
are common coin not only among them but among many
young whites as well (three of whom I have interviewed: trombonist Roswell Rudd, bassist David Izenson, saxophonist Frank
Smith).

Of course the spread of political nationalist ideas among
young black artists can be understood only in the context
of the steady growth of nationalism itself in the ghetto, as

---

ing in jazz" (*Down Beat Record Reviews,* vol. VI, pp. 229-30). A
more flagrant attempt at political repression by what is ostensibly
a music magazine would be difficult to conceive of. See also the
contribution of Gitler and others in a panel discussion, "Race Prejudice in Jazz: It Works Both Ways," *Down Beat,* March 15 and 29,
1962; the letters of Gitler, Martin Williams, Don Schlitten, Willis Conover (who runs the Voice of America jazz program), and others
to *Jazz* magazine during the latter half of 1965 and first half of 1966;
and Gitler's baiting of LeRoi Jones in a letter to the editor of *Down
Beat,* September 9, 1966, for additional instances of the antiradicalism and antinationalism of the white critics.

Not long after the controversy centering around Roach and Miss
Lincoln erupted, political and artistic censorship at *Down Beat* reached
such intolerable levels that both Ralph Gleason and this writer were
compelled in good conscience to resign from its staff.

illustrated by the increasing appeal of the Nation of Islam prior to the split between Elijah Muhammad and Malcolm X, the immediate support for Malcolm's Organization of Afro-American Unity up until the time of his assassination, the formation of the all-black Freedom Now Party for the 1964 elections, and, most recently, the steady swell of the membership rolls of the Black Panther Party, notwithstanding the most vicious and violent repression by the police. I have not gone into detail regarding these developments because I assume they are well enough known to the reader. Nonetheless, it would be well to keep them in mind, as a kind of historical counterpoint to the narrative that follows this introduction. In no other way will we be able to comprehend the early maturation of both cultural and political nationalist ideologies within the hothouse environment of the jazz world.

The last point is directly germane to the purpose of this portion of the introduction — to give backing to the assertion that there is an intimate relationship between the black community as such and the smaller jazz milieu, a relationship that exerts its influence on jazz by helping to shape the course of the music's evolution (aesthetically and sociopolitically). The larger issue at stake, as raised at the outset of this section, was whether it could be concluded that the black community offers physical and moral support for jazz. I have not sought to "prove" the affirmative in any quantitative way, because, as already stated, my feeling is that such attempts were bound to be fallible, and therefore futile. On the other hand, having surveyed the unprecedented upsurge of cultural nationalist ideas in jazz following the release of Miles Davis's *Walkin'* in 1954, it seems clear to me that to deny the two-way flow between the jazz world and the black ghetto would leave us at a total loss as to how to explain this impressive flowering of nationalist sentiments. On that statement I am prepared to rest my case.

III

Through the years, as I've listened to music and collected records, I think it's a very simple deduction that the music is Negro music to begin with; and for these guys [critics] to write about the music as though it's an American music, that everybody plays equally, and that we all love one another and we're all brothers —

to me, really, that's a lot of horseshit. I mean, I read critics even today in 1968 who say that in the old days, the Negro musicians were never unhappy and they didn't complain about the social conditions in the country, I think they forget that in those days it just wasn't done. A Negro musician just couldn't come out and say, "Hey! the situation stinks."

Bob Thiele, producer from 1961 to 1967 for the late John Coltrane

Jazz has no particular social content; specifically, it in no way pertains more closely to black experiences, perceptive modes, sensibilities, than it does to white. Jazz is not "protest music" and black jazz musicians have been either unwilling to or incapable of concerning themselves with social issues. These propositions comprise the final argument in the divine trinity that guides most white jazz critics in the discharge of their craft.

Since even the most refractory of white critics has had to recognize the Afro-American foundations of funky and soul jazz (too many black musicians made the point too explicitly for any other course to be feasible), the usual critical bit of sleight-of-hand consists of making the concession for the post-cool period, only so that it can better be retracted for the remainder of the history of jazz. Of course, not every period in the evolution of jazz is as unmistakably nationalist as were the immediate post-cool period and its successors. Nevertheless, as the preceding section sought to show, there is an intense cross-pollination process that goes on between jazz and the black community, the net effect of which is to guarantee that jazz — the music and the musicians — will either anticipate or reflect the mood, concerns, and aspirations of Afro-Americans. It is just this thesis that white jazz critics go out of their way to deny.

By way of illustration, I will quote from a letter written by one of their number, Ira Gitler, during the course of a heated exchange with the author; it should be kept firmly in mind, however, that there is nothing whatsoever unique about Gitler's views, and that if we substituted for his name that of almost any other prominent white critic — Leonard Feather, John S. Wilson, Martin Williams, Gene Lees (a past editor of *Down Beat*), Willis Conover — the outcome would not be significantly different.

One of the subjects of my dispute with Gitler was what I

called the "obvious social implications" of the bebop revolution in jazz; to buttress my argument, I pointed to the title of a Charlie Parker blues, *Now's the Time*. The bebop movement, it should be remembered, took place during the years of World War II, which saw Afro-American workers organize for a massive March on Washington for equal employment opportunities; the insurrections in Harlem and Detroit; the "Double-V campaign" for victory over racism at home as well as abroad; "innumerable clashes both on and off the military posts" as black servicemen protested Jim Crow treatment;[11] the work stoppage of Afro-American Seabees to compel a cessation of racist propaganda issued by the U. S. government ("yellow-bellied Japs") as a means of whipping up sentiment for the war in the Pacific; the involvement of Afro-Americans with the formation of the United Nations as an organization that could conceivably intervene in the struggle against racism in the United States, Union of South Africa, and elsewhere — all these and other developments were contemporaneous with the genesis of bebop. It was because of them that I was fairly confident that the title of Charlie Parker's *Now's the Time* meant just what it said it meant: now's the time to abolish racism, discrimination, oppression and Jim Crow. Gitler's reply to my point is both representative of his peers and instructive: "I deny the 'obvious social implication.' The title refers to the music and the 'now' was the time for the people to dig it."[12]

Now it is not outside the pale of possibility that the title of Parker's piece did have the meaning that Gitler assigned to it; but if so, it had this meaning only in addition to the one that I have supplied — or so I have been assured by every black musician with whom I have ever discussed the question (the most frequent occurrence, incidentally, is simply for the musician to burst into laughter when Gitler's statement is read). For the fact of the matter is, as the widely respected British economic historian E. J. Hobsbawm (writing pseudonymously as Francis Newton) has asserted, that "race relations" is "a factor in the coloured jazz musician's life which has steadily grown in *conscious* importance" [emphasis added]. "No bar of coloured jazz," he continues, "has ever made sense to those who do not understand the Negro's reaction to oppression." Especially was this the case after the 1930s, when the "political awakening of all the oppressed and underprivileged . . . put a new tone" into the black musician's instrument: "open resentment." Thus "from the late thirties the coloured jazz musician became increasingly ambitious, both to establish his superiority over the white musician . . . and to raise the status of his music . . . ." [13]

For the reasons adduced by Hobsbawm, there can be little question among serious students of the music that jazz has inevitably functioned not solely as music, but also as a vehicle for the expression of outraged protest at the oppression of Afro-Americans as a people and the specific exploitation to which the jazz musician, as black artists, have been perennially subjected *in an art of their own creation*. Nor is there much room to doubt, Gitler to the contrary notwithstanding, that the "open resentment" of which Hobsbawm writes was an important consideration in bringing about the bebop revolution of the 1940s. A black bebop musician thus confided in the German critic Joachim Ernst Berendt:

> You see, we need music; we've always needed a music — our own. We have nothing else. Our writers write like the whites, our painters paint like them, our philosophers think like them. Only our musicians don't play like the whites. So we created a music for ourselves. When we had it — the old type of jazz — the whites came, and they liked it and imitated it. Pretty soon it was no longer our music . . . .
>
> You see, as soon as we have a music, the white man comes and imitates it. We've now had jazz for fifty years, and in all those fifty years there has been not a single white man, perhaps leaving aside Bix [Beiderbecke], who has had an idea. Only the coloured men have ideas. But if you see who's got the famous names, they're all white.
>
> What can we do? We must go on inventing something new all the time. When we have it, the whites will take it from us, and we have to start all over again. It is as though we were being hunted. [14]

Bebop can therefore be viewed in its social aspect as a manifesto of rebellious black musicians unwilling to submit to further exploitation. Unfortunately, this manifesto had to be proclaimed primarily in musical terms and its social correlates left tacit — a situation that today allows Ira Gitler to maintain that *Now's the Time* had only musical implications. As is made clear by the quote at the head of this section from (white) producer-executive Bob Thiele, whose career in music spans three decades, blacks, artists or not, were until very recently not permitted to speak out regarding their own plight or that of their people; in Thiele's words: "in those days it just wasn't done. A Negro musician just couldn't come out and say, 'Hey! the situation stinks.'" [15] In consequence, a black musician learned to resort to subterfuges. The young Afro-American players of the late 1930s had witnessed the fate of the black bands of that decade, and resolved that theirs would be different. As Professor Leslie B. Rout, Jr., has written of the career of black composer Fletcher Henderson: "As early as 1928, this bandleader had worked out the basis of the jazz style known as Swing. By the early thirties he had assembled an outstanding aggregation — but it was still a black orchestra. A compromise of sorts resulted: Benny Goodman became the 'King of Swing' — everywhere except in Harlem and other urban ghettos — and Fletcher Henderson became his chief arranger." The swing bandwagon had ample room for the white orchestras of Glenn Miller, the Dorsey Brothers, Artie Shaw, Woody Herman, and others, despite the fact that, according to Professor Rout, "black powerhouse battalions led by Count Basie, Chick Webb and Jimmy Lunceford . . . played better jazz" while earning "less than half as much as their white counterparts." Nor did the occasional hiring of black musicians by white bandleaders such as Goodman materially improve the situation, in black eyes; instead, it only served to generate "increased black discontent, because from the [black musician's] point of view, acceptance into white orchestras demonstrated how badly black swingsters were needed! Why, then, be satisfied with a few crumbs, while 'Whitey' took cake?" Why indeed? The logical move for black players — especially appropriate by the early 1940s, since "Swing had then passed its inventive peak" — was "the creation of a jazz form that whites could not play! Ideally, this would insure for black jazzmen the recognition they craved, plus a lion's share of the profits." [16]

However esoteric originally, bebop did not accomplish the liberation of the black musician from white plagiarism and expropriation. For one thing, as I have written earlier in this essay, the economic decline of the postwar period made it impossible for the bebop players to consolidate their initial hegemony; and by the time recovery had begun, bebop had been prematurely undermined by the new cool style. The advent of the funky and soul modes of playing was, at least in part, a renewed attempt — and a more explicit one, at that — to establish a black monopoly in the music on a lasting basis. But notwithstanding its greater outspokenness, the funky/soul

approach was not totally successful, though it undoubtedly
did alter somewhat the distribution of rewards within jazz.
(Ironically, many of the white cool players driven out of jazz
with the onset of funk and soul probably earn more now in
the studios, on the West Coast at any rate, than they ever
did from strict jazz playing. Blacks, on the other hand, never
had the refuge of the studios to fall back on when bebop and
the economy collapsed simultaneously; and even in 1969 only
a tiny handful have gained admission to the much-prized studio
work. All of which only goes to underline how convenient it
is to be the possessor of a white skin in this society).

The reasons why funk and soul failed to be more effective
are easy enough to comprehend; some have already been
alluded to. There were, as we have seen, built-in limitations
of the funk/soul movement, arising from the nature of its
cultural nationalist assumptions. That is to say, the thrust and
logic of the funk/soul style was to go past the point of mere
self-affirmation ("black is beautiful") into meaningful action
aimed at negating the (musical and social) status quo. That
step, however, was beyond the resources of the funk/soul movement as a whole; it was only subsequently taken, as the remainder of this work attempts to demonstrate, by the succeeding wave of (for want of a better term) avant-garde innovators,
many of whom are explicitly black nationalist in a *political*
sense.* Meanwhile, any efforts of funky/soul players to maintain their particular style in vogue indefinitely were doomed to
come to naught, as the hallmarks of the movement underwent
the gradual evolution from innovation to painful cliche. Funk
and soul jazz, once a breath of fresh air following the pre-

---

* Since the charge is often made that politically radical black nationalism means nothing more than "Hate whitey!" and that the new
jazz is therefore nothing more than "hate music," it must be emphati-
cally stated that the new music groups, in general the most nationalistically inspired, are also the *most* integrated ones. To be specific,
the bands of Cecil Taylor, Archie Shepp, Marion Brown, Albert
Ayler, and Ornette Coleman—certainly among the leading figures
of the new music—usually have at least one white member. The
analogy for the conventional jazz of this period would be for the
groups of, say, Miles Davis, Dizzy Gillespie, Cannonball Adderly,
Thelonious Monk and Horace Silver to have one white member
apiece, which is not ordinarily the case (though Gillespie, Davis
and Adderly have on occasion hired white sidemen). Here one sees
the difference between the political nationalism of the new musicians
and the cultural nationalism of the funk/soul rebellion against cool.

ciousness of the cool period, ultimately became cloying as the single ingredient on the musical bill of fare. By the nadir of the movement, around 1962-63, the jazz public was avid for a change.

Then, too, it would be extremely naive to think that any given set of purely *musical* innovations would suffice to emancipate black musicians from the grip of white entrepreneurial domination. To bring about a change of that magnitude would necessitate not only aesthetic revolution, but social upheaval as well. Because the funky/soul musicians attempted little or nothing in the social sphere, the preexisting distribution of power was left undisturbed; which meant, of course, that there was no new allocation of the economic benefits. True, the eventual conquest of funky/soul styles very likely did cause some white musicians to leave jazz for greener pastures, and may therefore even have created a modicum of additional work for black artists. But the extent of such gains should not be exaggerated. Jazz tastes are notoriously idiosyncratic: even if Dave Brubeck were never to play another engagement, it is highly improbable that all of his followers would shift their allegiance to, say, Thelonious Monk. What I am arguing is that, regardless of what many black musicians may believe, their suppression is due less to competition from white players than to the fact that ownership of the leading economic institutions of jazz are vested in the hands of entrepreneurs whose preeminent goal is not the enhancement of the art but the taking of a profit. And it will surely continue to be so as long as the artists do not themselves exert any control over the nightclubs, booking agencies, recording companies and, in short, the terms of their collective employment. This contradiction the pioneers of soul and funk never fully faced (whereas, by contrast, several avant-garde players, Cecil Taylor and Bill Dixon most notably, have sought to organize musicians' cooperatives to circumvent the customary white business channels). Consequently, and not surprisingly, their aspiration went

---

Hence even as the Archie Shepps and Cecil Taylors are being denounced — as I have heard them denounced by white nightclub owners, recording executives, and other business personnel — for their ostensible race bias, the hard fact of the integration of their respective groups is conveniently overlooked. The real offense of the new musician, one thus concludes, is not the racism that has been alleged, but that they have the temerity to protest against exploitation and degradation. *That* is the unpardonable sin.

partially unfulfilled, their liberation remained incompletely attained.

The purpose of this section of the introductory essay was
to illustrate the persistent presence of a social content — a *black*
content — within jazz. Contrary to what the white critical consensus has maintained, such a content has been a permanent
feature of the music since the 1930s. More than that. Continuity between the bebop period, the funky/soul period after
1955, and the present avant-garde period can be seen to exist,
in the form of repeated attempts of black musicians to assert
their primacy in an art of their own making. That such efforts
have not been more explicit or visible cannot be interpreted,
as most white critics have done, as the absence of discontent
with the prevailing situation. Rather, the muted or symbolic
nature of black protest within jazz, as the comments of Bob
Thiele should remind us, springs directly out of the economic
conditions that characterize the jazz world — conditions that
have continued to exist to this very day.

The truth is that *there has never been sufficient employment
within jazz to keep all the musicians playing who wanted to
play.* It is as simple as that. The jazz musician, the black musician especially, has always been forced to sell his services
in a buyer's market. The most famous groups and individual
artists can secure all the work they want; their problem is that
they are unable to play every engagement they are offered.
But there have never been more than a dozen or so groups
that fell into this category. The journeyman jazz musician,
on the other hand, is in no such privileged position. He takes
what work he can get and, if not exactly grateful, is at least
relieved to have it; it certainly is an improvement over sorting
mail at the post office, which is the usual alternative. The consequences of this state of affairs ought to be obvious, particularly to any student of the labor movement. It is well known
that unions are virtually never organized successfully during
a period of high unemployment; and for black jazz artists as
a whole, it has almost always been the Great Depression (the
period of World War II is probably the only significant exception).

As a result, the black jazz musician has concluded that he
must be extremely guarded in his utterances if he is to survive, let alone flourish. All he need do — unless he has attained
the status of a Miles Davis or Thelonious Monk, in which case
he can be relatively free from fear of reprisals — is let it be

suspected that he is not quite "right" in some way, and — poof!
— his career has gone up in smoke. For once the entrepreneurial powers-that-be have decided that a black man is unemployable, unemployable he becomes and unemployable he
remains. In all likelihood, this accounts for the recent disap-
pearance from view of Max Roach and Charles Mingus, "bad
niggers" both; and it is as certain as anything can be that it
accounts for the all but complete dearth of the new music in
the established jazz nightclubs, such as *Shelly's Manne-Hole*
in Hollywood.* The constant dread of permanent unemployment — the "average" jazz musician already spends a good deal
of his time without work — is enough to make all but the most
stalwart radicals cautious and equivocal in their public statements.

I have witnessed this often enough with my own eyes. A
black musician will accost me: "Hey, man, I dug your piece
on_____. That was really telling it like it is!" Fine. May
I quote him on this? "Well, man, . . . you know how it is."
If I didn't know before, by the fifth or sixth time this has
happened, I am no longer in ignorance. Or again, I am tape-
recording an interview on the subject of black nationalism and
the jazz avant-garde. The subject of the interview is uneasy.
He mumbles; he scratches; he shuffles his feet; he becomes
extremely uncomfortable. Finally, it emerges: "Look, man,
I told this dude I'd meet him uptown. . . ." These are not
imaginary scenarios; they are not isolated events. Names could
be supplied — but why impose further hardships? Doubtless
the participants involved will recognize themselves, should they
happen to read these pages. I merely wish it to be understood
why the continual undercurrent of protest in jazz has historically
been advanced in a highly convoluted, symbolic, even Aesopian form. [17] After all, black men have been speaking to white

---

* Certainly it is not lack of a potential audience that keeps these
new musicians unemployed. To quote Bob Thiele once more: "You
know, we all try to be realistic and the only reason you make records
is to sell records, and Coltrane happened to sell an awful lot of
records. Most of the musicians in the new movement happen to sell
records, too. I don't say that they sell in the quantities that Coltrane sold, but they do sell records and there is a market for them,
not only in the United States but all over the world" (interview, February 1968). As the former head of Impulse, the ABC Records jazz
subsidiary, and probably the single individual most involved with
the production and sales of recordings by avant-garde black musicians, Thiele's qualifications to speak on this point could scarcely
be improved upon.

in riddles ever since slavery, when *Bye, Bye Blackbird* signaled
the impending departure of a slave via the Underground Railroad. Have we any reason for believing things are substantially different now, or that our treatment of black jazz musicians
has been so generous as to exempt them from the constraints
felt by other Afro-Americans?

Under these circumstances, it took considerable courage for
those black musicians — Archie Shepp, Cecil Taylor, Bill Dixon
are among the most prominent — to speak out for truth and
against injustice — not once, but repeatedly.[18] And, of course,
their careers have suffered because of it — of that there can be
no doubt. One can only hope that someday, in some possible
better future, we will have achieved sufficient humanity to attempt a partial and very inadequate compensation for the dam-
age that has been inflicted, by according these prophets a portion of the honor that they, and those like them, so richly
deserve from their country. Only would that more could be
done now!

IV

I'm saying that essentially there is no difference, as
long as you're black, where you come from; that the
thing that unites us is the sameness in the oppression
that we have undergone at the hand of the white man,
no matter where we are from. That's one of the things
that binds us.

Cecil Taylor

Some of us are more bitter about the way things are
going. We are only an extension of that entire civil
rights-Black Muslims-black nationalist movement that
is taking place in America. That is fundamental to
music.

Archie Shepp

There was a time — and not so long ago, at that — when one
could not begin a book on jazz without an obligatory attempt
at defining it. These definitions were almost invariably worth
next to nothing, however, for what they had in common was
their utter disregard for the well-established dialectical principle
that it is impossible to formulate any static definition that will
contain something so dynamically evolving as jazz (or art,

or life) and yet exclude with finality everything else. Fortunately, I do not consider myself similarly compelled to provide definitions; but I do not see how, in any event, I could possibly improve on Archie Shepp's statement that we ought to regard jazz from the perspective that it is "one of the most meaningful social, esthetic contributions to America. It is that certain people accept it for what it is, that it is a meaningful, profound contribution to America — it is antiwar; it is opposed to Viet Nam; it is for Cuba; it is for the liberation of all people. That is the nature of jazz. That's not far-fetched. Why is that so? Because jazz is a music itself born out of oppression, born out of the enslavement of my people. It is precisely that."[19]

The essays that comprise this book were written between 1961 and 1969, though the earlier ones were updated for publication — when that proved possible — in 1965 and thereafter. Some that have appeared previously — in *Jazz* and *Monthly Review*, primarily — are presented here in somewhat condensed form and with minor revisions, but much of the material is receiving its baptism in print in these pages. All of the writing, I would like to believe, is informed by the point of view that the above quotation from Archie Shepp presents with such eloquence.

In closing, I should like to give the reasons for the inclusion of the final essay, on Malcolm X, in what is nominally a book on music. As Archie Shepp points out in one of the quotations heading this section, the new Afro-American innovations in music "are only an extension of that entire civil rights-Black Muslim-black nationalist movement that is taking place in America. That is fundamental to music." In my own interviews with Afro-American jazz artists, conducted mostly in New York during the last three years, I have consistently found that Malcolm X, as a one-man distillation of the essential nationalist movement, is the single political figure to whom the greatest number of musicians (including some whites) are responsive; he is the one to whom most would dedicate a composition (if they were to dedicate one to anybody at all). Indeed, Archie Shepp's poem, *Malcolm, Malcolm — Semper Malcolm*, on his *Fire Music* album, is among the earliest efforts by an Afro-American artist that I know of to commemorate the assassinated leader; but it will not be, I expect, the last by a black jazz musician, for clearly Malcolm's memory is an inspiration to this generation of black artists; his words come the closest to articulating their needs, their frustrations, their hopes, their problems. Without exaggeration, moreover, it does appear that there is an extraordinary parallel between the curve of Malcolm's personal history — his evolution from dope, numbers, and ghetto racketeering in general to become (in actor Ossie Davis's words) "the shining prince" of black nationalism — and the history of jazz itself during the past two decades. Where Afro-American musicians of the generation of Charlie Parker often fell into the quicksand trap of narcotics addiction, the new breed of black artists has renounced addictive drugs for the more humanizing activity of political commitment. In that sense, jazz as a social creation has taken the same course as that marked out by Malcolm X. *

If young black jazz musicians have been drawn to the image of Malcolm X, it is equally true that Malcolm himself was always attracted to jazz as one expression of the soul of his people. This point has often been overlooked or denied outright by some commentators on his career; but Malcolm himself left the matter in no doubt. In his all-important address to the founding meeting of the Organization of Afro-American Unity (OAAU), June 28, 1964, he made a powerful analogy between the black man's ability to improvise musically and his ability to devise new political and social forms when allowed to function in "an atmosphere of complete freedom where he has the right, the leeway, to bring out of himself all of that dormant, hidden talent that has been there for so long."

> And in that atmosphere, brothers and sisters [Malcolm continued], you'd be surprised what will come out of the bosom of this black man. I've seen it happen. I've seen black musicians when they'd be jamming at a jam session with white musicians — a whole lot of difference. The white musician can jam if he's got some sheet music in front of him. He can jam on something that he's heard jammed before. But that black musician, he picks up his horn and starts blowing some

---

* Thus Professor Stephen E. Henderson writes in "Survival Motion: A Study of the Black Writer and the Black Revolution in America": "What Coltrane signifies for black people because of the breadth of his vision and the incredible energy behind his spiritual quest, Malcolm X signifies in another way — not as musician, but simply and profoundly as black man, as Black Experience, and that experience in the process of discovering itself, of celebrating itself." Mercer Cook and Henderson, *The Militant Black Writer in Africa and the United States,* University of Wisconsin Press, Madison, 1969, p. 110.

sounds that he never thought of before. He improvises,
he creates, it comes from within. It's his soul; it's that
soul music. *It's the only area on the American scene
where the black man has been free to create.* And he
has mastered it. He has shown that he can come up
with something that nobody ever thought of on his
own [emphasis added].

Malcolm's understanding of the musical creative process
among black artists would be a difficult one on which to improve — the above passage could stand unaltered as a perfect
description of the work of John Coltrane or Pharoah Sanders,
for example.

It is fascinating to speculate whether Malcolm's paean to the
creative powers of black musicians was inspired by the presence
of musicians in the audience on that occasion. (We know from
the interview in Chapter 12 that John Coltrane, for one, was
present at one of Malcolm's later speeches.) Be that as it may,
what is abundantly clear, certain writers to the contrary notwithstanding, is that Malcolm had a warm rapport with the
black musician. So much so, indeed, that he could project the
black artist's improvisatory prowess into the political and
social realms, to complete the analogy begun above. The black
person, he believed, could "likewise . . . do the same thing"
as the black musician,

if given intellectual independence. He can come up with
a philosophy that nobody has heard of yet. He can
invent a society, a social system, an economic system,
a political system, that is different from anything that
exists or has ever existed anywhere on this earth. He
will improvise; he'll bring it from within himself. And
this is what you and I want.

You and I want to create an organization that will
give us so much power we can sit down and do as we
please. Once we sit down and think as we please, speak
as we please, and do as we please, we will show people
what pleases us. And what pleases us won't always
please them. So you've got to get some power before
you can be yourself. Do you understand that? Once
you get power and you be yourself, why, you're gone —
you've got it and gone. You create a new society and
make some heaven right here on this earth.

In the light of Malcolm's great symbolic significance for the new generation of black musicians and his own evident identification with the black jazz artist, it strikes me as only fitting to end this book with an essay on him, and this introduction with Archie Shepp's poignant words:

Malcolm, Malcolm – Semper Malcolm

Photo by Frank Kofsky

NORRIS JONES (L), MARION BROWN (R)

PART I

THE SOCIETY, THE MUSIC, THE CRITIC

Photo by Frank Kofsky

JIMMY GARRISON (L), ELVIN JONES (R)

Chapter 1
CRITIQUING THE CRITICS

THE STATE OF JAZZ CRITICISM

*I don't know, by any stretch of the imagination,
how the music I heard that night could be called
musical. . . . I think we're getting away from
musical values that have been established for
centuries.*

Jazz critic Ira Gitler
(In a discussion, "The Jazz Avant Garde: Pro
& Con," *Down Beat Music '65*; ellipsis in original.)

*. . . Art is a means of communication. But it
doesn't try to communicate anguish, horror,
hate and war; it tries to communicate beauty. . . .
[In] art we're trying to create out of the havoc
of living and of the world something beautiful. . . .*
 *What I'm saying is that, when the form and
the content [of art] is [sic] thrown out, the end
result has to be beautiful.*

Jazz critic Don Schlitten
(Also a photographer and record producer,
Schlitten's comments appear in the same discussion as Gitler's; Schlitten is identified by the
editors of *Down Beat* as a man whose "love
and understanding of jazz are deep.")

The immediate occasion of these comments was an article
by Joe Goldberg, "The Personal Basis of Jazz Criticism," which
appeared in *Down Beat* for February 11, 1965; but it should
be added for completeness that some of the ideas advanced

SOME OF THE MATERIAL IN THIS CHAPTER ORIGINALLY APPEARED IN
JAZZ, MAY AND OCTOBER 1965, APRIL AND MAY 1967.

below are those on which I have been mulling for a considerable time.

I would begin by observing that the majority of those who style themselves jazz critics have, until the very recent past, done so despite a lamentably large number of defects in their preparation for that role. Here I am referring not merely to the question of an extensive technical knowledge of music. Such a background neither guarantees that its possessor will utilize it to enhance his reader's critical understanding and appreciation of the music, nor does lack of it automatically disbar the critic from a perceptive appraisal of what he hears. No one, after all, demands that the theatre critic be a successful playwright.

But if a musical education is not an absolute prerequisite to the critical craft, it does not at all follow that there are *no* particularly relevant skills for the would-be critic to acquire. Quite the contrary: it is possible to conceive of numerous ways of apprenticing oneself for a career in criticism. Were all critics possessed of at least a solid grounding in the theory of aesthetics, to take one example, much of the lack of clarity and repetitiousness which characterize critical discussions might readily be avoided. At the very minimum, it should become possible for us to arrive at reasonably meaningful working definitions of terms and a rough consensus as to what should comprise the canons of taste in each historical era of the music.

To this it may be objected — rightly, I should say — that a magazine such as *Down Beat*, which is representative of its species, is not suited to serve as the vehicle for weighty philosophical treatises better left to the academic journals. Very well, then, the point is conceded; still, there are myriad other valuable functions which a perspicacious critic might legitimately be expected to perform. The instance that comes most readily to mind concerns the impending Negro revolution and the simultaneous and related aesthetic revolution taking place in jazz. Now it should be obvious to an observer with even the most rudimentary sociological intuition that these revolutions are interconnected and interdependent. That is to say, rejection of the conventions of bebop, which are perceived by the younger generation of jazz musicians as unnecessarily restrictive, is a manifestation of the same social forces that have produced a repudiation of the values of white middle-class America in the urban ghettos of this country. But if this be the case, do not anticipate seeing it discussed in the pages of any "jazz" magazine. Such topics are too far outside the pale to be encompassed within the parochial confines of jazz journalism (save as they occur in the laconic asides of a LeRoi Jones, an A. B. Spellman, or a Robert Levin).

The exceptions all turn out on closer examination to be of the rule-proving variety: a panel discussion sponsored by *Down Beat* in which Max Roach and Abbey Lincoln (Mrs. Roach) were confronted with a group of white jazz critics, all of whom save one (Nat Hentoff) showed themselves unalterably hostile to, and constitutionally incapable of, understanding black nationalism;[1] an article on *soul* — by a white writer, naturally — two years ago in the same magazine; and more of the same. By no stretch of the imagination can these occasional articles and discussions on jazz and race be accounted an acceptable substitute for a consistent policy of diligent and objective inquiry unmarred by dogmatic preconceptions. And in point of fact, not a single jazz periodical has made an effort to meet this most elementary responsibility to its readership by presenting a broad analysis of the effect of contemporary social developments in the Negro ghettos on jazz.[2]

For that matter, are there more than two or three white writers who have bothered even *to try* and transcend their indoctrination and subjective prejudices to the point where black nationalism appears as something more intelligible than the "reverse Jim Crow" to which it is so ubiquitously equated (and thus dismissed) by the white critical fraternity? Merely to raise the question is to answer it. Judging by the gross manhandling and ludicrous distortions to which LeRoi Jones's *Blues People* was subjected by white reviewers in the jazz press, such men are too thoroughly enslaved by their conditioning and insecurities as white interlopers in a predominantly Negro subculture to recognize reality — even when it glares up at them from the printed page.

That this state of affairs prevails is, as the phrase goes, not accidental. For one thing, consider the institutional restraints operative. How many jazz magazines — or magazines of any sort, as far as that is concerned — are going to jeopardize a segment of their advertising by undertaking a dispassionate appraisal of black nationalism as it pertains to jazz? (To point out the disastrous probable consequences of printing "radical" material, by the way, is not to indulge in any "conspiracy theory" of history; that advertisers exert control over the contents of a periodical, albeit through subtle and often indirect channels, is one of the fixed first principles of the publishing business. Not that such control is all that necessary:

the vast majority of publishers have never distinguished themselves by marked tendencies toward unorthodoxy on questions
of "race relations," economic policies, or what have you.)

But the matter only begins at the publisher's desk; it does
not end there; the jazz critic himself must also be taken into
account. In order to formulate the kind of sociological analysis of jazz and its environment which I have been discussing,
the rank-and-file critic would have to be a vastly different
animal than he is at present. The fact that such an analysis
would require a certain irreducible minimum exposure to the
social sciences — my own preference would be for a combination of sociology and history — in itself suffices to disqualify
easily three-quarters of the practicing jazz critics.

One of the areas in which our knowledge of the sociology
of jazz is most deficient is that dealing with the critic; but from
what we do know, it is probably a safe generalization that the
preponderant number of established critics — those whose names
are recognized by the literate public at large — have graduated
into their present line of endeavor not from a background in
social science or even the humanities, but from journalism.
Their perspective, therefore, most often tends to be the parochial
and narrowly circumscribed one of the reporter, and the white
reporter at that. What such critics are missing in the way of
training, whether musical, philosophical, or sociological, they
attempt to compensate for with raw enthusiasm, usually without even being aware of their deficiencies. Any glimmerings of
their personal inadequacies (as nonmusicians, for example,
or as whites) which threaten to emerge into consciousness are
readily repressed; the attendant insecurities are then dissipated
through a strident display of self-importance and officiousness,
the more vigorously advanced the less the inner certainty. (I
am here reminded of the *Down Beat* correspondent who, when
the management of a prominent jazz festival refused to pay
the cost of his rather astronomical liquor bill *in addition to*
his lodging costs, retaliated by giving the festival an unmerci-
ful panning. Apparently neither the fact that he did not stay
to witness the entire series of concerts nor the all-around agreement on the festival's excellence by audience and critics alike
were allowed to interfere with his obtaining balm for a case
of badly bruised pride.) All of which perhaps goes some distance toward accounting for the stultifying miasma of anti-
intellectualism which permeates the jazz-critical milieu in its
every crevice. [3]

But even were jazz critics to be recruited from the ranks of

sociology Ph. D.s, because of the peculiar relationship to the
recording industry in which most of them stand — a relationship
not duplicated in any other artistic field — the situation would
not be materially altered. For the fundamental datum from
which any investigation of jazz critics and criticism must pro
ceed is that the majority of those who bear the name of critic
do not, speaking strictly, merit that title.

Arguments about *the* correct definition of criticism, like attempts to find the line of demarcation between art and nonart,
are legion; but on one thing probably all disputants would
agree: the critic should be free to arrive at his verdicts without
being coerced, overtly or otherwise, by influences external to
the work of art *per se*. Yet this condition, which — let me stress
it again — is the basic prerequisite of all artistic criticism, is not
even remotely approached so far as jazz is concerned.

More than likely, the average jazz devotee has never given
much thought to how a critic goes about procuring his livelihood. If the critic's name appears often enough in the right
magazines or on the jackets of enough LP records, that es-
tablishes his legitimacy. Hence it is all the more essential to
make the point explicitly that *only a very small fraction of
the men known as "critics" derive the major portion of their
income from criticism; the remainder are, in one fashion or
another, dependent for their livelihood on the recording industry.* The distinction between a critic and an employee of the
recording industry is elementary. The absence in actual practice of this distinction results in a number of consequences,
all of which, however, have one thing in common — a pernicious effect on the practice of jazz criticism.

That this is indeed so emerges from an examination of the
way in which all but a privileged few jazz critics earn their
living, and the pivotal role which economic connections with
the recording companies play in shaping critical views. Within the United States only a very small minority of the best-
known critical figures live primarily off the revenues which
writing aesthetic commentary brings in. Included in this number might be, say, columnists such as Ralph J. Gleason of the
San Francisco Chronicle, the permanent editorial staff of *Down
Beat*, etc. Clearly, the number of these positions which enable
a man to survive by functioning solely as a jazz critic (or,
more broadly, as a commentator on popular culture) is severe-
ly limited. Those U. S. newspapers which retain a jazz columnist *on full salary* can be counted on one's fingers; likewise
for the slick magazines. The corollary is that the less fortunate

writers (i.e., the majority), must seek elsewhere for their support if they hope to concentrate all their energies on jazz;[4] and here is where the recording companies enter the picture.

As circumstances would have it, there are vastly more opportunities awaiting an ambitious young man with the recording industry than there are in writing criticism. Unless it has changed since 1962, the price for a single record review in *Down Beat* is $4; but payment for a set of notes for the back cover of an LP begins around $75, and may climb up to three or more times that amount for those who occupy the top niches in the jazz Establishment — the presumption, of course, being that the critic's famous name helps the record to sell. It requires something less than the mental apparatus of an Einstein to perceive the blatant moral: between $4 and $200 there cannot be any hesitation.

But what ludicrous incongruities this arrangement involves! No one would ever dream of having the interested producers vote to select the outstanding play of the Broadway season; yet it is deemed permissible for men who maintain themselves primarily through their activities as publicists (writing album notes or advertising copy) or executives (artists-and-repertory men) for recording firms to vote in the International Jazz Critics Poll which *Down Beat* conducts each year. To believe that these economic activities do not exert an influence, even if unconscious, on the critics would take a degree of innocence or naivete — I am not sure just which — that I, for one, am unable to muster.

Possibly the clearest example of how this influence is mediated can be witnessed even as I write. A few years ago there was a splenetic outburst on the part of a few writers who damned the then embryonic jazz revolution with the epithet "antijazz"; and although the term was nowhere further defined, the pejorative connotation was unmistakable to even the most casual reader. While the initial manifesto of counterrevolution did not originate with him, Leonard Feather, one of the most renowned of the jazz critics — and a man who is, incidentally, musically quite expert — gave his public endorsement to it in *Down Beat*.[5] Three years later this same critic is to be found writing the album commentaries for several members of the jazz avant-garde; in one instance he has even had the temerity to contribute the notes to a record memorializing the late Eric Dolphy, who was among the chief targets of the initial "antijazz" diatribe to which Feather himself subscribed.[6]

How is this striking reversal, which still awaits its acknowl-

edgment in print, to be accounted for? The fact that we are
unable to adduce an answer with absolute certainty need not
prevent us from suggesting the most plausible interpretation.
During the intervening period since the publication of the first
"antijazz" polemic, there has occurred a fairly significant shift
in the tastes of the jazz public, sizable enough to make it profitable for several recording companies to have released albums by avant-garde performers. Blue Note Records, one
of the firms that has taken the initiative here, coincidentally
happens to be a frequent employer of Leonard Feather as an
author of liner notes. Now if there is an axiom among "critics," it is that a chance to earn a ready $100 or $200 by doing
an album commentary is *never* turned down — regardless of
what the critic may actually think of the artist in question. [7]
Inasmuch as the critic is being paid in good coin to sell records, it is highly unlikely that his notes will be found acceptable by his employer if they do not praise the LP they are
intended to accompany. [8] Thus whatever may have been the
critic's original sentiments, by a process of retroactive ration-
alization he soon comes to convince himself that the paeans
he has inscribed reflect the convictions he held all along.

Could a greater travesty on the idea of aloof and unbiased
criticism be found? The hapless record purchaser is left totally in the dark as to which critical view represents the genuine one: Was Feather sincere in his 1962 denunciation of
"antijazz" or are his later panegyrics to the avant-garde [9] to
be accepted as his true views? But isn't it rather the case that
both opinions are spurious, both the results of considerations
that ought to be extraneous to any type of aesthetic criticism,
properly so called?

Exclusive responsibility, however, ought not to be placed
on the recording executives and the critics for the inequities
which I have been discussing. They are, in actuality, caught
up in a complex matrix of social pressures whose nature they
only dimly perceive; the evils they unwittingly perpetuate have
long since been institutionalized beyond the reach of any such
small and relatively powerless group of individuals as these.
Indeed, it is not unreasonable to believe that the majority of
recording firms would prefer to produce art of a high calibre
rather than *kitsch* — but what if there is a greater market for
kitsch? Similarly, no one doubts that the publicist whose sensibilities have not already been dulled beyond the point of
protest experiences a surge of revulsion when faced with the
task of writing the umpteenth album jacket in the same month

for yet another organ-and-tenor-saxophone group. The natural temptation is to chuck the record into the wastebasket
and be on to something more constructive. Alas! There is
still the pressure of economic necessity to be reckoned with.
So that umpteenth set of notes ultimately gets written — but
not without much gnashing of teeth en route. [10]

The real villain is not the individual producer or writer,
but the form of social organization which insists that art, like
birth, death, and marriage (see *Bride* magazine and *The American Way of Death*), be huckstered as a commodity; and that
only those commodities (be they artistic or otherwise) that
pass the test of profitability have won the right to survive.
The system of art (one should really say *life*) as a commodity
demeans everyone and everything with which it comes into
contact. In jazz, it means that the musicians are forced — either
by outright coercion or through their own internalization of
the criteria of the market — to orient their output in commercial-
ly acceptable directions; that the recording executives are left
no choice but to place these restrictions on the musicians; that
writers, instead of being encouraged to practice objective criticism, find themselves employed primarily in glorifying a "product" to which as often as not they can feel no positive commitment whatsoever. [11]

A long-term solution to rectify the status quo can only take
shape as a basic structural change of society. For the short
run, some amelioration, insofar as criticism alone is concerned,
might lie in the direction of bringing pressure to bear on newspapers and magazines to create positions for capable writers
that would emancipate them from the incubus of the recording
industry. (Wouldn't it be astonishing to discover our leading
drama critics lending their name to the sale of theatre tickets
by composing laudatory comments for the back cover of the
program?)

Even in so modest a proposal as this, implementation would
probably not be easy. It is hardly a secret that jazz has been
a music of the dispossessed and disinherited. Even among
whites, it has had an appeal to the more recently arrived (and
hence more heavily exploited) ethnic minorities, particularly
Italians and Jews, beyond their numerical proportion in the
population at large. These, however, are not the elements to
whom the upper-middle-class-oriented carriers of what passes
in the United States for culture — the *New York Times*, the
Saturday Review, *Harper's*, etc. — have traditionally felt most
responsive; while I suspect that the periodicals read by the
rank and file of the jazz audience are not about to subsidize

esoteric disquisitions on jazz by iconoclastic authors of the
LeRoi Jones stripe. This has to be recognized as part of the
historical dues which the jazz subculture as a whole has had
to pay (and continues to pay) as the result of the music's
being the art of the infraproletariat. In any event, as Jones
has repeatedly made clear, there are some more than com-
pensating advantages in being excluded from the dubious benefits of the pallid white Anglo-Saxon middle-class mode of
existence that predominates in this country.

In the last analysis, it is perhaps to the ongoing Negro revolutionary movement that we must look for a curative to the ills
that assail the jazz body politic. It is virtually impossible to be
unaware that this incipient upheaval poses on the agenda the
question of a root-and-branch overturn of U. S. society, the
ramifications of which will — if the effort be successful — certainly
extend to culture in general and jazz specifically. Is it too much
to hope that one of the attendant gains that the revolution will
bring in its wake will be the opportunity to enjoy America's
only genuinely popular art freed from the economic straitjacket in which it has until now been restrained?*

JAZZ CRITICISM AS SOCIAL CONTROL

Leonard Feather, Michael Zwerin

Why the critics?

That is a question I get asked fairly frequently, by friends
and correspondents who want to know why I expend so much
energy on this particular aspect of the jazz Establishment.

The answer is really quite simple. My point of departure is
to analyze what services the jazz critic might be performing

---

* Writing in 1969, I am able to add as evidence a bit of personal
documentation that was lacking when this essay was originally undertaken in 1964-1965. From 1967 to 1969 I was unable to obtain
a fulltime academic position. During this period I did freelance work
as a writer and/or photographer. If I had any illusions about the
opportunities open to one who would list his vocation as "jazz critic,"
these two years were more than sufficient to dispel them. Thus I
found that I might manage to survive by writing five to eight sets
of album notes per month (average fee — $75), but I doubt that my
combined earnings from reviews, essays, and other critical endeavors
in the field of music journalism netted as much as $1,000 over the
two-year period. I am therefore unhappily able to reaffirm that in
nine out of ten cases jazz criticism can only be an avocation, not
a vocation. The consequences for the practice of such criticism are,
of course, dismal.

for the music (which means for the musicians and their audience). I then compare this with the actual accomplishments of the critics. Since the balance thus struck is so wholly unfavorable to the major critical figures — Leonard Feather, Martin Williams, Dan Morgenstern, Michael Zwerin, and the entire editorial staff of *Down Beat*— I conclude that it is my duty to the jazz community to expose — to use a good 1930s leftist word — their failings, to prevent them from leading their readers even further astray.

The place to begin the discussion is with an inquiry into the power of the jazz critic to alter the present state of the jazz scene. Some musicians believe that, collectively, the critics hold the keys to economic success. For better or worse (probably for better, given the current state of criticism), this is simply not so. True, critics can strew the path of a determined innovator with unnecessary obstacles, as they have in almost every case that comes to mind. But they cannot "make" their favorites top dog, no matter how hard they try. (If I give Vol. II of the *The Heliocentric Worlds of Sun Ra,* for instance, my most enthusiastic endorsement, will this cause the sale of even ten additional albums? I doubt it.) And even the critics' ability to obstruct the flow of history is fairly narrowly limited, as the recent surge in popularity of John Coltrane, Ornette Coleman, and Cecil Taylor should demonstrate.

What then *can* the critics do? For one thing, they can muckrake — they can lay bare the sordid conditions that prevail within the jazz milieu. Should they so choose, the critics could probably bring about a fairly substantial degree of integration in the recording, TV, and movie studios, simply by a consistent public assault on the existing policy of whites-preferred. The same methods might also be employed to remedy the ghastly situation in the nightclubs, where exorbitant charges to the clientele are coupled with hyper-exploitation of the artists (even the major ones, though with them the exploitation is more subtle and indirect than with the lesser-known men). A picket-line in front of the *Five Spot*, say, initiated and led by Martin Williams, Dan Morgenstern, and Michael Zwerin would, you can be sure, produce the most salutary results in that club's pricing and employment practices in short order!

(The objection that this is the work of journalism rather than criticism is not very germane. Most self-styled jazz critics are in reality nothing more than glorified journalists to begin with — and not very glorified at that. For that matter, what in itself is wrong with journalism? A little less insipid "criticism" and a little more crusading journalism would, at this particular stage of the game, very definitely be A Good Thing.)

A second and related task the critics could undertake, were they so minded, is that of relating the present revolution in jazz to the changes in society that have helped shape it. In the long run, of course, the success of any radical movement in the arts depends on its reception by the community of practicing artists, especially the younger ones — which is, by the way, why the triumph of the jazz revolution is assured (assuming my observations in the East to be correct). Nonetheless, the critics have it in their hands to smooth the way for the innovators, by mediating between them and their public. This in turn would require that the critics abandon their own preconceptions and biases in the attempt to comprehend what motivates the youthful iconoclasts, how their art has been molded by the social and aesthetic environment. It was precisely this which was *not* done in the 1940s; with the result that the bebop revolution of that decade produced a number of acrimonious splits that haunted the music for many years thereafter.

When we go to score the leading critics on their performances of these two tasks, what we find is a record of almost total negligence — or worse. I have yet to read a column by Leonard Feather, Martin Williams, Dan Morgenstern, Michael Zwerin, or any of that crowd, which makes the least attempt to decry the virtually total segregation of the studios; nor has there been any protest on their part regarding the abominable practices of nightclub owners like the Termini brothers of New York's *Five Spot* cafe.

If their performance as journalists of the expose is dismal, the way in which these men treat the social components of the jazz revolution is nothing short of criminal. There is, in fact, a certain logic involved here. The easiest way to summarize the status quo in jazz is with the two words *white supremacy.* Themselves being the beneficiaries of the existing order, the foremost critics, all white, are blind to its inequities; they accept them, that is, as natural and even inevitable. But the jazz revolution, in its social aspect, is an indictment of the very inequalities of class and race that have given these critics their privileged position. Hence it would be genuinely astonishing were they able to offer their readers an objective account of the revolution and the conditions that provide it with its fuel. Need I add that the critics make no such attempt? (The only exception to that rule worth mentioning is *San Francisco Chronicle* columnist Ralph J. Gleason, whose constant pressure on union

officials provided much of the impetus for the abolition of segregated locals in the Bay area not too many years back. But
Gleason is, as I say, the *exception.*)

It is easy enough to document these charges *ad nauseam.*
Consider Michael Zwerin of the *Village Voice*, for one. While
with the Earl Hines band on a State Department tour of the
Soviet Union, Zwerin bombarded his readers with a baleful
account of the unhappy plight of the citizen on *that* side of the
Iron Curtain. But he has never written a line on the exclusion
of black musicians from the studios, never done a column on
working conditions for musicians in the dingy toilets known as
jazz clubs — and this despite the fact that he is one of the few
men who could describe these things from first-hand experience.
Or take Martin Williams. Instead of trying to assist his white
audience in understanding the integral role of black nationalism (and other forms of social radicalism) in the jazz revolution, he continues to prate away in *Down Beat* about alleged
"black supremacists" (e.g., issue of June 30, 1966), thus en-
couraging the unthinking, gut-level white racism that he should
be at great pains to extirpate. More than that, he strives to
discredit those writers who would point out the central relationship between radicalism and the new music, condemning them
for espousing, in his words, "opportunistic Marxist cliches de-
livered with a slightly Peking-ese accent" (*Saturday Review*,
April 30, 1966).

But for the title of champion "misleader of the people," to
invoke another old-radical phrase, no one can take a back
seat to Leonard Feather. A year ago he asserted in *Down
Beat* (December 16, 1966) that musicians weren't interested
in discussing such things as black nationalism and Vietnam —
it was all a plot of certain white writers (guess who?) who
were trying to convince Negro musicians that they too were
soul brothers. (He really did say this; I have not taken it
from a HUAC publicity release.)

Later, however, he had an eyeball-type confrontation with
Archie Shepp, when the latter played *Shelly's Manne-Hole* in
Los Angeles. Apparently, this was enough to convince Feather
that musicians *were* involved with those questions that he felt
should be placed off limits. But far from revising his opinions
after discussing them with Shepp in his abode in the lily-white
Hollywood Hills, Feather took another tack: he sought to convince his following that Shepp and those who thought like him
were racists.

In the first of what I am afraid will not be a short-lived

series in *Cavalier* (December, 1966), Feather, in rapid succession, implies that (1) Shepp is a phony who plays and
dresses one way in public, another way in private; (2) that
his poetry is part and parcel of Shepp's efforts to "find more
work and sell more records"; and (3) that he is antiwhite.
What is the truth? Need you ask? When I visited Shepp at
his home last spring, he was wearing the same "eccentric out-
fits and Benjamin Franklin shades" that are, Feather would
have us believe, "a part of his stage shtick." (Thanks for the
Yiddish, Len — it lets us know you're hip. Too bad your
hipness doesn't extend to familiarity with East Village dress
mores.) Only Shepp can fathom the motivation behind his
poetry; but somehow Feather leaves me unconvinced that poetic dedications to Malcolm X and the late black Marxist intellectual W.E.B. Du Bois are the best way to go about securing
increased employment from Joe Termini and the likes!
  As for Shepp's alleged antiwhite proclivities, here Feather's
unscrupulousness surpasses the credible. Shepp has always
had at least one white member, trombonist Roswell Rudd, in
his group since he started working semiregularly (none of the
new musicians work regularly). When he played Los Angeles,
where Feather resides, another white, bassist Charlie Haden,
had been added, and since then, Haden has flown east to work
with Shepp.
  None of which, however, is of the least importance so far as
Feather is concerned. Articulate and militant black radicals
like Shepp threaten Feather and his ilk, psychologically and
socially. For that reason, they must be destroyed. Or so Feather
hopes. . . .

  *"Mister X [an anonymous correspondent] is right about
  aesthetic and social theories being something apart from
  music. As a matter of fact, I think a number of avant-
  garde jazz musicians would be better suited in politics —
  it would be a more direct expression for them."*—Michael
  Zwerin, *The Village Voice*, December 15, 1966.

  *"Art without ideas is like a man without a soul: it
  is a corpse."*—Belinsky

  The two quotations above illustrate diametrically opposed
ideas about the relationship between art and society. The first
of these, of course, is today's critical orthodoxy insofar as

jazz is concerned; with only a couple of exceptions, it is subscribed to by all the big-deal critics like Leonard the Feather.
(That it is also endorsed by Michael Zwerin, jazz writer for
the *Village Voice*, is ample comment on the presumed "hippi-
ness" of that journal.) Essentially counterrevolutionaries, these
men labor long and hard to convince their readers that the
best art is devoid of content, apolitical, divorced from all social
realities. Perhaps the clearest statement of this position comes
from Feather, who, writing in *Down Beat's Music '67,* misreads
the course of jazz history in such a way as to "prove" that it
would be "a basic denial of freedom" were the music not "to
remain art, pure and inviolate." Which is only another way of
saying that art should never contain anything that might cause
Leonard Feather even a momentary discomfort.

Ideologues can spew forth their "theories" until blue in the
face — but so much the worse for them if reality does not cor-
respond to their constructions! There may have been a time
when the Zwerins and the Feathers might have appeared half-
way persuasive; but those times are long past, probably for
good. As Isaac Deutscher, the masterful Marxist biographer
of Leon Trotsky and Stalin, writes in *Ironies of History:*

"An attitude of non-commitment [in art] can crystallize and
become accepted only in a stabilized society where the foundations of national existence are generally taken for granted and
where social conflict runs at a tension so low that it fails to
communicate itself with art."

Any moderately perceptive observer of the scene will have
to agree that there is damn little "stabilized" about American
capitalist society; and it is precisely the "foundations of national existence" which *cannot* be taken for granted by the
black artists who produce the new music. Hence to expect the
vapid kind of "art" which would please Feather & Co. under
the irrational and chaotic conditions of today is like trying to
find a quiet spot for a picnic in the midst of a raging artillery
battle. Lots of luck!

Nothing demonstrates more clearly the intertwined nature of
politics and the new music than a concert that I had the good
fortune to be able to attend over the 1966 holidays. The concert was in New York's *Village Theatre*, and it featured, besides the artistry of Jackie McLean, Marion Brown, Archie
Shepp, and their respective groups, a short speech by none
other than Stokely Carmichael.

What Carmichael had to say has already been reported
and would be stale now, so I need not go into that. And in

one sense, the contents of his brief remarks were of secondary importance to the mere fact of his presence at the concert: a leading advocate of black nationalism being publicly united with some of the leading figures in the new music. One could hardly ask for a more vivid instance of the relationship that joins the two.

At least as fascinating as Carmichael's appearance in tandem with the new jazz was the way in which the presentation came about. Poet A. B. Spellman, who served as master of ceremonies, made it a point to announce that the idea for a jazz benefit for SNCC had originated with Jackie McLean, who wanted some way to put his work at the service of the black liberation movement — something which Michael Zwerin, who devoted half a column to reviewing McLean's performance, somehow managed to omit (*Village Voice,* December 29, 1966).

McLean's decision to take the initiative in sponsoring a benefit for SNCC and Black Power is of particular significance because heretofore, as far as anyone knew, he was simply another one of the Establishment's good niggers in jazz. Though his playing had been tinged lightly with some of the ideas of John Coltrane and Ornette Coleman, McLean's roots were still in bebop, and he had not committed himself wholeheartedly to the Jazz Revolution. More important to the Establishment, he had never given any indication of "unreliability" — never, that is, taken to seasoning his discourse with talk of exploitation, nationalism, radicalism, Vietnam, boycotting the jazz business, organizing musicians' cooperatives, or any other contemporary heresy. That makes his desire to be of value to SNCC and the cause of Black Power so much the more notable. After all, no one would have been particularly surprised had the benefit been planned by Archie Shepp or Cecil Taylor or Marion Brown or Bill Dixon. But *Jackie McLean?*

That Michael Zwerin could review the concert without mentioning this salient fact is, in its own way, a significant social act: it reveals, even if the omission were merely "accidental," Zwerin's unwillingness to put jazz — and I mean *all* jazz, not just the new music — in its proper social perspective. But Zwerin's "sin" is at least only one of omission. What can we possibly think of this distorted account of the Bebop Revolution given us by Leonard Feather in the article cited earlier:

"Neither in the sounds produced by Gillespie, Parker, Kenny Clarke, and their contemporaries, nor in the titles or the arrangements, is there a relation to the brutal conditions that persisted through the bebop years."

One wonders. Jackie McLean was one of the musicians to be in on the ground floor of developments in the music during the bebop period. If jazz were really as removed from social reality as Feather would like us to believe, is it conceivable that McLean would be in the Black Power camp today? Apparently Feather finds it easier to "forget" that Charlie Parker — McLean's earliest mentor — wrote a blues with obvious social implications called *Now's the Time*, to "forget" that Parker himself said: "Music is your own experience, your thoughts, your wisdom. If you don't live it, it won't come out of your horn." (Ironically, this statement is quoted by Nat Hentoff, attacking the proposition that "jazz can somehow be insulated from life," on the page following Feather's warped version of bebop history!)

Feather and Zwerin or no, jazz has *always* flowed out of the circumstances of the musician's existence. In this respect, the critics could well stand to absorb a few lessons from Charlie Parker, not to mention his latter-day descendants. It is neither tenable nor realistic to assume that the black men and women of this century who have given us the music called jazz were any more unaware of their oppressive environment than the slaves who in the last century produced the spirituals, work-songs, and other protestations against their condition. Nothing could be more vain than to hope to sunder jazz and politics; the two have continually been wedded, and the closeness of the union must grow rather than shrink. For that reason, Jackie McLean's concert for SNCC can only be the beginning.

Down Beat

In what follows I intend to go beyond mere individuals, to make clear the pivotal *institutional* role played by *Down Beat* magazine in helping to perpetuate the reign of white supremacy in jazz.

As a handy rule of thumb, you can estimate the stature which any art enjoys in a modern nation by the calibre of the journals devoted to it. Such being the case, you would never have to hear a single note of the music to be made aware that the powers-that-be are convinced of the inferiority of jazz; all you need do is glance at a few issues of *Down Beat*. If the art it purports to discuss were considered "serious" (i.e., European, i.e., white), there would be no room for the existence of a periodical like *Down Beat*. That the magazine not only exists but has the largest circulation of any of those dealing with the music offers the weightiest evidence I know of for the continued second-class artistic citizenship of jazz.

If jazz were the movies, *Down Beat's* name would be *Silver Screen*—that's the quickest way to convey the essence of the magazine to the nonreader. And yet for all its blatant triviality, it has a greater degree of influence than any rival periodical. Owing to its aggressive sales of advertising, it has been able to outlast and outstrip all its competitors. *Metronome, Jazz Review, Record Changer, Jazz Quarterly*—all these and others whose names I have forgotten have come and gone, while *Down Beat* has hung on since the late thirties, riding out each new development in the "music business."

Its very longevity in a field where failure and quick demise is the dismal rule has made *Down Beat* a force to be reckoned with. Musicians like to pretend (with good reason, I might add) that they are indifferent to what these days passes for "criticism" and therefore don't read the magazine; but secretly they all do. Even Miles Davis, whose independence and outspokenness are bywords in jazz circles, has his awards from *Down Beat* mounted in his living room. (Davis's proffered explanation, which writer Nat Hentoff naively repeats at face value, is that the trumpeter "has a particular liking for 'good wood'"!) Hence the views which *Down Beat's* editorial staff and conservative publisher disseminate are a subject of more than passing importance.

"There hasn't been one time where I have been prevented from saying what I wanted to say—or has anyone, for that matter, been prevented from expressing his opinion."

That pious sentiment came from the mouth of *Down Beat's* New York editor, Dan Morgenstern (*Down Beat Music '66*). Unhappily, it is a prescription honored more in the breach than in the observance. In point of fact, *Down Beat* is quite cavalier in its mishandling of the truth, and is more than eager to suppress dissenting opinions. Since this is a basic aspect of its *modus operandi*, it is worthwhile to establish the point at the outset.

Item: In 1960, Ralph Gleason wrote a column for *Down Beat* drawing a favorable comparison between the political winds of change, as represented by Fidel Castro, and the musical ones, as represented by Ornette Coleman and others. Though the column somehow managed to see the light of publication, the publisher and advertisers were aghast, and the word quickly came down to Gleason from On High: No more of that Commie shit! Next, Gleason's columns and record

reviews (both signed) began to be subjected to persistent censorship, leaving him no choice but to resign. Shortly thereafter, my own reviews for *Down Beat* were altered without my
consent, and I followed Gleason within a matter of months.
This, however, did not bring the issue to a close. When Gleason
related these incidents in the pages of the *San Francisco Chronicle*, Don DeMicheal had the insufferable gall to write the *Chronicle* denying the whole thing and accusing Gleason — one of
the few honest writers in the field of jazz reportage, incidentally
— of "scrambling . . . facts and truths"! (A copy of this letter,
dated August 13, 1962, is in this writer's possession.)

Item: In its December 16, 1966, issue, *Down Beat* carried
a scurrilous column by Leonard Feather, in the course of
which Feather denounced "two or three white critics" for "trying
desperately to prove . . . to Negro musicians . . . that they
think just like soul brothers," by, among other things, "rail[ing]
and rant[ing] about the white power structure" and "shedding
crocodile tears for Malcolm X." Though Feather's insulting
polemic was evidently directed at yours truly — my name was
mentioned twice in the column — *Down Beat* refused to allow
me even one line to reply. So much, I trust, for Morgenstern's
contention that "there hasn't been one time" when "anyone"
has "been prevented from expressing his opinion"!

I believe that the editorial staff of *Down Beat* is thoroughly
ingrained with the precepts of white supremacy — so much so,
indeed, that they are an integral part of the magazine's frame
of reference which can be taken for granted without continual
reiteration. That is why black nationalism, as well as other
forms of radicalism, which threatens to disrupt the status quo,
are anathema to its editors, why they are at such pains to
discredit all radical ideologies. (Archie Shepp has related that
when he submitted an article to *Down Beat* declaring himself
a compatriot of Fidel and Ho Chi Minh, he received a phone
call from the editor, who told him: "This article frightens me."
One can be certain of that!)

Before going on to describe what I believe to be *Down Beat's*
systematic attack on nationalism and radicalism, however,
the nature of the magazine's antiblack bias should be eluci-
dated. A couple of representative incidents will serve.

Item: In its August 11, 1966, issue, *Down Beat* carried an
article about the modern painter Larry Rivers, who also happens to be an amateur saxophonist and has on occasion sat
in with groups led by drummer Elvin Jones, an old friend.
More recently, Dan Morgenstern wrote a brief essay on the

paintings of clarinetist Pee Wee Russell (December 1, 1966),
who began working in oils about a year ago. But the magazine has never printed word one about the fact that the exciting new music composer and flugelhornist Bill Dixon has had
four one-man shows in New York City. Why not? Well, it
might just have something to do with Russell and Rivers being
white and Dixon black . . .

Item: In the same discussion from which I've already quoted
editor Dan Morgenstern's sanctimonious disclaimer of censorship at *Down Beat*, Cecil Taylor made a quite explicit accusation of racist practices on the part of Morgenstern and the
magazine which employs him:

"I refer to you, Dan Morgenstern [Taylor said], in your
selection of artists representing the new music in the *Museum
of Modern Art* garden series just last summer [1965], when
you knew very well the creators were ready, at whatever terms
you suggested, to play. And what did you do? You ignored
us and hired a former [white] sideman of mine, a man named
Roswell Rudd, who was never heard of in the modern musical
context until the record I made for Impulse in 1961."

How did Morgenstern deal with this accusation? Did he attempt to clear himself of the charge of racism by concrete
deeds? Not in the least. First, as permanent consultant to the
Jazz in the Garden series — which is, according to Morgenstern's employer, "co-sponsored by *Down Beat*" (July 28, 1966;
also October 20, 1966) — he once more refused to extend an
invitation to Cecil Taylor or any of the other seminal black
artists involved in originating the new music: second, he enhanced this sin of omission by rubbing salt in Taylor's wounds
with the following bit of hypocrisy, incorporated into a review
of the pianist's 1966 *Town Hall* concert:

"This is music that, for lack of better venue, belongs in the
concert hall. Yet, while academic hacks and fashionable mod-
ernists reap the necessary grants and fellowships without which
no 'serious' musician can sustain himself in our time, Taylor,
regarded by the establishment [!] as a 'jazz' musician, is left
to shift for himself. . . .

"Given his rightful opportunity to create and perform with
that minimum of security that our society now grants talents
much lesser than his, there is no telling what Taylor might
accomplish, considering what he already has achieved in spite
of the unfair odds against him."

What crap! While Morgenstern throws around all this "radical"
language about "the establishment," "our society," and "unfair

odds," he fails to do the one thing within his power to aid Taylor — provide him with a job. Actions speak louder than words. Morgenstern's actions in excluding radical black artists like Taylor from the Jazz in the Garden series drown out his devout protestations about the pianist's talents and make manifest the white-supremacist preconceptions on which he — and the magazine for which he writes — operates.

In the good old days when niggers knew their place and tended to keep to it, social discipline in the jazz world was fairly easy. If you were a conservative white concerned about black nationalism, all you had to do was unleash a tirade in *Down Beat* about the evils of "reverse racism" — like, you know, black musicians wanting to hire other blacks instead of whites, and other highly significant manifestations of black oppression directed against hapless and helpless whites — and the situation would soon be set right. To a degree, this sort of thing still can be found especially among the older established critics.

But this tactic is crude and, worse yet, even ineffectual. For that reason it has given way among the more astute white conservatives to a new policy: divide and rule. Actually, there is nothing very novel in this approach; the British were using it early in the last century to retain their hold on India. In essence, the technique is simplicity itself: you merely find members of the oppressed group who, for one reason or another — venality, stupidity, naivete — are willing to work with the masters against the slaves; you then appoint these "cooperative" and "responsible" slaves to be the "leaders" of the remaining masses, and control the masses through the instrumentality of the "leaders."

Thus the new *Down Beat* response to black nationalism. At first, a few years ago, the editors of *Down Beat* sought to wipe out nationalism and other radical proclivities among the musicians through a campaign based on direct attack. Recently, however, the more sophisticated methods of divide and rule have been employed to the same end. At least a few of these methods deserve some comment, since they demonstrate the cleverness of white conservative liberalism (or liberal conservatism, there being no appreciable difference).

If, for example, you wish to scuttle the radicalism of the Jazz Revolution while it's still a-borning, you needn't stoop to dirtying your own hands. Instead, you can get a nice, safe, domesticated neobebopper like Kenny Dorham who feels economically threatened by the new developments — "If this thing

isn't quarantined, we'll all be in the garment center pushing
wagons," was Dorham's response in *Down Beat* (July 15, 1965)
to an Albert Ayler recording — and he can do the job for you.
That way, no one can accuse *you*, a white critic, of hostility
toward the young black radicals: "What the hell! The musicians
themselves don't dig it, right?"

Or again, if your aim is to counteract the increasingly leftist
sentiments that prevail among the new musicians, you can best
accomplish it by finding some atypical men to interview, palm-
ing off their statements as wholly representative. A good place
at which to begin might be with, say, John Tchicai, who, although of African-European descent, has lived almost all of
his life in the comparative racial utopia of the Scandinavian
countries. Sure enough, what do we discover if not our old
acquaintance Dan Morgenstern, *Down Beat's* New York City
editor, doing an article on "John Tchicai, A Calm Member of
the Avant-Garde" (February 10, 1966) — the clear implication
being that the *other* avant-gardists are screaming maniacs.

As if that title weren't sufficient, Morgenstern goes out of his
way to make the point, telling us, for example, that Tchicai
"seems more relaxed and more at peace with himself, less aggressive [a favorite word!] and aggrieved, than the self-appointed spokesmen and standard-bearers [read: uppity niggers]
of the new music." Later on, Tchicai gets quoted by Morgenstern as saying: "I think there is also a tendency among a lot
of Negro musicians to only look at this — that they are Negroes
and that there will always be more opportunities for white
musicians. But I think that is wrong . . ." (Hear that, Archie
Shepp, Bill Dixon, Cecil Taylor?) And in an effort to deny
the primacy of black artists in the creation of all the major
stylistic innovations in jazz: "I've heard Negro musicians talk
about 'black music.' The music doesn't have any color. You
can't see music, so how can you give it a color." That bit of
profundity certainly ought to tell those niggers where to get
off!

That this utilization of isolated black artists to create disunity
among the new musicians and prevent the spread of radical
ideas is standard *Down Beat* policy is indicated by the fact
that articles, such as the one I've just quoted from, are ubiquitous in the magazine's pages. Another illustration, from which
I shall not quote this time, is Morgenstern's interview with
Freddie Hubbard (December 1, 1966). Hubbard, you must
understand, is not at all a full-fledged participant in the Jazz
Revolution; his position is closer to that of an ambivalent ob-

server located somewhere on the periphery. As you can readily learn from a few minutes conversation, he is a very amiable young man who is as yet uncommitted to any hard and fast doctrines, be it in political or aesthetic terms, and above all doesn't want to be considered *too* unconventional by his mates. More than that, by virtue of his temperamental caution and his reluctance to align himself fully with the Jazz Revolution, a variety of employment opportunities are open to him that are denied to many of his less equivocal peers, so the grinding poverty that bears down on the shapes and views of men like Marion Brown and Archie Shepp are absent in Hubbard's case. To ask this man to evaluate the contributions of the Jazz Revolution is therefore somewhat like asking Kerensky what he thinks of the Bolsheviks. Yet is is precisely because of this ambivalent stance that Hubbard's views are so highly prized by Morgenstern and his employer, *Down Beat* magazine.

So far, the instances of *Down Beat's* antiradicalism which I have cited have been of a "mixed" character, both social and aesthetic. This is a reflection of the fact that in jazz especially it is impossible to discuss the music without reference to the social context (though this doesn't seem to have stopped the majority of critics from trying), and vice versa. Nonetheless, there are cases, particularly frequent lately, in which the magazine has endorsed social pronouncements as such, without even seeking to give them the figleaf of a musical "cover." That these pronouncements have been blatantly hostile to social radicalism goes almost without saying; but that *Down Beat* has been able to utilize the pen of a black man to compose them is something of a novel twist. (Until about 1959, *Down Beat* was as lily-white as the Ku Klux Klan, notwithstanding the overwhelming preponderance of black musicians in jazz and the sizable black readership which the magazine has always enjoyed.)

The black man in question is one Brooks Johnson, whose perspective on black nationalism in particular and radicalism in general can perhaps be inferred from the fact that his present employer is, according to *Down Beat* (June 16, 1966), the Governmental Affairs Institute in Washington, D. C. At any rate, his debut in *Down Beat* consisted of a denunciation of something he has dubbed "neo-neo-Uncle-Tomming," whose prime practitioner seems to be, according to him, Sun Ra. Sun Ra's nationalist militance and refusal to be a pawn for the white-owned recording industry is translated in Johnson's hands into irrational paranoia "about his relationships with

white people and the white race." (After all, what would happen if *all* black musicians were unwilling to allow themselves
to be exploited at the convenience of the recording firms?)
For the dullwitted, Johnson spells out the moral in blunt and
unmistakable terms: "Success is not based upon alienation,
but accommodation." Following this dictum, he offers his thesis
that the men who play what they call the "new black music"
can be dismissed as nothing more than "jive punks" who "have
to be more way out" on social and racial questions "to compensate for their lack of talent." Far from developing an art
that is "representative" of black people, the work of the jazz
revolutionaries is "based in ignorance and a talent void. Further, I have heard these same men"—it is fairly clear that
Johnson is talking about artists like Archie Shepp—"rant about
how they have been taken advantage of, and yet they have been
up on the stand faking it, taking advantage of the listeners."
It would be sufficiently easy to go on quoting from Johnson
ad nauseam. For example, he descends even lower in the rhetorical scale, describing the new musicians as an "unattractive,
negative element . . . in contemporary music," and referring
to poet-playwright LeRoi Jones as "their pimp"—certainly a
tasteful way of phrasing it! But enough has been said already
to convey the flavor (odor might be more exact) of Johnson's
opinions. A subsequent disquisition on "Racism in Jazz" (October 6, 1966) while adding nothing new, continues fulminating
in a similar vein, rehearsing the same tired complaints about
an alleged "perversion of black pride in jazz," condemning
nationalists as musical incompetents ("it is easier to be a racist
than it is to be a good trumpeter"), and painting the radicals
as "black phonies and musical panderers in jazz."
To what purpose?
It ought to be evident that this outpouring of vitriol can
have no other intent than to undermine the appeal of those
blacks who, like Shepp, Taylor, Brown, Dixon, *et al.,* are
uncompromising in their protests against all forms of exploitation. Ironically, if there is anyone engaged in "neo-neo-Tom-
ming," "neo-Tomming," or just plain old-fashioned Tomming,
it is Johnson himself, who has allowed his talents to be used
by *Down Beat* for such ignoble ends. The men he maligns
so intemperately are, as he might learn if he were to take
the trouble to search them out, inveterate enemies of all distinc-
tions based on class *or* race—they seek, as Ornette Coleman's
bassist David Izenson told me, to construct a "classless society."
Yet even so, the blame is not so much Johnson's as *Down*

Beat's, for attempting to brainwash its readers into accepting the perverse notion that radical opposition to a sick status quo is somehow to be equated with racism and charlatanism.

Happily, however, it looks as if the school of thought which *Down Beat* distills so accurately no longer has unchallenged hegemony in jazz. During the last few years there has emerged a group of young writers whose primary orientation is that of the *social* critic, rather than the jazz critic. Doubtless you will know who I mean — figures like poets LeRoi Jones, A. B. Spellman, and John Sinclair, playwright-essayist Robert Levin, and (I like to think) yours truly. In its short existence, this loose grouping has already produced: two of the finest and most important books on jazz ever written, Jones's *Blues People* and Spellman's *Four Lives in the Bebop Business;* and a number of stirring manifestoes, such as Robert Levin's incomparable article in the first issue of the now defunct *Sounds & Fury.* Besides that, the new movement has fixed a permanent mark on jazz journalism. That *Jazz* sponsored a public forum on *Jazz and Revolutionary Black Nationalism,* with Archie Shepp, LeRoi Jones, and others among the participants, is in part directly attributable to the pressures generated by these young writers. Paradoxically, the very fact that *Down Beat* now feels constrained to devote space to publishing diatribes against black nationalism is a measure of the influence which the group is capable of bringing to bear.

Behind the new authors there stand the new musicians, whose discontent provides the fuel in which we writers dip our pens.

IS JAZZ DEAD?

The premature lament for the demise of jazz is not a new one. Three years ago the pseudonymous Jean P. LeBlanc — in some ways an ironically apt disguise — began an article in *Esquire* entitled "The Happy Sound is Dying" with the mordant conclusion that:

"Jazz is sick. What was once, only a few choruses ago, the unspoiled child of the American arts is now a pain-ridden adult. Neurotic musicians [who wouldn't be neurotic, exposed to the social conditions under which jazz musicians are compelled to exist?] are serving up nerve-wracking music for nervous critics. With the help of the self-appointed experts, jazz has been manufacturing its own mausoleum."

The complaint then, is anything but novel.

Is jazz dead (or dying)? On the affirmative side we have

Frank Sinatra; on the negative LeRoi Jones, who persistently calls our attention to the development of a youthful avant-garde movement in jazz. The division is by no means fortuitous. It must be our basic point of departure to reaffirm that jazz is, above and beyond anything else, what Francis Newton has felicitously described as "a folk music gone urban"; it is, in short, "a people's music"; and the people involved are the ghettoized and Jim Crowed "blues people" who loom so large in Jones's groundbreaking theoretical opus of the same name. That being the case, the corollary should be quite obvious: jazz will persist at least as long as the separate existence of the American Negro is maintained, conceivably even after that.

Those who insist upon the moribund state of jazz, therefore, have shot extremely wide of the mark. Their tremendous *social* distance from the black ghettos of the United States has sufficed to remove them from the milieu in which the new jazz inventions are incubated; and as a result they tend to be loose with pontifications heralding jazz's imminent end. By the same token, conversely, LeRoi Jones, through his poet's sensitivity to the mood of the ghetto, is privy to all the most recent developments, currents and movements.

The fact of the matter is (and Jones's great unpopularity with the bulk of the white critical Establishment is an immediate instance in point) that notwithstanding certain superficial indicators to the contrary, the yawning gulf that separates white and black America is increasing rather than shrinking in magnitude. This is the real significance of the statement by Frank Sinatra that jazz has perished; and while its aesthetic worth is nil, taken as symptomatic of a widespread state of mind among whites who at one time had some liaison with the jazz (i.e., Negro) world, it is a valuable little scrap of sociohistorical data and should be apprehended as such. Sinatra's opinions on jazz are most unlikely to be of interest in themselves; but they are deserving of attention nonetheless for what they suggest about the workings of the American Dream as it has affected Negroes and whites.

Two generations or so ago Italian immigrants, such as the grandparents of Frank Sinatra, did not stand appreciably higher in the social order than Negroes. Asked, for example, if he considered Italians to be white men, an Anglo-Saxon construction boss replied: "No, sir, an Italian is a Dago." At the same time, the anti-Catholic American Protective Association, which flourished in the Midwest, opened its ranks to Ne-

groes; and at least one case is known in which Negroes participated in lynching Italians (which is certainly joining the
black bourgeoisie with a vengeance!).

Since that period in U. S. history, of course, things have
changed somewhat for the immigrant: the descendant of lace-
curtain Irish Catholics has become President, Italians have
reached Cabinet status, Jews are appointed to the Supreme
Court with machine-like regularity, and so on and so forth.
But for the black American there has been a less dramatic
altering of the pattern of ostracism, proscription and discrimination — a pattern which in any case has a far more stable
entrenchment in the traditions of America. Now as the third-
generation progeny of "new" immigrants myself, I am clearly
in no position to begrudge Mr. Sinatra and his peers the pit-
tance of *embourgeoisement* they have attained: I know too
well that a WASP's heaven can be a kike's (or Dago's, or
Mick's, or Polack's) hell. Yet I must still insist the very fact
of divorce from the misery of a ghetto existence renders the
preponderance of today's white Americans of *whatever* descent
unfit as objective commentators on anything which involves
the Negro.

Because, you see, despite the embellishments of a few shreds
of token integration here or there, the American Dream still
functions as a nightmare when it involves the Negro. Between
1955 and 1964, as C. E. Wilson has observed, the ratio of
nonwhite family income to that of white family income has
actually *declined* by two percentage points (55.4 percent to
53.4 percent); the fraction of white families with income under
$4000 per year (estimated to be the minimum for a decent
living standard for a family of four) has fallen off for whites
by two-thirds since 1945, while the comparable decline for
Negroes has been but half as much; and the ratio of Negro
unemployment to white unemployment has risen since 1955.
What these dry statistics — which are the only meaningful criteria for measuring "progress," let me emphasize — demonstrate
is that the socioeconomic position of the Negro in the United
States, far from improving, is in reality worsening.

Yet at the very same time, according to public opinion polls
taken on a representative national sample by Louis Harris,
81 percent of the American white populace opposes a quota
system that would guarantee Negroes, 10 percent of the population, 10 percent of the jobs; while *97 percent* of the whites
questioned were in agreement that Negroes should *not* be given
preference in new jobs. Rarely has white America ever displayed

the degree of unanimity that characterizes it when it becomes a question of "keeping the Negro in his place" at the absolute bottom of the social order!

Whatever whites may think of the foregoing reasoning, the Negro ghettos of America have not been slow to perceive the implications of these figures. The result has been a massive, if so far largely symbolic, repudiation of the American Dream; this is unquestionably the interpretation that must be given to such phenomena as the popularity of the late Malcolm X in Harlem, the disturbance which took place there (and in a number of other ghettos) during the summer of 1964, and the attractiveness of revolutionary black nationalism to young Negro intellectuals (and white dissidents).

The musical expression of Negro discontent has been the avant-garde revolution, just now becoming airborne; this much can be inferred from the published interviews with Cecil Taylor, Bill Dixon, Archie Shepp, the late Eric Dolphy and others. (It is worth remarking that the new generation of Negro jazz musicians is probably the most astute politically as well as being the most outspoken.) It follows of necessity that this accounts for the unpopularity of the avant-garde with the critical Establishment, whose self-appointed members, being white, are staunch believers in the American Dream. On the avant-garde which has removed itself from their culturally desiccated and spiritually barren middle-class world, the critics have pronounced the official verdict that jazz is "dead"; it remains to be seen, however, in which culture rigor mortis will develop first.

Be that as it may, black men and women in the United States are turning their backs on the racist disabilities imposed on them by the West; and inherent in that rejection is a disavowal of the traditional canons of Western culture. This is the key to an understanding of the avant-garde, which fully mirrors this anti-Western stance. Those whites for whom jazz music is an integral part of their life should take note, for the present trends promise to be with us for a long time yet to come.

Photo by Frank Kofsky

ORNETTE COLEMAN (ALTO, L), DAVID IZENSON (R)

Photo by Frank Kofsky

DONALD (L) AND ALBERT (R) AYLER

Chapter 2
THE BLUES PEOPLE
OF LEROI JONES

In due course, no doubt, emancipated American Negroes will have their own "New Orleans revival," being sufficiently distant from the old South to separate the original cultural achievement of their people from the conditions of oppression in which it took place.

Francis Newton, *The Jazz Scene*

From our current vantage point in the 1960s it has become vividly apparent that the white American Left has never adequately comprehended the nature of either Negro music or Negro nationalism.

With the honorable exception of Sidney Finklestein in the United States and Francis Newton in Britain, white radicals have been content to indulge in a preteristic cult of "folk music," an art of dubious content drenched in nostalgia for days gone by — but then, isn't this true of so much of the white Left today, whose primary public is comprised of alienated middle-aged intellectuals and momentarily rebellious white college youth? If ever there has been an art exhibiting beyond question all the properties of "bourgeois decadence," this — and not jazz — is it! Yet the single music that perhaps more than any other deserves the appellation "folk" has never been any further away than a switch of the radio dial: on the rhythm-and-blues AM stations (one in every urban center with a sizable Negro ghetto) and, more recently, on the all-jazz FM stations as well. But while jazz was evolving from the bebop and neobebop of the 1940s and 1950s into the contemporary extended improvisa-

---

THIS ORIGINALLY APPEARED IN *REVIEW 1*, ED. FRANCES KELLEY, NEW YORK, MONTHLY REVIEW PRESS, 1965.

tions of Miles Davis, John Coltrane, and Cecil Taylor, and as rhythm-and-blues underwent a tremendous revitalization at the hands of singers such as Ray Charles, the majority of white leftists were still to be found at the same shopworn stand: carrying that execrable hammer to the Cap'n!

The juxtaposition of jazz and black nationalism made in the initial paragraph has more than fortuitous significance — indeed, ·it is their intimate connection that makes the cultural abdication of white radicals in reality so shameful. As poet, jazz critic, playwright and *belletrist* LeRoi Jones makes transparently clear, jazz, like revolutionary black nationalist ideology, springs from the most oppressed stratum of United States society, the Negro working class, the "blues people," in the author's felicitous phrase.[1] And to the same degree that black nationalism implicitly poses on the agenda a thoroughgoing transformation of the American social structure, the aesthetic values of jazz cry out for a no less fundamental restructuring of this country's banal and tepid white middle-class cultural vistas.

But there is still another, more deep-seated sociological relationship linking jazz with black nationalism. Whereas Negro intellectuals and artists functioning in other areas must for the most part appropriate the canons of European, therefore white, culture, there are no such canons on which the Negro jazz musician can draw. On the contrary, the source of his inspiration can *only* stem from his racial subculture. Thus, even though the record companies, night clubs, and other means of jazz production/distribution are in white hands and much of the jazz audience itself is white, the Negro musician must perforce reflect the collective mind of the ghetto in the way that painters or *litterateurs* ordinarily do not.[2] That is why we find that long before the Muslims gained notoriety, as far back as the late 1940s in fact, "advanced" Negro musicians were renouncing Christianity and their Western "slave" names for Islam; the hard bop-funky-soul movement of the 1950s was likewise an early adumbration of the later mass-based black nationalism; and "Freedom Now," recently adopted as the name of an all-black political party, had its original debut in 1961 as the title of a jazz record (generally misunderstood by white critics and ignored by white radicals) featuring the music of nationalist-inspired drummer Max Roach.

For all that, we should not be misled into thinking that the reformulation of jazz in terms of a *deliberately* Negro aesthetic was either effortless or instantaneously achieved. "The

direction, the initial response, which led to hard bop," Jones
tells us, was:

> as much of a "move" within the black psyche as was
> the move North in the beginning of the [twentieth] cen-
> tury. The idea of the Negro's having "roots" and that
> they are a valuable possession, rather than the source
> of ineradicable shame, is perhaps the profoundest
> change within the Negro consciousness since the early
> part of the century. It is a re-evaluation that could
> only be made possible by the conclusions and redress
> of attitude that took place in the forties. . . . The form
> and content of Negro music in the forties recreated,
> or reinforced, the social and historical alienation of
> the Negro in America, *but in the Negro's terms.* . . .
> By the fifties this alienation was seen by many Negro
> musicians not only as valuable, in the face of what-
> ever ugliness the emptiness of the "general" culture served
> to emphasize, but as necessary. [Emphasis added.]

It is this "profoundest change within the Negro consciousness" that LeRoi Jones has set himself to elucidate in *Blues
People* — and far from the least delectable paradox of his highly estimable and immensely provocative book is that it is
a product of the very forces it attempts to delineate. Yet if
Blues People is impossible to imagine without an antecedent
shift in Negro consciousness, at the same time Jones has accomplished that rare feat of raising himself (as the authors
of the *Communist Manifesto* put it) "to the level of comprehending theoretically the historical movement as a whole." The
work, in short, is considerably more than a reflection of the
transitions that have taken place during the last two decades;
rather, it is a reasoned and reflective disquisition ("this book
should be taken as a strictly *theoretical* endeavor") on the
world-historical events that have led up to and produced those
changes. I can think of very few others capable of having
written it. [3]

Those who approach this volume as simply another tome
on jazz and its history should be forewarned that they are
likely to be disappointed. For, notwithstanding its author's
deserved repute as a jazz critic, *Blues People* is not concerned
primarily with jazz *per se*: its province is more accurately
conveyed in the subtitle: *Negro Music in White America.* What
Jones has in actuality done — a thing so disarmingly obvious

one wonders that no one has thought to carry it out before —
is to use Negro music as a sociological tool to analyze the
role and function of the Negro in United States society. In
his own words:

> If the music of the Negro in America, in all its per-
> mutations, is subjected to a socio-anthropological as
> well as musical scrutiny, something about the essen-
> tial nature of the Negro's existence in this country
> ought to be revealed, as well as something about the
> essential nature of this country, i.e., society as a whole.

And again:

> The most expressive Negro music of any given period
> will be an exact reflection of what the Negro himself
> is. It will be a portrait of the Negro in America at that
> particular time. Who he thinks he is, what he thinks
> America or the world to be, given the circumstances,
> prejudices and delights of that particular America.

To recount Jones's conclusions in full is, of course, beyond
the scope of the most ambitious review. Some of the salient
points, however, may be singled out for commentary.

Such an enumeration necessarily begins with an examination of one of the consequences of the continued exclusion of
the Negro from American society — an early chapter of Jones's
book bears the heading: "The Negro as Non-American" — except in his central role as superexploited subproletarian. Here
Jones undertakes to remind us that "adaptation or assimilation was not much of a problem for most Negroes in the nine-
teenth century," since there was always "a border beyond which
the Negro could not go, whether musically or socially. . . .
The Negro could not ever become white and that was his
strength; at some point, always, he could not participate in
the dominant tenor of the white man's culture." But by a rich
dialectical contradiction, it was precisely the existence of this
"boundary," this "no-man's-land" beyond whose confines Negroes
were forbidden to trespass, that occasioned the development
of a distinctive music vastly excelling (in the shared opinion
of author and reviewer) the pallid "culture" whose ideologues
were so unyielding in their rejection of the black man.

But if the Negro masses turned their imprisonment in white
America to good use by creating the most praiseworthy of

the indigenous American arts, this achievement went largely
uncelebrated by the black would-be bourgeoisie. Jones's emphasis on the schism along class lines in the Negro community is another aspect of his book that marks it unmistakably as an outgrowth of the black nationalist ferment. With
respect to the embryonic Negro middle class, Jones is on firm
ground in asserting that it "represented (and represents) not
only an economic condition," but a characteristic ideology
and *Weltanschauung*; it has consistently operated on the assumption:

> that it is better not to be black in a country where
> being black is a liability. All the main roads into Amer-
> ica have always been fashioned by the members of the
> black middle class (not as products of a separate cul-
> ture, but as vague, featureless Americans). . . .
>   It was the growing black middle class who believed
> that the best way to survive in America would be to
> *disappear* completely, leaving no trace at all that there
> had ever been an Africa, or a slavery, or even, finally,
> a black man. This was the only way, they thought, to
> be *citizens*.

The "middle-class black man" thus came to develop "an emotional allegiance to the middle-class (middlebrow) culture of
America," one that "actually made hideous" anything stem-
ming from without that narrow compass. In sum: "The black
middle class wanted no subculture, nothing that could connect
them with the slave."
  Jones's insight into the dynamics of antagonisms between
the essentially white-minded black bourgeoisie and the more
nationalist-oriented blues people yields an especially fruitful
interpretation of contemporary jazz styles in his closing chapter under the rubric of "The Modern Scene." Although previous
writers have hinted at the nationalist impulse that animated
many of the innovators of bebop, Jones adds another dimension to this thesis: bebop was not only a rebellion against
the white commercialization of jazz that had taken place during the swing era, but also a rejection of the stultifying "whiten-
ing" tendencies of the Negro middle class that had to be overcome if the music were to retain its vitality. (Moreover, the
development of bebop, which was protest music at an avow-
edly artistic, intellectual level, occurred simultaneously with a
rank-and-file revolt by the blues people against white middle-

class values in music, culminating in the postwar renaissance of urban rhythm-and-blues. Jones is, to this reviewer's knowledge, the first to have called attention to the underlying connection between bebop and the rhythm-and-blues revival.) Bebop was thus at one and the same time the only thing "that could have restored any amount of excitement and beauty to contemporary jazz" and "the idea that abruptly lifted jazz completely out of the middle-class Negro's life." Jazz, for this Negro, became "as it was for any average American, 'deep' or 'weird.'"[4]

Besides its repudiation of the Negro petty bourgeoisie, what Francis Newton has appropriately referred to as the "bebop revolution" additionally signified the first stirrings in recent years of an overt Negro nationalist consciousness. Tinged though it was by cultism and a predilection for the exotic, the music nonetheless contained "a deep emotional recognition . . . of the rudimentary sterility of the culture" that Negroes had "all their lives been taught to covet." Bebop musicians sought to compensate for this sterility by creating "a meta-culture as isolated as their grandparents', but issuing from the evolved sensibility of a modern urban black American who had by now achieved a fluency with the sociocultural symbols of Western thinking."

In this world nothing remains immobile for long—least of all, given the conditions of the Negro in America, jazz. Since the bebop revolution reached fruition now almost two decades ago, several notable developments have been recorded. The chasm separating the jazz musician as artist from the nitty-gritty folk of the ghetto has to some extent been bridged by the arrival in the last years of the 1950s of the hard bop-soul-funky genre, which had as its proclaimed goal the reaffirmation of black values in jazz music. But the exclusive hegemony of "soul music" turned out to be remarkably short-lived; within a few years the more adventurous figures—Miles Davis, Sonny Rollins, Charles Mingus and, above all, John Coltrane—were casting their muse in heretofore uncharted waters, liberated from the frozen orthodoxies of the soul cliches. (As for Thelonious Monk—he has never taken pains to hide the readily apparent Negro roots in his playing, and perhaps, for that reason, has felt under no compulsion to exhibit them in public during the orgy of soul-baring, nor to retract them after the halcyon days of soul music had passed.) These men have more recently been joined by a crop of younger iconoclastic jazz musicians, predominantly saxo-

phonists but with the other instruments also represented, among
whom the names of Ornette Coleman (alto saxophone) and the
truly formidable pianist, Cecil Taylor, may be most familiar.

No revolutionary movement, as Trotsky was fond of pointing out, ever advances along an unbroken ascendant. Some
of the innovations of what Jones has here and elsewhere de-
noted as the jazz avant-garde have resulted in less than devastating success; yet that is no reason for assuming that the
eventual triumph of the new conceptions is not in the long
run assured. In this connection, the intrepid defense of the
avant-garde from the attacks of the jazz Establishment — those
white writers who augment their income as record company
executives and publicists by composing jazz "criticism" as an
avocation — is not the least valuable function which *Blues People* performs, and performs well. Jones could not be more correct in writing, vis-a-vis the latter-day critical reactionaries:

> The same kinds of comment and misguided protest
> have greeted the music of [Ornette] Coleman and other
> young musicians that greeted the music of [Charlie]
> Parker and [Dizzy] Gillespie and [Thelonious] Monk
> in the forties. Where the music of Parker, et al., was
> called in *Downbeat* magazine "ill-advised fanaticism,"
> Coleman's music is called "anti-jazz."[5]

Another aspect of the bebop revolution which today bulks
large, albeit one that Jones does not explore to the fullest,
was the tremendous appeal of the then new music for disaf-
fected and alienated white nonconformists — with the prominent exception, naturally, of the political Left. This rejection
of "their own" culture by a relative handful of whites ("merely by being a Negro in America one *was* a noncomformist")
prefigured the much larger exposure to Negro music that the
generation which is just now coming to maturity has enjoyed.
Needless to say, such exposure can in no wise substitute for
a politically awakened and working-class-based radical movement capable of lending meaningful support to the Black Revolution. But at a time when all classes of whites have drunk
so heavily and long at the fount of white-supremacist ideology
— a point that requires weighty emphasis for certain Marxist
tendencies — this experience is not to be dismissed entirely out
of hand. I, for one, am quite convinced that when it comes
to the denouement, more than a few whites may find themselves on the "wrong" side of the barricades simply because

a Ray Charles or a Miles Davis has been instrumental in giving them a changed perception of reality that, under existing circumstances, could scarcely have been obtained in any other way. If the traditional Left in this country has fallen far short of its fundamental goal of imbuing white workers with a class-wide consciousness, it cannot be said that Negro culture has failed to make its vivid imprint on those young whites fortunate enough to have caught at least a taste of it. [6]

Moreover, although white radicals seem mostly unaware of it, spokesmen for the culture of the blues people like LeRoi Jones are, through their critique of the barbaric mores and values of white America, making a profound contribution to the eventual reconstruction of society on humanist (or just human) lines. Of course, cultural "criticism" *per se* is not an altogether novel phenomenon. Ever since the rise of widespread literacy in Western Europe and the attendant mass reproduction of the commodities of popular art, there has always been a certain stratum of the intelligentsia eager to inveigh against the degraded tastes of the swinish multitude. (Currently this position is perhaps most clearly articulated by Jacques Barzun.) Now there is no denying that much of what we are exposed to via the mass media is genuinely abominable; as Walter Benjamin and others have demonstrated, the necessary consequence of art, including "entertainment," dealt with as a commodity to be mass-produced for maximum profit is a rapid descent to the level of the least common denominator; with the result that a sort of Gresham's Law comes to prevail: bad art drives out good.

Thus far the intellectual critique possesses a measure of justification. But with what do the intellectuals hope to replace the much-excoriated "mass culture" (over which the masses have precious little control)? It is the answer to this question that, more surely than any other, reveals the bankruptcy of this ideology. For, by and large, the intelligentsia has nothing more substantial to offer than the desiccated, if not effete, works of the fashionable salons and academies over which they, as self-anointed cultural arbiters, reign. Isolated from the mainstream and hostile to it, these figures come to glory in their status, thus neatly transforming necessity into virtue. Because of their contempt for *all* popular art, they have lost the ability — if ever they had it — to distinguish the commendable from the merely trashy. To them, popular art is uniformly worthless — otherwise, how could it be popular? The clearest evidence of this attitude can be observed in the intellectual treatment

of jazz and Negro culture in general. Outside of an occasional nod here and there, the magazines of the liberal intelligentsia
— *Harper's, Atlantic, The Nation, New Republic, Commentary,*
etc. — either totally ignore jazz, or treat it as a manifestation
of "nigger exotica" (the recent *Time* cover story on Thelonious
Monk is symptomatic even though *Time* is not a "liberal" magazine), or else relegate it to the same obscurity as the cross-
word puzzle department and the astrology column. And in
this the Left has apparently found nothing better to do than
ape the liberals!

Fortunately, the whole issue is rapidly being taken out of
the hands of white liberals and radicals alike. The most telling
strictures against the insipidity of virtually every aspect of
white culture are now being put forward by black-nationalist-
influenced Negro writers; the names of Jones, Harold Cruse
(who occasionally lacks clarity), Robert Vernon (in many
ways the wittiest of the lot), and the staff of *Liberator* magazine come most immediately to mind. Outspokenly antipathet-
ic to the prevalent cultural sterility in the United States, these
writers have posed the most direct challenge yet to the norms
of middle-class America — in sharp contrast to the tendency
of all too many white radicals to acquiesce in the spiritual
aridity that is the status quo (remember "Communism is twentieth-century Americanism"?). What sets the nationalist (using
the word in its most inclusive sense) critique at opposite poles
from the liberal intellectual attack on "mass culture" is, that
the former is based not on narrow, elitist premises, but on
the democratic idea that art, to be meaningful, must maintain
its organic roots in the masses, reflecting their joys and their
travails, their aspirations and frustrations. To illustrate that
this is no idle fantasy, the nationalists can point to jazz and
the other manifestations of the "Negro soul"; for here are vig-
orous and flourishing arts that have retained their connection
with life without having sacrificed anything in the way of aesthetic worth. Armed with firsthand knowledge of a subculture
that has produced such remarkable creations as jazz music,
and repelled by the hollowness and sickening amorality characteristic of the majority civilization, Jones and his fellow writers are defying the liberal shibboleth of "integration" by demanding to know: into *what?* In so doing they have won for
themselves the undying enmity of liberals, white and black;
all the more reason, then, for genuine white radicals to tender
them appreciation and support.

At this point we have come full circle to this essay's opening lines. It is indicative of the nature of the times in which we live that even a book whose ostensible main concern is music cannot avoid ending on a political note:

> The American Negro is being asked to defend the American system as energetically as the American white man. There is no doubt that the middle-class Negro is helping and will continue to help in that defense. But there is perhaps a question mark in the minds of many poor blacks (which is one explanation for the attraction of such groups as the Black Muslims) and also now in the minds of many young Negro intellectuals. What is it that they are being asked to save? It is a good question, and America had better come up with an answer.

It is not to be supposed, if history affords any instruction whatsoever, that the present ruling class will take overmuch cognizance of even the best-intentioned warnings. Quite the contrary: in all probability, little or nothing will be attempted until the opportune moment has already slipped by — and this writer is profoundly in error if yesterday was not already too late. But if the white power structure has shown itself to be blind to all the auguries of an impending conflict, one may venture at least a timid hope that the much battered, fragmented, and disoriented American Left will not continue to insist on being similarly imperceptive to where its real interests lie.

Chapter 3
BLACK MUSIC: COLD WAR
"SECRET WEAPON"

Is black music an instrument of United States cold-war diplomacy?

Late in 1965 a controversy over that question erupted in the pages of *Jazz* magazine (now *Jazz & Pop*), set off by the revelation of Willis Conover, music consultant for the Voice of America, that a European musician had reported to him: "the uncommited people may very well indeed be attracted to the American [cold war] position by your broadcasts of American music." "And meanwhile," Conover himself added, "our music helps maintain contact with people already inclined to sympathize with the United States . . ."

Subsequently criticized for employing jazz to counteract the increasingly unfavorable impression created by U. S. foreign policy, especially in Vietnam, Conover issued a disclaimer: the conversation quoted above had taken place "some years ago, before we were in Vietnam." Leaving aside the fact that U. S. involvement in Vietnam goes back to 1948, when this country began to assume roughly 70 percent of the cost of France's war to repress the Viet Minh, Conover's denial is implausible on the face of it, as is made quite clear by an

---

* The title of this chapter derives in part from a front-page article in *The New York Times* of November 6, 1955, by Felix Belair,Jr. Datelined Geneva, Switzerland, Belair's story reported:

"America's secret weapon is a blue note in a minor key. Right now its most effective ambassador is Louis (Satchmo) Armstrong. A telling propaganda line is the hopped up tempo of a Dixieland band heard on the Voice of America in far-off Tangier. . . .

"American jazz has now become a universal language. It knows no national boundaries, but everybody knows where it comes from and where to look for more. . . ."

examination of his employer, the Voice of America. The VOA
grew out of the Office of War Information, a central ministry
of propaganda of the sort established by every wartime government, at the close of the Second World War. As the U. S.
began to transform its policy vis-a-vis the Soviet Union from
one of cooperation to one of military "containment," the VOA
was converted (in Conover's words) into "the radio arm of
the United States Information Agency," which, as is well known,
supervises the dissemination of pro- U. S. and antisocialist propaganda throughout the world. In short, the USIA is strictly
an outgrowth of the cold war, and were that war to end tomorrow, the USIA would soon vanish, taking with it the VOA.

Notwithstanding all the evidence to the contrary, Conover
still maintains that his efforts at the Voice of America do not
amount to cold-war propaganda: "my purpose in doing the
Voice of America program is . . . to show us as we are."
One may be permitted to express a modicum of doubt. Conover's version of the United States "as we are" will scarcely
be recognized by the reader. He insists, for example, that "what's
changed is the circumstances most of us live in, changed for
the better, and continuing to change for the better," and that
"in ten years at the most, there'll be nothing but a few illiterate
old diehard racists left in a few backwoods Southern shanties"
as the last vestiges of segregation. By way of supporting his
contention, he informs us that now "Sarah Vaughn and I can
dance at the White House," whereas twenty years ago, when
"Washington *was* a segregated Southern town, we had to go to
an illegal uptown after-hours club" [emphasis added.]

Conover's distortions of life in the United States are not
merely accidental; they are part of a larger USIA attempt
aimed at picturing this country, and its black-white relations
in particular, in the most roseate of tones. As I was completing
this article, I came upon deposed President of Ghana Kwame
Nkrumah's description of the USIA broadcasts in Africa as:
"the chief executor of U. S. psychological warfare, [glorifying]
the U. S. while attempting to discredit countries [like Ghana
under Nkrumah] with an independent foreign policy," and
"planning and coordinating its activities in close touch with
the Pentagon, CIA and other Cold War agencies, including
even armed forces intelligence centers." Dr. Nkrumah also reveals that when governments in Togo and the Congo (Leo-
poldville) wished to permit information centers from the Soviet Union as well as the United States, "Washington threatened

to stop all aid, thereby forcing these two countries to renounce their plan." 1

The evidence is that Dr. Nkrumah's picture of the USIA is an accurate one. The Deputy Director of USIA, Donald M. Wilson, told the House Foreign Affairs Subcommittee that his agency had "very close" relations with the CIA. "We have daily contact with them [CIA and other intelligence agencies] on a number of levels."2 The authors of *The Invisible Government* state that the VOA is "the official voice of the United States Government." "It should be obvious," they add, that its broadcasts "across national boundaries to other nations, particularly behind the Iron Curtain, are among the mechanisms of United States foreign policy."3 All of which disturbs Willis Conover not in the least. "What is wrong," he wants to know, "with presenting a good music program . . . ?" What indeed!

But, as was illustrated by a pair of recent events in such widely separated spots as Lisbon, Portugal, and Dakar, Senegal, the VOA-USIA complex is not the only official governmental agency to make use of jazz in furthering cold-war diplomacy. In the first of these incidents, reported in the jazz magazine *Down Beat* of March 10, 1966, under the headline "Jazz Halts Viet Protest," a scheduled demonstration by students at the Lisbon University Medical Faculty against U. S. intervention in Vietnam was "called off . . . after a concert at the University . . . by a jazz sextet from the *Springfield*, a U. S. Sixth Fleet cruiser in Lisbon for a five-day call."

The second item dates from a few weeks later. Again the headline (from a story in *The New York Times*, April 30, 1966) is most enlightening on the way in which Washington views the cold-war utility of jazz:

SOVIET POETS FAIL
TO CAPTURE DAKAR
Duke Ellington the Winner
in Propaganda Skirmish

The "win" of Ellington's referred to had taken place at Senegal's first World Festival of Negro Arts; and to underline the point that more was involved than merely art-for-art's-sake, the story's author, Lloyd Garrison, wrote that Soviet poet Yevgeni Yevtushenko "had been urgently summoned from Moscow to do

for Soviet propaganda what Duke Ellington had done for the
Americans . . ."

It is, of course, saddening that the works of artists of the
stature of Ellington and Yevtushenko are debased into ideological counters in the cold-war rivalry between antagonistic
social systems. What makes it even more disturbing, as far
as the United States is concerned, is the degree of hypocrisy
involved. For if the Soviet Union brings to bear its poets,
its dancers, and its musicians in the propaganda battle, it at
least pays these artists the elementary courtesy of giving them
a decent livelihood and an honored position in Soviet life.
Contrary to our own practice, the Soviets do not send their
artists and intellectuals abroad as roving ambassadors, only to consign them to second-class citizenship at home. Instead, there the artist is generally considered on a par with the
scientist, the professional, the government bureaucrat, and even
the Communist party member.

Would that this were true in the United States! If the *Times*
had wanted to be more thorough (not to say more ironic),
it could have followed up its account of Ellington's "triumph"
in Dakar by pointing out that the same Ellington had been
rejected for a Pulitzer Prize in music less than a year ago.
This juxtaposition — not atypical, just more glaring than most —
exemplifies the unwritten rule that jazz may be eminently serviceable for cold-war campaigns abroad, but when it comes
to winning acceptance *at home*, the prospects are more grim.
So far as the cultural-intellectual Establishment is concerned,
jazz is the unwanted stepchild of the arts. It is utilized for
Voice of America broadcasts, its practitioners are eagerly sought
for State Department tours; yet should it be proposed to the
representatives of the Establishment who are so concerned
with the worsening U. S. "image" that a jazz musician should
be the recipient of a foundation grant, a visiting professorship, or a Pulitzer Prize, the response would be one of shock
and dismay.

Possibly the best way to get a perspective on just where
jazz stands with respect to the Establishment is to look at
the position it occupies — or rather doesn't occupy — in the university. The reason I say this is that the university is in some
ways a microcosm of the Establishment as a whole. As we
now know from studies produced during free-speech contro-
versies at campuses all over the country, universities are gov-
erned by boards of regents, trustees, etc., on which sit representatives of the dominant business groups in the community. [4]

In a general way, the curriculum of the university is molded
so as to conform with the desire of this corporate elite to turn
out mid-level technicians with all the approved social attitudes
(an idea most frequently propounded by Clark Kerr in his
concept of the "multiversity"). Consequently, if one wishes to
see the value which the corporate elite — that is, the pinnacle
of the Establishment — places on jazz domestically (as opposed
to the value placed on it as a cold-war instrument), one could
do worse than look at the university curriculum.

With this in mind, I carried out a short survey of fifty college
and university catalogs chosen at random. Of the fifty institutions, only three offered courses in jazz (though no course title
mentioned jazz by name, the more respectable euphemism "stage
band" being preferred). It should be emphasized, moreover,
that the dearth of jazz on the campus is not to be explained by
its relative newness. As forms of art, photography and jazz
are of roughly the same age; but photography — perhaps because its origins cannot be traced to "niggers" — has been able
to breach the walls of the University, whereas jazz, aside from
some very rare exceptions, has not. In the same fifty colleges
and universities referred to, there were eight with courses in
photography, almost three times the number of those giving
courses in jazz. UCLA, for instance, has an entire graduate
department in cinematic arts, while Yale now offers a course
in the aesthetics of film-making — but neither one makes any
mention of jazz in its catalog. At California State College at
Los Angeles, where I taught in 1964-65, one may take up
to seven courses in photography, including one in motion picture photography, a technique less than a half-century old. Of
jazz courses, however, there is not a one. For that matter, the
opportunities for music students to play jazz for academic credit
are so limited at Cal State L.A. that alto-saxophonist Jimmy
Woods preferred sociology to music as his major.

There are no grounds for believing that conditions elsewhere
are any better, as the experiences of John Handy at the other
end of the state (San Francisco State College) attest. Despite
the fact that he was regarded by his music professors as their
outstanding student and a model for the others, Handy, an
inventive saxophonist who worked with bassist Charles Mingus
before forming his own group, found that his insistence in
trying to obtain courses that offered credit for jazz playing
resulted in nothing more than a head-on collision with the department.

For every case of a university (North Texas State, for example) that offers a jazz-oriented education to the tyro musician, Handy's story could, I am sure, be repeated several times over. And the bias against jazz extends beyond the music department. Every four-year college and university presents a series of performances and lectures by visiting artists and writers — but virtually never jazz. There is, for instance, a Committee on Arts and Lectures (CAL) which plans such programs at the University of California, and well do I remember the hour of fruitless wrangling I spent with one of the upper-echelon administrators of CAL on this subject. Why, I wanted to know, were jazz artists never featured in the CAL programs? That was simple: jazz was "entertainment" not art. Against this arbitrary verdict I expostulated in vain, until sensing the futility of that approach, I shifted ground. Perhaps there was an explanation I had overlooked as to how the inclusion of comedienne Anna Russell [famous for her operatic spoofs] in the series for the coming year could be justified under the heading of "art." If Anna Russell, why not the vocal trio of Lambert, Hendricks, and Ross? At this juncture the conversation disintegrated completely. My opposite began spluttering about how "everyone" loved Anna Russell . . . one couldn't take these things too seriously . . . of course you understand . . . perhaps next year . . . and so on, until finally unable to bear any more, I excused myself. Thus jazz had to wait for its introduction on the Berkeley campus until the spring of 1960, when the Students for Racial Equality sponsored a concert to benefit what was later to become the Student Nonviolent Coordinating Committee. (Naturally, the Kerr administration refused to let us take the money off campus to aid our fellow students in the South — but that's another story, whose narration properly belongs in an introductory chapter to a history of the Berkeley Free Speech Movement.)

For brevity's sake I have concentrated on the university, but other, equally meaningful indicators could have been employed instead. One might look, for example, at the Establishment "intellectual" magazines — periodicals like *Harper's, Atlantic, The Saturday Review, The New York Review of Books*, the *New York Times Magazine* — and compare the amount of space devoted to jazz with that given over to European music, painting, books, or any other art which the Establishment deems of value. The results of such a survey would not be much different from what has already been stated with respect to the Academy. Very few of these periodicals discuss jazz at all, and fewer yet with any regularity. Contrary to what might be expected, moreover, the smaller-circulation journals of the liberal and radical left offer no dissent from the Establishment view of jazz; if anything, there is less coverage of jazz in such journals as the liberal *Nation* and *New Republic*, or the radical *Monthly Review* and *National Guardian*, than can be read in *Harper's* or the *Saturday Review*. But the differences are in any case negligible in the face of the overwhelming lack of respect for jazz which all of the above-named periodicals exhibit.

Why this intransigent hostility to jazz on the part of Establishment educators, administrators, arbiters of culture, and patrons of the arts? The answer, as I have previously hinted, lies in the origins of jazz, particularly its black origins. Regardless of whether jazz came up the river from New Orleans or was born at Harlem rent parties, the popular stereotype of it is — bluntly — "nigger" music. Attitudes of white intellectual supremacy and European ethnocentrism are so thoroughly ingrained that it is impossible for many whites, even "intellectuals," to conceive of a Negro art as equal in aesthetic value to a white one. To be sure, one may occasionally find a piece of African sculpture in the home of some white intellectuals; that is "quaint," or "primitive." Undeniably, it is now fashionable to own the recordings of Negro performers like Lightnin' Hopkins or Big Bill Broonzy; that is acceptably "folksy." But what is absolutely too threatening for most of us to bear is the notion that American Negro artists can produce a music which rivals European music in its complexity and demands on the listener's intellect. So when the grants are handed out, the visiting professorships dispensed, and the awards announced for the American artists judged outstanding, one will scan the list from beginning to end without encountering the name of a single jazz musician.

I don't deny that there are occasional exceptions to this rule, but these are more apparent than real. Almost always the musicians so honored will be white, and therefore their triumphs will be exceptions and nothing more. It is extremely important to understand why rewards for white musicians cannot be taken as a vindication for the music itself. It is not that whites are incapable of playing jazz. Clearly this is not true, although nearly all whites (of necessity) choose Negro models to imitate. The point is, however, that whites are not now and have never been a seminal force in *developing* the music. Two or three white jazz musicians at most have been able to leave a permanent imprint on the jazz that came after them; the major innovations have always stemmed from the black ghetto. This generalization is as applicable today as it was in New Orleans in the 1920s, in Chicago in the 1930s, in New York in the 1940s. A simple tabulation of the more than 200 instrumentalists listed by name in the 1965 International Jazz Critics Poll [5] shows that over 70 percent of the most distinguished jazz artists are Negro—and even that statistic probably understates the case. Nonetheless, for the same causes that have prevented jazz from assuming its rightful place among the other arts, whenever the Establishment seeks to acknowledge the achievement of a jazz musician, almost invariably it is a white band that reaches out to grasp the prize. Most Negroes involved in the music rightly view such occasions as a victory not *for* jazz, but *over* it. *

By way of illustration, take the case of two jazz musicians whose versatility and schooling in the European masters are roughly comparable. Pianist Cecil Taylor and trumpeter Don Ellis can both boast of an extensive "legitimate" education; insofar as they differ, it is because Ellis is white, Taylor black. Need I say which one received a visiting professorship at UCLA, a Rockefeller Foundation grant, and regular employment at *Shelly's Manne-Hole* in Los Angeles to boot? With all due appreciation for Ellis' talent, his good fortune must be held a monstrous injustice to Taylor and to jazz. The history of jazz in the 1960s cannot be written without pages devoted to the influence of Cecil Taylor; in that same history, Don Ellis would merit a footnote. Yet it is Ellis who obtains the academic appointment and who works steadily, while Taylor is deprived of all but sporadic employment and thus the opportunity, so necessary to the creative jazz musician, to have his music interact with an audience.

Invitations to the White House for jazz musicians provide a second index of the way in which the Establishment channels its rewards primarily to whites. To my knowledge, the jazz performers who have received such invitations in the last few

---

* "At this point a couple of questions that are asked time and time again can be interjected. Why the almost systematic exclusion of qualified Negro jazzmen from collegiate and [music] clinic jazz programs? Why in a list of 30 clinicians listed for a summer jazz clinic are there only three Negro clinicians? Even more ridiculous is the low percentage of Negroes teaching jazz in the colleges and universities that offer or specialize in jazz courses." Dave Baker, "Jazz: The Academy's Neglected Stepchild," *Down Beat,* September 23, 1965, p. 29. The author, needless to say, a Negro, played trombone with an avant-garde sextet led by George Russell and is presently a music educator at the college level.

years are Sarah Vaughn, Duke Ellington, Gerry Mulligan, Paul Winter, and Dave Brubeck, the latter three being white. While I have respect for all of these artists, it is simply a willful perversion of reality to argue that they represent a cross section of the best or most interesting or most vital or most relevant that the music has to offer. Why Gerry Mulligan or Dave Brubeck, when the contributions of either Thelonious Monk or Miles Davis have been universally proclaimed (in jazz circles) of much greater significance? Why Paul Winter, of whom nine out of ten jazz followers have probably never even heard (his outstanding accomplishment to date being a State Department trip to Latin America), rather than the revolutionary innovations of John Coltrane? I don't have foolproof answers to these questions, but my hunch is that the groups that were invited were judged to be more acceptable on both musical and *social* grounds. After all, one can sit and appear to be enjoying Paul Winter's music without ever really paying much attention. But can you imagine responding that way to Coltrane or Miles Davis, who are so preoccupied with their art as actually to *sweat* while they play? (Really! *Sweat* at the White House?)

This pattern of whites obtaining a disproportionate share of whatever fitful recognition the Establishment is willing to bestow on jazz is anything but a new one. Regardless of the almost exclusive creation of the music by Negroes, they have never been the ones to reap the most lucrative returns. In the 1930s it was Benny Goodman, instead of Count Basie or Duke Ellington, who grew wealthy on the craze for swing music; and two decades later it was Goodman and his sometime drummer Gene Krupa who had movies made out of their lives — not Ellington nor Basie, not Jo Jones nor Lionel Hampton, though all of these men had more to do with the genesis of swing than Goodman or Krupa. The situation has not changed appreciably in the interim. In the fifties Dave Brubeck preceded Thelonious Monk on the cover of *Time* magazine by several years, despite the fact that Monk's music antedates Brubeck's by at least a decade and has exerted a much more powerful pull on the ultimate critics of the music, the musicians themselves.

Furthermore, when *Time* magazine finally did get around to doing a feature on Monk, there was a marked difference in the way it treated him as compared to Brubeck. The latter was handled as a respectable middle-class citizen with all the conventional bourgeois attributes and only one minor idiosyncrasy — that of being a jazz pianist. Monk, on the other hand, was presented to *Time's* readers as a combination of mad savage (the funny hats, the ritualistic dances) and some sort of pharmacological eighth wonder of the world. The closing paragraphs of *Time's* story on Monk then went on to depict several other Negro jazz luminaries as if they were performers in a side show: Coltrane was protrayed as a vegetarian mystic; Miles Davis, it was implied, teaches boxing to his children so they can attack whites; and so on.

It is worth stressing that more than mere honorifics are involved in the differential reception of whites and blacks by the Establishment: a performer's whole way of life can be altered, depending on the response his music obtains. Benny Goodman has been able to retire from the ignoble occupation of jazz musician to the rarified heights of Mozart clarinet concerti; but Duke Ellington and Count Basie are forced to continue presenting their artistry in dance halls and dingy nightclubs under a schedule of one-nighters that no self-respecting "legitimate" artist of their stature would dream of accepting.

A great deal of jazz's history can thus be summarized with the observation that despite the sweeping changes in the music which have occured since the time of Goodman, the distribution of economic benefits has not been substantially altered. Notwithstanding the repeated assertion of many white jazz journalists that all artists (or all avant-garde artists, if they are the ones under discussion) have "the same problems," there is little basis for this inane bit of conventional wisdom. Bill Dixon, an avant-garde trumpeter, composer, and the principal organizer of a short-lived musicians' cooperative, the Jazz Composers Guild, states unequivocally that white avant-garde musicians are treated "significantly better . . . than are black musicians," adding: "White players have a leverage which Negro players do not. Many of them also play in symphony orchestras or work with other avant-garde white musicians in a nonjazz idiom and get grants and subsidies from that. Those [white] cats may be criticized a lot, but they are recognized as artists."

Dixon's argument has particular relevance to the area of "studio work," i.e., semipermanent employment by one of the large recording firms, television studios or motion picture corporations in New York City or Hollywood. Studio work is highly valued among jazz musicians because it provides a safety net of economic security against the possibility of hard times, and also because it enables the musician to avoid the

hazardous and debilitating experience of going "on the road."
But with some minor exceptions (Clark Terry, Richard Davis
in the East; Harry Edison, Benny Carter in the West), employment in the studios for jazz musicians is, in general, restricted to whites. Alto saxophonist Sonny Criss, a Negro,
told a reporter from *Down Beat*: ". . . talk about Los Angeles,
I lived here since I was twenty-five [a period of twenty years]
and never saw the inside of a movie studio. In France, within
six months, I was on the Riviera playing in and for a high-
budget film . . . with Tony Perkins — making $200 a day!"*
   It would be no trouble at all to compile a prodigious catalog
of experiences of black musicians similar to those of Criss.
For example, George Russell, a talented and much admired
avant-garde composer and theoretician now an expatriate in
Europe, has written of "dreary subway trips to Macy's or
scrubbing floors or washing dishes in a Harlem, Bronx, or
Brooklyn luncheonette" to keep alive. "Until last year," he continues, "I held a membership card in Local 1199, Retail Drug
Workers' Union of New York" — a statement that few white
musicians of *any* persuasion could duplicate. Indeed, the situation for Negro avant-garde jazz artists has become so bleak
that one of them, the gifted and iconoclastic pianist Andrew
Hill, has been reduced to the expedient of calling on readers
of *Down Beat* to send him one dollar each "so I can survive,
and that will be appreciated in the true sense of brotherhood
. . ."
   One concludes from this chilling survey that the attempt of
the Establishment to utilize jazz to win cold-war propaganda
"victories" like that of Duke Ellington at Dakar has not resulted in fundamental improvements in the jazz musician's
social status or economic well-being. On the contrary, this is
but the most recent in a series of expropriations by which the
black community has been deprived of the fruits that should
have accrued to it from its musical innovations.
   Although the status quo has not materially altered, the response of the black artists has. Consciousness of the exploitative conditions under which jazz musicians are forced to create

* Criss had more reasons than the simple availability of studio
work to explain his enthusiasm for France: "People listen here. And
racially . . . oh, man, racially, it is the greatest feeling over there . . .
I must admit, for the first time in my life — and that means from
my childhood in Memphis right up to Los Angeles — I was completely relaxed. . . . Result? I played in a way that I never played
before."

has, of course, always been present; but it has been only recently that protest against those conditions has become explicit
and unremitting. In the early fifties an anonymous California
musician bemoaned the plight of the black man in jazz to
German critic J. E. Berendt in despairing tones:

> You see, as soon as we have a music, the white man
> comes and imitates it. We've now had jazz for fifty
> years, and in all those fifty years there has not been
> a single white man, perhaps leaving aside Bix [Beider-
> becke], who has had an idea. Only the coloured men
> have ideas. But if you see who's got the famous names:
> they're all white.
>   What can we do? We must go on inventing something
> new all the time. When we have it, the whites will take
> it from us, and we have to start all over again. It
> is as though we were being hunted.[6]

Now the tone of despair is gone, replaced by one which min-
gles militant discontent ("We are not angry young men," tenor
saxophonist Archie Shepp told one interviewer, "we are
enraged.") and political radicalism in equal proportions.

   "The black people are becoming more and more dissatisfied.
And if changes don't take place within ten years, there'll be
a revolution." Those are the words not of some "aggressive" —
a favorite term among white writers — upstart, but of trumpeter
Dizzy Gillespie, one of the most popular and widely respected
jazz musicians ever to put horn to lips — and incidentally,
one most often chosen by the State Department to go on tour.
As shocking as Gillespie's statement has seemed to some in
the jazz world, it pales beside the sentiments heard from the
younger generation of black avant-garde artists. It is widely
rumored, for example, that prominent avant-garde musicians
on the West Coast have affiliated themselves with the W.E.B.
DuBois Clubs; while in New York Archie Shepp voices his
denunciation of "these United States, which, in my estimation,
is one of the most vicious, racist social systems in the world —
with the possible exceptions of [Southern] Rhodesia, South
Africa, and South Viet Nam."
   "For the moment a helpless witness to the bloody massacre
of my people on streets that run from Hayneville through
Harlem," Shepp demands of his readers:

   Don't you ever wonder just what my collective rage

will . . . be like, when it is — as it inevitably must be — unleashed? Our vindication will be black as the color of suffering is black, as Fidel is black, as Ho Chi Minh is black. It is thus that I offer my right hand across the worlds of suffering to black compatriots everywhere. When they fall victim to war, disease, poverty — all systematically enforced — I fall with them, and I am a yellow skin, and they are black like me or even white. For them and me I offer this prayer, that this twenty-eighth year of mine will never again find us all so poor, nor the rapine forces of the world in such sanguinary circumstances. [7]

Here speaks the new radicalism of the black jazz musician. Given this degree of political sophistication and the willingness to articulate it, one suspects that as an Establishment weapon in the cold war, jazz may yet turn out to be a double-edged sword.

Photo by Frank Kofsky

ARCHIE SHEPP

PART II

BLACK NATIONALISM AND
THE REVOLUTION IN MUSIC

Photo by Frank Kofsky

ALBERT AYLER

Chapter 4
REVOLUTION IN BLACK MUSIC: ORIGINS AND DIRECTIONS

At the climactic moment of LeRoi Jones's allegorical drama *Dutchman*, the author has the enraged hero (Black America) denounce his blond would-be "seductress" (i.e., enslaver) in a scathing passage, a portion of which runs as follows:

> Old baldheaded four-eyed ofays popping their fingers
> . . . and don't know yet what they're doing. They say,
> "I love Bessie Smith." And don't even understand that
> Bessie Smith is saying, "Kiss my ass, kiss my black
> unruly ass." Before love, suffering, desire, anything
> you can explain, she's saying, and very plainly, "Kiss
> my black ass." And if you don't know that, it's you
> that's doing the kissing.
> Charlie Parker? Charlie Parker. All the hip white
> boys scream for Bird. And Bird saying, "Up your
> ass, feebleminded ofays! Up your ass." And they sit
> there talking about the tortured genius of Charlie
> Parker. . . .[1]

This speech has a reality which transcends the question of whether or not Jones is "factually" correct in a narrow sense (the truth is the whole, as Hegel long ago put it). Regardless of what Bessie Smith was actually singing, or even what she thought she was singing, or what Bird intended with his music, the view which Jones enunciates is coming to be increasingly characteristic of the sentiments of the current crop of Young Turks in jazz, and of course not just in jazz: the avant-garde generation, if you will. Indeed, I am deliberately understating the case from what I believe to be prevalent; my intuitive suspicion is that the alienation from the Wasp Amer-

SOME OF THE MATERIAL IN THIS CHAPTER ORIGINALLY APPEARED IN *JAZZ*, JANUARY 1966.

ican Dream of thinking young Negro radicals — among whom many of the avant-gardists must be numbered — has proceeded considerably further than the white reading public is cognizant.

As for the reasons behind this massive repudiation of the Dream, let it suffice here to remark that the Negro was never meant to be anything in American society but a slave. The freeing of Negroes in the Civil War was widely regarded in the North as a regrettable but unavoidable consequence of the military struggle against the South. In his Emancipation Proclamation — which, it should be recalled, specifically exempted loyal slave states from its provisions — Lincoln justified it on the grounds of military necessity three times. Even before that internecine conflict, the life of the quarter of a million free Negroes of the North had been made a hell; all the institutions of Jim Crow and second-class citizenship were, in fact, brought to perfection not in the magnolia-scented South, but in the more austere climes of the ante-bellum North. So inconceivable in the U. S. social structure was the notion of a creature who was both free *and* Negro that either the freedom had to be destroyed or the Negro had to be harried out of the land. Under these conditions it comes as no surprise to learn that Negro nationalism — black rejection of an oppressive white-dominated culture — sprang up as early as the decade of the 1850s among these free Negroes. [2]

Nor did any marked departure from these precedents take place after the Civil War; there was, that is, no intention in either the South *or* the North of allowing Negroes to attain anything approaching genuine equality. [3] The voters of New York State, Professor Litwack recounts, turned down a constitutional amendment to enfranchise Negroes in 1869 — *four years following the conclusion of the Civil War;* and the New York electorate was in no wise atypical.

The white American consensus on excluding the Negro from its rights and abundance has never been decisively shattered, for there was nothing in the American experience that would undermine it, no influential vested interests concerned with altering the status quo. On the contrary, the ruling powers all more or less aligned themselves with the policy of subordination of the blacks. (In the political sphere this was most apparent: Woodrow Wilson was an ardent segregationist, and Teddy Roosevelt and Herbert Hoover both sought to build up a "lily-white" Republican party in the South. Northern industrialists, the economic group that after the Civil War converted the South into an economic appendage of the North,

concurred: cheap labor — Negro and white, since low wages
for the one inevitably affected the status of the other — meant
high profits; and besides, Negro strikebreakers could always
be put to good use in deciding labor disputes in favor of the
corporation owners — mute but eloquent testimony to the racist
predilections of the white workers.) In this way, racism was
maintained in the position it had always held: a staple item
in white American life. [4]

The association of racist philosophies with the Axis foes during World War II brought about an epochal change in the
United States: for the first time it became unfashionable to
profess white-supremacist sentiments in public. Pressured by
Negro militants and white radicals and anxious to avoid the
embarrassment that would result from such projected anti-
discrimination protests as the 1941 March on Washington,
a Roosevelt administration that had on several occasions permitted antilynching bills to be talked to death in Congress
reluctantly moved to prohibit the most blatant manifestations
of Jim Crow. For those old enough to remember the overtly
racist character of the government's wartime anti-Japanese
propaganda ("dirty Japs"), the sincerity of this belated conversion to the side of the angels is open to question. Indeed,
Negro Seabees found this propaganda so repugnant that they
engaged in a series of strikes to compel the federal government to withdraw it from circulation. Nevertheless, it cannot
be denied that the combination of increased demand for industrial labor and the official U. S. ideology of a "victory
over racism" did produce some tangible wartime benefits for
black Americans.

It proved impossible to restore the full range of Jim Crow
practices following the conclusion of peace in 1945. For one
thing, a minority of young and idealistic whites, perhaps
touched by the social radicalism prevalent in the 1930s, took
the slogan of a "victory over racism" seriously. Still more important, the U. S. cold-war policies placed crucial significance
on wooing the nonwhite, formerly colonial nations away from
a possible rapprochement with the Soviet Union; and to this
end it was required that the United States divest itself of the
more obvious trappings of racism. Ultimately, such was the
logic that prompted the 1954 Supreme Court decision on "desegregation" of the public schools: not a root-and-branch overturn of the pattern of second-class noncitizenship, but a propaganda gesture intended primarily for foreign consumption.
Thus the U. S. Attorney General's supporting brief in this case

quite openly proclaimed that: "It is in the context of the present world struggle between freedom [sic!] and tyranny that the problem of racial discrimination must be viewed. . . . Racial discrimination furnishes grist for the Communist propaganda mills."

"Within a few hours after the Supreme Court's decision was read in 1954," Professor C. Vann Woodward of Yale University relates, "the Voice of America had broadcast the news to foreign countries in thirty-five separate languages." The decision, however, was principally for overseas consumption; implementation in the United States was something else again. The Court, according to the same author, made no secret of its

> acknowledgement of the many difficulties that would be involved in doing away with segregation and its evident tolerance of a gradualistic approach toward a solution. It was quite evident that a long transitional period was inevitable. . . . The possibilities of delaying tactics were large, and it is well known that many things that have been declared unconstitutional have continued to exist for a long time. [5]

Nothing, in short, has ever wrought a meaningful alteration in the "place" to which white America wishes to consign — and has more or less successfully until now consigned — "its" Negroes. This is as true today as it was a generation ago or more. And in reality, some comparative statistics which I adduced in Chapter I would indicate that the Negro's relative economic position has not improved in the last decade or so, but has worsened: the shibboleth of "Negro progress," as C. E. Wilson has astutely pointed out, is a myth and nothing more. The cold, hard economic facts of life all contradict the comforting illusion that things are getting better miraculously of themselves without human intervention ever being required. [6] For that matter, white America is determined — and by a substantial majority — to keep things pretty much the way they have always been, with the Negro confined to the bottom. The most authoritative recent survey of white attitudes on this question demonstrates that: "white people are . . . adamant that there should *not* be a strict 10 percent quota for Negroes in job hiring (rejected by over 40 to 1) or that Negroes should actually be given job preference over whites (turned down by a staggering 31 to 1 margin.)" [7] The implication is that, for all

white America cares, Negroes may continue to fester forever
in pestilential urban slums — as they surely will unless provided with massive economic assistance of just that type which
whites find so objectionable. So long as no white skin has
to suffer for it, a tepid "Negro revolution" is permissible; beyond that point, however, nothing.

This is the framework within which black disaffection with
the white American consensus is reaching ever more vocal
proportions. It is in terms of this disaffection that such social
phenomena as, for instance, the indisputable popularity of the
late and much-mourned Malcolm X in the ghettos of the North
is to be comprehended. Like all radical agitators attuned to
the needs and aspirations of their constituency, Malcolm articulated what others felt but, for a variety of reasons, were unable to speak. He was nonpareil at voicing the discontent of
the "blues people," their lack of faith in the ability of the American Dream to provide a decent life style for them, their fervent
wish for an existence of their own without the suffocating painful foot of Whitey crushing in on their chest.[8] The Muslim
doctrine of a separate state for Negroes, so ubiquitously de-
rided in the white press, was only another tacit recognition
of the intense yearning emanating from the ghetto for a social
and political system in which the destinies of black people
would be placed in the hands of blacks themselves.

But it should not be thought that the domestic aspects of the
Afro-American freedom movement are the sole ones, for this
battle for liberation is being connected with greater and greater
frequency by politically concerned young Negroes (including
not a few musicians) with similar struggles of the former colonial nations around the globe to rid themselves of white imperialist overlordship. Indeed, by now it has become a commonplace to observe that the emergence of many of the nonwhite
peoples as independent nation-states, particularly in Africa,
has had a dramatic effect in altering the "self-image" of Negro
Americans and imbuing them with a sense of pride in their
ancestral heritage and achievements heretofore unprecedented.[9]
All of the political concomitants of this process, however, have
still to be enumerated. One especially illustrative corollary, as
yet unremarked, of the appearance of these new nations on the
world stage is that Negroes in the United States now realize,
possibly by intuition, that there are other viable alternatives
available to them besides that of transforming themselves into
carbon copies of the white man. The importance of this devel-

opment can scarcely be overstressed, because in effect it opens a door for a Negro movement of mass dimensions based on an explicit rejection of the American Dream.

What I have been saying, therefore, comes down to this: that as the futility of relying on white largesse as a means of attaining substantive equality for Negroes becomes increasingly undeniable, whites can anticipate that Negro estrangement from the American consensus will grow apace. Malcolm X's Organization of Afro-American Unity, which had taken on only rudimentary form at the time of his mysterious assassination, represents, in fact, an early attempt to crystallize this mood of alienation and rebellion in a political form. In jazz music this estrangement had also already progressed quite some distance; here the vehicle through which it is finding expression is, as you might imagine, none other than the youthful avantgarde movement (coupled with the efforts of a few of its better-established precursors). But in all cases the central point is that this malaise *does* exist among those imprisoned within the ghetto; it is not merely a product of Black Muslim rhetoric; it will not vanish with the corpse of Malcolm X; it is a stubborn fact which must be reckoned with in any more than superficial examination of contemporary Negro culture in general or jazz in particular.

There is one additional idea which I wish to advance before leaving this subject. To many white Americans it may be nearly incomprehensible that there can be any connection between anticolonial liberation struggles, such as those waged in Vietnam or the Dominican Republic, and the Negro freedom movement in the United States. Nonetheless, the parallel is there, and it is increasingly being dwelt upon with each passing day by genuine spokesmen for Negroes. Just to begin with, could there be anything more transparently absurd than the contention that the government of the United States is fighting for the freedom and democratic rights of the nonwhite population of Vietnam, when it permits those identical rights to be violated with complete impunity by any KKK redneck who takes it into his head to raise his status among his peers by "getting him a nigger"? To Negroes, that is to say, the Marines are needed to intervene not in Santo Domingo or Saigon but in —Selma: democracy, like charity, ought best to begin at home.

Secondly, the very fact that the U.S. military juggernaut is using the Vietnamese people as raw material for its military "experiments"—as has been admitted by virtually all the major news sources—serves at once to strip away those

virtuous fig leaves with which the current administration strives
to clothe its policy of naked aggression, and betrays more
accurately than could anything else that very real contempt
which white America harbors for all nonwhites. 10 Thus it is
only logical that the United States now follows the path marked
out by Nazi Germany, which also maintained an ideology
of superior and inferior races and took full advantage of its
undeclared participation in the Spanish Civil War to test the
most advanced means of human destruction then known against
one of the "inferior" peoples. 11 To whites, this comparison
of the United States with Germany may appear ludicrous, if
not downright obscene; but Negroes do not view it that way.
"There is a favorite joke among many black people," writes
Ossie Sykes, "that states that Martin Luther King, Jr., is going
to be the one to lead us to the gas chambers singing *We Shall
Overcome*. This writer fails to see the humor because it can
happen here just like it happened in Germany . . ." And in
the same issue of this journal another black author asserts
that "[this] culture is fully prepared to isolate, incarcerate, and
kill, if need be, those [Negroes] who are too proud and too
daring to submit to the current level of dehumanization and
destruction. . . ."12 Clearly, then, while whites reject with horror the idea that their society could ever verge in the same
direction as that taken by Nazi Germany, politically sophisticated black thinkers are already forearming themselves against
an American version of the "final solution."

The reader may ask what relevance to jazz the preceding
remarks bear. I would simply answer by asserting the proposition that today's avant-garde movement in jazz is a musical representation of the ghetto's vote of "no confidence" in
Western civilization and the American Dream — that Negro
avant-garde intransigents, in other words, are saying through
their horns, as LeRoi Jones would have it, "Up your ass,
feeble-minded ofays!"

Before proceeding to defend this thesis, however, certain obvious qualifications have to be noted. I am *not* contending,
first of all, that every avant-gardist has affiliated himself with
this musical persuasion out of the direct desire to undermine
and overthrow the status quo, or because he hates whites,
or because he is choking with the suppressed rage of the down-
trodden. Such a mechanical formulation would really be untenable, for the simple reason that human psychology is not
that neat, and total consciousness of motivation is only rarely vouchsafed us; indeed, many of our most consequential

actions may be impelled by motives of which we are but dimly aware. (On the other hand, certain of the avant-garde fraternity have left no doubt that to them the aesthetic revolution is closely linked with the social-political one.) Beyond
that, some of the avant-gardists, though a minute fraction,
I would guess, may be truly apolitical: they are involved in
the movement out of aesthetic considerations alone, and by
and large are impervious to the influence of social currents
external to the narrow sphere of art.

Secondly, my argument does not stand or fall on the question of white participation in the avant-garde movement. There
have been in every generation a handful of white dissidents
who in one way or another have repudiated their society's
racist institutions and values and gone over to the side of
the "enemy." In the pre-Civil War years such a man might
essay the role of a John Brown; in the 1930s he could, like
Mezz Mezzrow, turn his back on co-racialists and become an
expatriate to Harlem; similar figures today might be found
in the ranks of the white field workers of SNCC, or among
the few white partisans of Malcolm X. Regardless of the form
the rebellion takes, the existence of these "deviant" types indicates that the Negro "cause" will always attract a scattering
of white adherents; but these adherents do not in and of themselves suffice to alter the character of the movement which
they penetrate (as the evolution of jazz, to which the white
man's contribution has been of strictly marginal significance,
demonstrates).

These qualifications noted, it is legitimate to ask what objective evidence can be brought forward to support the idea
that avant-gardism is a manifestation of Negro disaffiliation
from the American consensus. Here I shall be the first to admit that we are treading over extremely treacherous ground.
There is no question in my mind that, given ample time and
patience, and blessed with the kind of research endowment
that the affluent foundations prefer to lavish on comparatively trivial and irrelevant problems, a definite answer favorable to my thesis would ultimately be forthcoming. But revolutions have a habit of unfolding too rapidly for the social
scholars and their elaborate behavioral methodologies; and
this epoch is supremely one of revolution in all corners of
the earth. The unpleasant but inescapable fact is that we are
reduced, for want of anything more immediately serviceable,
to utilizing what the distinguished Norwegian sociologist Svend
Ranulf called with some disdain "the method of plausible guess-

es."[13] That the "plausible guess" is anything but wholly satis-
factory, that it can readily lead one astray, I will not attempt
to deny; the rationale for employing it nonetheless is that the
risk of error pales beside the penalties we must inevitably
pay if we do nothing but keep a discreet silence on social
questions of immeasurable gravity.

Perhaps one must live with the avant-garde for a prolonged
while before it begins to become intelligible. It was, at any
rate, only after I had listened to Archie Shepp's most recent
recording, *Four for Trane*, for what must have been the tenth
time, that the thought struck me: this is simply not European
art; it has moved wholly away from the traditional canons
of Western music. Once one begins to toy with that seemingly innocent notion, whole new vistas suddenly open up — vistas which reduce the superficially chaotic diversity of the avant-
garde insurrection to at least a kind of order.

Suppose, for example, that one continues along the same
line and poses the question: in what way is this music non-
Western? The answer lies not in any reputed "atonality" of the
avant-garde performers, because (for one thing) the music
of the avant-garde is tonal and (for another) atonality has
been, since Schoenberg at least, a staple feature of the European musical landscape. Rather, the peculiarly non-Western
character of the avant-garde would appear to reside in its presumably deliberate abandonment of the diatonic scale; for
once the diatonic scale is given up, the entire harmonic foundation of European music — which can be deduced as a logical corollary from diatonicity — is headed for the historical
scrap heap.

An immediate and obvious consequence of the departure
from diatonicity, of course, is the atrophy of the piano in
avant-garde groups since if one is going to avoid playing
in any of the conventional Western modes or scales, then the
presence of a piano in the background can only serve as a
distraction. This may explain why, amidst the profusion of
avant-garde musicians, such a small segment of that number are pianists. Not that the abolition of diatonicity necessarily signals the end of the piano in jazz with absolute finality. John Coltrane, to name one prominent example, has
found it possible to incorporate a piano in his group and still
employ a nondiatonic conception by having the piano remain
mute during those portions of his solo in which he dispenses
with the diatonic framework. In a different approach, pianist
Cecil Taylor (and to a lesser extent, Andrew Hill) utilizes

tonal clusters to give his playing an anti-diatonic cast. But notwithstanding these exceptions, on balance it would probably be a reasonably safe prognostication to venture that the status of the piano in jazz is heading for a precipitous decline when the avant-garde takes the ascendant.

Can we predict with like certainty one direction in which the avant-garde is traveling? This is no easy task. While it requires relatively scant effort to discern what the avant-gardists are opposed to, what they favor remains shrouded in considerable obscurity. Yet I do believe that two main tendencies are coming to the fore: one of these would bring jazz out of a semi-Western European context into an Asian or African setting; the other tendency also seeks to divorce jazz from its current ambience, but it points deeper into the urban Negro ghetto. The separation between the two is actually somewhat arbitrary. Both tendencies symbolize the effort to escape from the confines of the Western prison, and to that degree are obverse sides of the coin. Where they differ is over the question of what route is to be taken; but on the exodus itself there is fundamental agreement.

Let me comment on the latter tendency first. It has been written so often as to be a cliche that the avant-gardists are striving to simulate the sound of human speech in their playing. Even a casual audit of a few of their recordings will illustrate the validity of this dictum; but what has not been stated is the *kind* of discourse that is being reproduced. Naturally I would have difficulty in proving the point, but if one drops one's preconceptions and listens with care, what one will hear in the music of John Coltrane, Eric Dolphy, Sam Rivers, John Tchicai, and especially Archie Shepp is not speech "in general," but the voice of the urban Negro ghetto. This, I well realize, may verge on mysticism; certainly it defies any "objective" demonstration at the moment. Yet my intentions are anything but mystical; and I would continue to maintain, in the absence of decisive evidence to the contrary, that Archie Shepp's growling, raspy tenor saxophone locutions, for example, distill for your ears the quintessence of Negro vocal patterns as they can be heard on the streets of Chicago, Detroit, Philadelphia, Harlem, or wherever you choose. Although the speech-like attributes are conceivably less palpable in their work, this is also the significance of Coltrane's eerie shrieks and *basso profundo* explosions, the jagged clarinet squeals of Eric Dolphy, even the more stately and oblique lamentations of John Tchicai: all invoke, to one degree or another, those cadences and

rhythms that are unique to the lives of black people in the
city milieu. [14] Seen from this perspective, the avant-garde functions as the logical artistic culmination of, and successor to,
the self-conscious search for musical roots in the gospel and
blues tradition — a movement known initially as "funk," later
as "soul" — that was so conspicuous in the jazz of the second
half of the 1950s.

I fully expect to be told that the presence of sounds resembling Negro speech is nothing new in jazz music; that it goes
back to Louis Armstrong and Duke Ellington in the twenties,
if not before. Quite so — and quite immaterial. What happened
in the twenties cannot meaningfully be compared with the contemporary situation because so many of the pertinent historical factors have undergone mutation in the intervening decades. It is not surprising that Armstrong and his peers took
the inspiration for their music from the sound of Negro song
and speech; as self-taught and largely unlettered men, excluded from white culture since the time of their early youth, it
was most improbable that they could have done otherwise.
Much the same holds good for the bulk of the musicians in
the early Ellington orchestras, [15] if not for the Duke himself.

But this is a far cry from what one finds at present, when
the possession of a baccalaureate by the tyro jazz musician
is looked upon as run-of-the-mill, and his ability to read at
sight even the most complex scores is taken for granted. [16]
If today's innovating jazz radical faces toward the ghetto and
away from the European experience, rest assured that this
attitude springs not at all from any limitation of technique
or educational deficiency. Whatever the similarities with the
speech-inflected music of the twenties, the differences between
it and the current avant-garde movement are in the final analysis of greater relevance.

The other trend in avant-garde jazz, toward an assimilation of Afro-Asian contributions, is not as widespread as the
ghetto-directed tendency I have been discussing, nor is it entirely restricted to the hard core of the revolutionists. For that
matter, as soon as one begins to poke around in the corners
of this subject, one can't help but be made aware of the futility of such abstract definition-mongering as would erect im-
permeable barriers between musical "schools." Any classificatory
scheme is really nothing more than an heuristic device; a means
of apprehending reality more fully. It should not be allowed
to become reified to the point where it imposes itself as a substitute for that reality. So it is for the two musical categories

"avant-garde" and "mainstream." Supposedly, Miles Davis belongs in the latter; yet some of his associates, namely, Herbie Hancock, Anthony Williams and Ron Carter, are more or less identified with the avant-garde. Are we to assume that these men possess multiple musical personalities which, chameleon-like, they slip on and off at will, "avant-garde" one moment and "mainstream" the next? Or, for an even more puzzling dilemma, consider John Coltrane. Here is an artist who stands with one foot in either camp but whose work transcends them both. Is he mainstream or avant-garde or some yet unnamed hybrid? Clearly, nothing is to be gained by this species of neo-scholastic logic-chopping. Coltrane synthesizes the best from both aesthetic generations — it is as simple as that. To try and compress his music into one or another narrow pigeonhole can only result in distorting the essential nature of what he is doing, thoroughly obfuscating the salient issues in the process.

As matters stand, the incorporation into jazz of African and Asian musical strains by avant-gardists has been mostly restricted to John Coltrane and his group, plus a few of Coltrane's more devoted disciples (though other avant-gardists have expressed an interest in non-Western musics, as the recent spate of articles on Ravi Shankar goes to indicate). Here too this trend cannot properly be appreciated in isolation. The retreat from Western canons was gathering momentum even before the avant-garde began to draw notice: in the African drum adventures of Art Blakey, the Mideastern effects to be heard in Yusef Lateef's compositions, the excursions of Miles Davis into flamenco and *cante hondo*, and of course Coltrane's hypnotic Indian-flavored dithyrambs on soprano saxophone. Taken en masse these aesthetic departures from the West signal the exhaustion of European musical thought as a potentially fructifying stimulus to the further evolution of jazz. But more than that, they signify the non-Western or anti-Western stance of the musicians themselves — a posture that will, as I have earlier suggested, become even more blatant in the days ahead.

But is this particular interpretation of the impulse away from the West the best one? Is is not conceivable that these developments are merely artistic phenomena, and should therefore not be projected onto the larger social matrix? Although the extent of our present knowledge does not enable me to advance any concrete evidence by way of refutation, I reject this line of argumentation as inadequate; the reasons for doing so are set forth below.

Basically, my motivation for discarding the hypothesis that the avant-garde movement is an aesthetic revolution only, not possessed of any broader social ramifications, have to do with the nature both of historical change and of jazz. The fundamental premise in my reasoning is that major alterations in the nature of jazz improvisation do not "just happen"; that because of the intimate symbiotic relationship between jazz and the urban Negro community, such profound modifications in the jazz aesthetic occur primarily as the outcome of a simultaneous (or antecedent) shift in the collective consciousness of the ghetto. This is not the usual approach to the study of successive waves of jazz innovation, I readily acknowledge; but it is my contention that the conventional treatment — which largely divorces jazz from its social setting and "explains" the decay of one style and burgeoning of another as the result of a happy series of accidents that throw together an isolated coterie of individual geniuses — obscures more than it illuminates. When we are dealing with an art such as European concert music or avant-garde painting, where the primary public is small and the role of a relative handful of collectors, middlemen, academic authorities, lay patrons and the artist's own professional contemporaries is influential, then it perhaps makes sense to describe those aesthetic mutations which take place without relating them to contemporary socio-political trends and events. But surely this has not been the situation in jazz, nor is there much to indicate that it is about to become so.

In the particular instance which I have been analyzing, the revolution of the avant-garde, I think that we may at this juncture attain an additional degree of insight by conducting a sort of contrary-to-fact "thought experiment." Let us ask ourselves what the outcome would have been, so far as jazz alone is concerned, had a substantial measure of racial integration been achieved by this time — that is, had Negroes been incorporated *at all levels* of the economy in proportion to their number in the overall population (rather than, as is currently the pattern, disproportionately relegated to the absolute bottom positions in the economic pyramid). In these hypothetical circumstances we would certainly anticipate that differences between (urban) Negro and white musics would become increasingly blurred as the two ethnic groups took on more nearly

identical ways of life. With respect to jazz, it seems a plausible
speculation that some kind of hybrid music would ultimately
emerge from the melting-pot process of integration and mutual
assimilation: in short, a variant of what we now call *third-
stream music.*

And yet nothing could be more striking than that the viability of third-stream music appears to be on the decline with
the passage of time rather than the opposite. To date it has
failed to generate a sizable audience. Of still greater import,
those young black musicians with what one would suppose
the greatest aptitude for this music — men of the calibre and
background of Cecil Taylor, Archie Shepp, Eric Dolphy, Bill
Dixon, Ken McIntyre, Ron Carter, Richard Davis, Jaki Byard
and numerous others — have generally been holding themselves
aloof from the attempt at artistic fusion. With the single possible
exception of Ornette Coleman, the musicians active in promoting
the third stream have been either white composers such as Gunther Schuller, or else Negro performers like John Lewis whose
ties, emotionally and aesthetically speaking, are with the previous generation. If the leading avant-garde insurgents have
been of significance in this endeavor to create a new "middle
way" for jazz, it can only be by their continued absence. One
thus concludes that much of the abortive character of the third
stream has been dictated by the futile effort (if you will forgive
the pun) to swim against the prevailing currents.

Chapter 5
THE NEW BLACK RADICALISM

Sometime in the autumn of 1964, a series of avant-garde jazz concerts were held in New York's *Cellar Cafe*. Although the music itself was of vital significance, no less important was the title chosen for the series — the October Revolution.

To be sure, most of the reporters present missed the implications in the reference to the triumph of Bolshevism in 1917 — an interesting commentary on the degree of political awareness of jazz journalists — but this was not at all the case with the participating musicians. Subsequent developments have shown the October Revolution to be only one of a number of signs of a thoroughly radical upheaval, musical and social, taking place among young Negro jazz artists.

In every respect the combined social-musical revolution in jazz amounts to a repudiation of the values of white middle-class capitalist America. This is most obvious from the statements of the musicians themselves; but it is also apparent (to those who trouble to listen with open ears) in the wild and exciting music which the revolution is producing.

Among the leaders of the revolution, three names top the list: John Coltrane, Ornette Coleman, Cecil Taylor. These triumvirs are (to continue the metaphor of October) the Lenin, Trotsky, and Luxemburg of the new wave in jazz.[1] To name the leaders, however, is simpler than to describe the movement they head. The substance of the music, for one thing, is too elusive; the range of styles, for another, is too great. Still, beneath the apparently endless diversity there are common themes that unify the various aspects of the revolution.

On a strictly musical level, one of the common themes is the attempt of the revolutionaries to replace the static rhythmic pulse and unvarying cycle of chords that jazz artists have used as a basis for their improvisations since men such as Charlie Parker and Dizzy Gillespie first pointed the way in the mid-1940s. The new musicians have been moving away from these now-stale devices toward a fresh concept of group, as opposed to individual, improvisation. The reasons for this shift are, as I have said, both musical and social. Let it suffice here to say that collective improvisation symbolizes the recognition among musicians that their art is not an affair of individual "genuises," but the musical expression of an entire people — the black people in America. In any event, that the subordination of the individual to the group has been an important element in the work of John Coltrane, Ornette Coleman, Cecil Taylor, and their numerous followers is no longer seriously disputable. [2]

A second and related unity underlying the "new black music" — a name bestowed by poet-playwright-critic LeRoi Jones, who himself functions as an unofficial spokesman for the musicians — is a rejection of Western musical conventions. Such a rejection, as has been suggested, possesses obvious social implications above and beyond the artistic ones. In point of fact, it mirrors the larger decision of the Negro ghetto to turn its back on an exploitative and inhumane white American society. Thus tenor saxophonist Coltrane draws on the nonwhite world, especially Africa and India, for inspiration (his compositions bear titles like *Africa/Brass, Dahomey Dance, India*); while alto saxophonist Coleman explains to one interviewer: "I came up with a music that didn't require European laws applied to it," a "revolutionary breakthrough" for jazz.

If the nonwhite world abroad has been influential in shaping the new music, the same applies to the nonwhite world at home — Watts and Harlem. "The greatness in jazz," pianist Taylor told Nat Hentoff, "occurs because it includes all the *mores* and folkways of Negroes during the last fifty years." Despite outraged denunciations from white writers who argue that statements such as Taylor's are "racist," there is not much question that Taylor is correct. His remarks, moreover, illustrate a growing trend for jazz artists to draw on the ghetto environment for their material.

Nowhere is the indebtedness of the jazz revolution to the vocal patterns of the ghetto more manifest than in the huge, raucous sounds that emerge from the tenor saxophone of Archie Shepp, a student (and employee) of Cecil Taylor before branching out with his own quartet. Jazz, he maintains, is "one of the most meaningful social, esthetic contributions to America. . . . It is antiwar; it is opposed to Vietnam; it is for Cuba; it is for the liberation of all people. . . . Why is that so? Because jazz is a music itself born out of oppression, born out of the enslavement of my people."

A second spokesman for this unprecedented radicalism in jazz is trumpeter-composer Bill Dixon, the chief organizer behind the 1964 October Revolution. Like Shepp, Dixon writes both poetry and prose.[3] Also like Shepp, Dixon is an uncompromising enemy of the racial and social status quo. The experience of the October Revolution led him to realize the need for an organization that could "protect the musicians and composers from the existing forces of exploitation." He was convinced that if radical black musicians were willing to reject "the crumbs that up to the present they have been forced to accept," they could drive out many of the absentee owners from what is accurately called the jazz *business.* In the aftermath, Dixon was able to persuade Taylor, Shepp, and several other avantgarde musicians to form an integrated cooperative, the Jazz Composers Guild.

The Guild, it turned out, was a noble experiment which failed. Its quick demise could in part be said to reflect the unshakeable position of the white businessman in jazz. But it was also due to racial frictions that developed between the members. Dixon told writer Robert Levin, one of the few whites in sympathy with the aims of the jazz revolution, that there was "a subtle, but apparent, indignation on the part of the white members . . . that a black man . . . could conceive and execute an idea that would be intelligent and beneficial to all."

Despite its failure, the Guild remains an omen of things to come. To understand why this is so, one need merely examine the circumstances under which these proud musicians are forced to create. Three representative incidents—out of the hundreds that might be selected—serve to lay bare the inner workings of the jazz world.

Robert Levin writes in the first issue of the new music magazine *Sounds and Fury:* "Anyone present at [Cecil] Taylor's March 17th concert at Town Hall [in 1965] will tell you that at least 500 people were in attendance. Norman Seaman, who runs the Hall and is in charge of delivering the artists their percentage of the gate, claimed a count of only 247 ticket stubs. Would he have dared to do that to a white artist? To, say, Bill Evans?"[4]

To most devotees of jazz, John Coltrane possesses a stature roughly equivalent to that of Vladimir Horowitz in the field of "legitimate" music. As some token of Coltrane's achievement, consider his awards in the single year of 1965: named to the "Hall of Fame," his album *A Love Supreme* (Impulse 77) selected as "Record of the Year," and elected to first place in the tenor saxophone category by the voters in the *Down Beat* Readers Poll; honored as "Jazzman of the Year," for the "Jazz Composition of the Year," for the "Jazz Album of the Year," and with a first place among tenor saxophonists by readers of *Jazz* magazine; *A Love Supreme* voted "Record of the Year" and Coltrane awarded one first prize (for tenor saxophone) and one second prize (for "miscellaneous instrument" — soprano saxophone) in the *Down Beat* International Jazz Critics Poll; *A Love Supreme* chosen as both "Jazz Composition of the Year" and "Jazz Album of the Year" by the writers responding to the Jazz Album of the Year Poll sponsored by *Jazz*. Small wonder that one jazz periodical dubbed 1965 as "The Year of John Coltrane"! [5]

Yet for all of these tributes, John Coltrane remains "just another nigger" to the jazz Establishment. Toward the end of March, 1965, Coltrane and his group played what was ostensibly a benefit concert for LeRoi Jones's Black Arts Repertory Theatre/School. I say "ostensibly" because in retrospect it appeared as if the main function of the concert was to provide Impulse Records, which transcribed the performances and later released them on an album titled *The New Wave in Jazz* (Impulse 90), with an opportunity to turn an effortless profit from the jazz revolution. [6] Thus three times the Coltrane quartet began to play, only to be interrupted each time by the recording engineer's insistence on rearranging his equipment and the instruments themselves. Finally, on the fourth attempt, the engineer allowed the musicians to proceed — the dictates of high-fidelity and the profit system had been met. Here a paraphrase of Robert Levin's question comes to mind: Would any record company have even dreamed of treating a "legitimate" (or white — the two are nearly synonymous) artist in such a contemptuous manner? Can you imagine the reaction of Glenn Gould or Fritz Kreisler under these circumstances? But then, Gould and Kreisler are not jazz musicians. For the latter, the blatant implication is that, as "niggers," they will take what the Establishment sees fit to give them and jolly well like it.

Finally, the case of Archie Shepp. As late as 1965 Shepp could say: "I've been in this music for fifteen years, and I've never worked [as a musician] for a solid week in this country. I've never made my living playing jazz. I work now as a merchandiser for Abraham & Straus." A break came early in 1966 when he was offered a two-week engagement at a new San Francisco club, the *Both/And*, followed by another two weeks at *Shelly's Manne-Hole* in Los Angeles. But notwithstanding the packed houses he drew in California, Shepp returned to New York only to find himself without musical employment once more — and this time without a job at Abraham & Straus to cushion the fall. In desperation, his saxophone was pawned.

Now lacking both job and horn, Shepp came across an advertisement in which the Selmer Company, a manufacturer of musical instruments, had used his name to promote their products.[7] Perhaps Selmer would provide him with a horn in exchange for the privilege of featuring him in their ads? "We never give our instruments to musicians," was the answer Shepp received from Selmer. (Again one wonders: Would Steinway mention Van Cliburn in one of their ads without the pianist's permission? And then dare to refuse him a piano?) Enraged at this high-handed treatment without even a hint of compensation, Shepp checked with Impulse Records (where he is under contract) to determine what legal recourse was open to him. At this point it seemed for a brief moment as if the gods were about to intervene in his behalf: Shepp was told that Impulse, one of the more beneficent and enlightened firms, would buy a new saxophone for him from Selmer. Naturally, this was too good to be true. A few days later he learned that the saxophone's cost was more than Impulse was willing to bear; only if he consented to write, say, half-a-dozen compositions and copyright them through Impulse could the purchase be arranged.

When I left New York at the end of April 1966, Shepp was still slaving over the compositions; his group, which had begun to hit its artistic peak during its stay on the West Coast, had already gone several weeks without rehearsing. And yet the representatives of the jazz Establishment have the nerve to protest their innocence when Shepp writes "with some authority about the crude staples (clubs) where black men are groomed and paced to run till they bleed, or else are hacked up outright for Lepage's glue."

Painful to relate, the incidents recounted above are all too typical of what the dedicated jazz artist must endure in order to find an audience for his music. Taken en masse, they go far toward explaining the mood of bitter revolt sweeping through the fraternity of black musicians, particularly the younger ones.

Cecil Taylor, for one, has become so disgusted with the prevailing conditions in the world of jazz that he has publicly
called for "a boycott by Negro musicians of all jazz clubs in
the United States. I also propose that there should be a boycott by Negro jazz musicians of all the record companies, . . .
all trade papers dealing with music . . . and that all Negro
musicians resign from every federated union in this country."
He concludes: "Let's take the music away from the people who
control it."

But this is not to suggest that the artists involved in the jazz
revolution aim only at redressing their own grievances. At
bottom it is recognized that the problems facing the creators of
the new music are no different than those which beset the black
ghettos that have produced them. As Archie Shepp observes,
the white entrepreneurs who dominate the music business "are
only the lower echelon of a power structure which has never
tolerated from Negroes the belief that we have in ourselves,
that we are people, that we are men, that we are women, that
we are human beings. That power structure would more readily
dismiss me as an uppity nigger or a fresh nigger than to give
me my rights."

The hope, then, is that the music will prove itself relevant to
the plight of the ghetto. Indeed, Cecil Taylor is convinced that
the jazz Establishment wishes to keep radical musicians from
steady employment for just this reason. Were these artists to
work regularly (which almost none do), he argues, "they would
be able to operate at maximum capacity on all levels," thus
becoming "an engaged part of the community." In this event,
because the jazz musician is "so close to reality, he would be
able to spell out in language the community could understand
exactly what his work is about and how it has relation to them
— how it comes out of perhaps the same problems they're
struggling with.' Saxophonist and critic Don Heckman, who
speaks from the vantage point of a participant, puts the matter
even more succinctly when he writes: "Some of today's players
conceive of jazz as a symbol of social change — even social revolution." Such is the state of mind that today obtains among
the men who play the new black music. No one save the fatu-
ous expects that it will be dispelled before the prison walls of
the ghetto are themselves shattered.

Chapter 6
THE "JAZZ CLUB":
AN ADVENTURE IN
COCKROACH CAPITALISM

When Cecil Taylor spoke at a panel discussion at the University of Pittsburgh prior to his concert there, it apparently came as a shock to his collegiate audience that he and his fellow musicians no longer wish to undergo the demoralizing experience of presenting their music in nightclubs. How could the musicians not want to play in nightclubs? The students wanted to know. What was going to happen to jazz then?

This naive attitude illustrates the propensity of white middle-class Americans to view the artist, particularly the Negro jazz artist, as some kind of disembodied entity who has no existence except at the moment of artistic creation. If you are a jazz musician, you are expected to get up on the stand and create on demand, simply because the audience has paid its money for the purpose of seeing you do so. You may have to go home to rats, roaches, and poverty, but that won't bother your listener in the least, for as far as he is concerned, you cease to exist the moment you lay down your horn.

Such narrowness would be inexcusable with regard to any group of artists, but it is downright insane in the world of jazz. Much more so than the painter, say, or the sculptor, the Negro jazzman is attuned to the needs and aspirations of a specific community — the black ghetto community. This, in fact, is what imparts such overwhelming vitality to his art. So with what logic do we ignore the circumstances with which, every day, he must contend?

Which brings me back to the nightclub situation. "Crude stables where black men are run until they bleed, or else are hacked up outright for Lepage's glue" — Archie Shepp's totally accurate description of a jazz nightclub. Amazing that, for all the years he has been going to them, the average jazz fan will

SOME OF THE MATERIAL IN THIS CHAPTER ORIGINALLY APPEARED IN
JAZZ, FEBRUARY 1967.

never once step outside of his own frame of reference for a moment and try and see the club as it must appear to the working musician. All he knows, all he cares, is that the nightclub is there whenever he has some spare cash and wants to take in some jazz. The musicians? They're gettin' paid, ain't they? What more do they want?

What more, indeed! Suppose we start this particular Cook's tour with the *Village Vanguard* in New York. In the course of interviewing about two dozen musicians I had occasion to spend several sets in the backrooms of the *Vanguard*, so I suppose that I can speak with some authority. The first thing that struck me was that there was simply no place for the artists to go when they weren't playing — an all too typical condition. What this means in more precise terms is that the musician has his choice of spending his between-set breaks in a variety of unsatisfactory ways: (1) he can take a table and drink — if he doesn't mind having the drinks, at regular prices, deducted from his wages; (2) he can amble about in back, either rubbing up against a greasy stove in the kitchen or lounging on an equally dirty staircase while watching the traffic in and out of the men's room; or, finally, he can go sit in his car or, weather permitting, wander outside. Of course in this event the musician may end up, as Miles Davis did when he was playing *Birdland* a few years back, by having one of New York's finest trying out his nightstick over his skull. What happens, I keep wondering, when John Coltrane works the *Vanguard?* Coltrane's sets consume so much of his energy that he likes to sleep during his breaks — obviously impossible within the confines of the *Vanguard*.

Or consider this instructive tableau, observed at the *Vanguard* in the course of a vain attempt to obtain an interview with Charles Lloyd. Lloyd has just removed a bottle of soda from the refrigerator, stage right; in from stage left strides a tuxedoed and bow-tied waiter, a particularly vicious martinet who would make Mussolini appear a libertarian by comparison. The following dialogue ensues:

Waiter ("jokingly"): I see you're at it again, eh, Charles?
Lloyd (in earnest): That's right. Nigger's in the refrigerator again.

Above and beyond their lack of even elementary facilities for the performers, nightclubs are just not suitable for artistic creation. The white jazz audience may not be aware of this —

may not even consider that what they are privileged to hear
is art — but black (and some white) musicians are. In the same
series of interviews that I've already mentioned, tenor saxophonist Pharoah Sanders told me that he didn't want to see
his music utilized as an adjunct to the sale of whiskey. John
Coltrane, Pharoah's employer, objected to the noise ("Who
needs that cash register rung during Jimmy Garrison's [bass]
solo?") and to having himself hustled on and off the stage at
the convenience of the owner. Besides the indignity of being
ordered to shape his creations to the whim of some cockroach
capitalist who probably knows less about music than I do
about scuba diving, Coltrane was upset because he realized
that it was costing his listeners a small fortune to see his group,
and he wanted to make sure they went away well satisfied.

Yet it is inherently part of the present nightclub scene that
Coltrane is not allowed to play as his muse dictates; that the
things I have been discussing are not the fortuitous "abuses"
of a basically sound system, anymore than the suppression of
social revolution in Vietnam is an aberration of American
foreign policy, blundered into in a fit of absent-mindedness.
No, these episodes are inextricably part of the day-to-day
business of operating a jazz nightclub.

For instance, that matter of forty-five minute sets. No accident is involved here. Almost all clubs have a certain minimum
number of drinks that must be consumed by each member of
the audience every set; hence the shorter the sets, the more
drinks sold. It's as simple as that. Bassist Buell Neidlinger,
who used to be with Cecil Taylor a few years ago, explained
this in great detail to poet-writer A. B. Spellman, in a taped
interview that Spellman includes in his marvelous book, *Four
Lives in the Bebop Business:*

"Trying to make a living playing with Cecil is absolutely
unbelievable," Neidlinger told Spellman, "because there is no
economic advantage to playing music like that. It's completely
unsalable in the nightclubs because of the fact that each composition lasts, or could last, an hour and a half. Bar owners
aren't interested in this, because if there's one thing they hate
to see it's a bunch of people sitting around open-mouthed with
their brains absolutely paralyzed by the music, unable to call
for the waiter. They want to sell drinks. But when Cecil's playing, people are likely to tell the waiter to shut up and be still.

"We used to run into this all the time at the *Five Spot.* For
some reason, I guess because I'm white, the owners considered
me, like, the one to talk to whenever there was trouble. We'd

be playing along for an hour or so and I'd get the old radio signal — the hand across the throat. Cut 'em off! Cut 'em off!"

In a system based on production for profit — which means production of art for profit, as well as anything else — it's the profit that counts; everything else can be subordinated. And it is profitable, rest assured of that. Some estimates I made on one of my New York trips should indicate just how profitable the business side of jazz can be — if you happen to be an entrepreneur, that is, and not a musician. Buell Neidlinger mentioned the *Five Spot* in the interview by A. B. Spellman. By coincidence. I was there in the summer of 1966 and had the invaluable opportunity to observe the workings of the system from its heart, so to speak. There is a *three*-drink minimum per person per set at the *Five Spot*, with each drink $1.20. Assuming 150 people per set and five sets a night (conservative estimates on both counts), this means that the owner, Joe Termini, grosses an amount equal to: 3 x $1.20 x 150 x 5 = $2400 in a single evening.

What do the musicians take home for their night's work? On the Monday evening that I was there, Elvin Jones, McCoy Tyner, Frank Foster, and Paul Chambers were playing. It would be nice to believe that the musicians received $500 for the night; I suspect that $300, however, is considerably closer to the mark.

Now for Termini's other expenses. Payroll for two bartenders, two waiters, and a cook — $250 at most. Cost of liquor and food consumed, utilities, and rent — about $250. Total expenses I estimate as follows:

Musicians $300
Payroll 250
Other overhead 250
Total expenses $800

Net profit = gross income — expenses = $2400 — $800 = $1600. Even economist Joseph Schumpeter would have to agree that $1600 (or even $1000) is a pretty penny for one night's entrepreneurship!

There are some interesting implications that emerge from this analysis. First and foremost, it can be seen that the biggest obstacle to expanding the audience for the music, especially the new music, is the structure of the music business which delivers such enormous profits to the likes of Termini (the man who, be it recalled, told Archie Shepp that he didn't think jazz musicians were artists, and then compounded injury with insult by having Shepp ejected from his club). As long as prices continue at this astronomical level, the people who are most interested in the new music — blacks, students, artists, political radicals — are precisely the ones who are least likely to be able to afford it. Ordinarily, two sets are the absolute minimum if the listener wants to get an adequate exposure to a particular artist; but who has $7.20 (exclusive of tips) to spend on a single evening? And should one wish to take a wife or girl — well, I presume you can do the addition for yourself.

But even if one were willing to pay the $7.20 for two sets — and for two sets of Coltrane or Cecil Taylor it would be a bargain — these are not the men whom Termini is about to hire, because they are unwilling to accept his restrictions and he is unwilling to allow the requirements of their art to take precedence over his unquenchable thirst for profits. On this point Buell Neidlinger has given ample testimony.

Parenthetically, the Establishment critics, to no one's surprise, have maintained an absolute silence on the mode of operation of the jazz nightclubs. Not that they have been adverse to complaining *per se*. On the contrary. Leonard Feather, for one, in his attempt to stifle the new breed of socially conscious writers, has promulgated a long diatribe against what he calls "critical infighting" (see *Down Beat*, December 16, 1966); only to turn around and condemn fellow critics Ralph Gleason and Whitney Balliett as hypocrites for revising previous views on Bob Dylan and Archie Shepp (*Cavalier*, December, 1966).

Feather's eastcoast sidekick, Martin Williams, is a protester too. He devoted almost one whole *Down Beat* column (June 30, 1966) to exposing the machinations of the "black supremacists" who wanted Ornette Coleman to hire a Negro bass player though that didn't stop him from opening his book with the statement that "it is in a sense almost mandatory . . . to consider jazz as an aspect of Negro American life and of the far-reaching and little understood effect of Negro American life on American life in general." We don't mind recognizing Negroes as artistic innovators — just so long as they don't demand commensurate rewards.

Then there is Michael Zwerin of the *Village Voice*, who, as a player as well as a writer, is uniquely competent to deal with the club milieu from the inside. Zwerin, it must be admitted, is tireless in detailing the suppression of artists — provided, of course, that it takes place on the other side of the Iron Curtain (e. g., *Village Voice,* October 30, 1966). But why expect anything more from the Establishment critical fraternity? After all, it's undoubtedly been years since any one of them had to pay for his own drinks in a club.

The conclusion, then, is that so long as the present situation is maintained intact, so long will both the audience and the musicians suffer at the hands of the nightclub capitalists and their attorneys, the co-opted Establishment critics. Private ownership has always been implicitly incompatible with the creation of art; but it is now becoming (or has already become) absolutely intolerable in the realm of jazz. Something must be done to enable the musicians and their followers to recapture the music from the hands of the Terminis and their ilk.

As a first step, it is time to begin discussing the formation of organizations like the Jazz Composers Guild, which could utilize boycotts and other appropriate tactics to bring these exploiters to their knees. Simultaneously, we should be exploring the potential for cooperatives like the Detroit Artists' Workshop. If carried out on a large enough scale, cooperatives could provide support for the newest and most impoverished musicians by promoting a series of concerts, happenings, poetry readings, etc., at the same time undermining the oligopolistic position of the clubowners by presenting the music at prices that non-Madison Avenue people can afford to pay.

Heretofore, the jazz enthusiast has had the best of two worlds: he has assumed that he has a God-given right to enjoy the music without assuming the least responsibility for its continued production. The moment for a change in this particular status quo is long overdue. It remains to be seen if the enthusiast can translate his oft-professed love for the music into something more tangible and useful. What we need now are not words but a weapon.

In the three years since the preceding essay was written, nothing I have seen has caused me to believe that it was in error save, perhaps, by understatement. In Los Angeles, for example, Shelly Manne's *Manne-Hole* is operated with as rank a disregard for the welfare of artists and patrons as any New York "club." The last time I was in the *Manne-Hole* — probably the last time I shall ever be in it — was in the winter of 1969, when Elvin Jones's group was playing an engagement there. Admission was, as I recall, $1.50 per person, with a two-drink minimum per person per set (drinks at about $1.20 each).

Thus for two people staying a single set, an expenditure of at least $7.80 not including tips.

The first night I saw Elvin at the *Manne-Hole*, I stayed several sets and managed to leave behind about $15 by the time of my departure. The bulk of the audience was overwhelmingly young, predominantly black. How they managed, I'll never even be able to imagine. Nor is this the worst of it. On weekends the prices go up and the waitresses, so I've heard (not being so rash as to go on a weekend myself), hustle the audiences even more diligently than during the week — a feat of no mean proportions. To add insult to injury, weekend visitors to the *Manne-Hole* have to suffer through the unbelievably insipid playing of Manne himself and his quintet.

The list of offenses committed by this "club" — which, I suppose, is probably representative — can easily be expanded. First of all, as regards the artists. There is a continual stream of harassment, much of which I witnessed myself, directed at the musicians by the management (so much so that Archie Shepp, for one, reportedly refuses to return). "Don't be here too late." "Don't make your sets too short." "Don't make your sets too long." "Don't have your piano player hit the keys as hard as he did, it's bad for the instrument" (which, as you might guess, is near decrepitude). This harassment extends to the point of actually dictating which local musicians shall be used if a visiting artist should arrive without a full complement of sidemen. Musicians are encouraged to drink, and the drinks are deducted from their wages — the old "company-store" policy as applied to the jazz situation. Those in the musician's party, even if they have been driving him from his hotel to the club and back, are forced to purchase drinks, whether they want them or not, for each set.

It was the cumulative impact of witnessing all of this oppression and exploitation of the artists by the management of the *Manne-Hole*, supplemented by what many musicians have told me of their experiences in that dank room, that decided me never again to return to the aptly named "Hole."

Even this is not the end of the story, however. To the foregoing must be added the fact that the *Manne-Hole* is blatantly discriminatory — some would say racist — in its hiring policies for local musicians. Most of the time, the *Manne-Hole* books "name" groups from out of town. Occasionally on the other hand, there is a week (or a part of a week) in which no out-of-town group can be obtained; in such a situation, the schedule is filled out with local musicians. Almost invariably, these are white; usually, they are drawn from the same clique of white studio musicians with whom Manne ordinarily works. As a result, there are many excellent and well-known local black musicians — Harold Land and Bobby Hutcherson, to name only two — who probably have not worked at the head of a group of their own at the *Manne-Hole* ten days out of the past ten years. (I know of only *one* night in which Land was allowed to bring a band into the *Manne-Hole*.)

But besides established artists such as Land and Hutcherson, there are a number of newer black artists who play in the avant-garde styles of the late sixties — men who are just now beginning to record: John Carter on reeds, trumpeter Bobby Bradford (who was with Ornette Coleman for two years when Coleman was not making records), pianist Horace Tapscott (one of the few men on his instrument worthy of mention alongside Cecil Taylor). If the management of the *Manne-Hole* had even a scintilla of public spirit or sense of obligation to the jazz community, it would make available at least one evening a week for promising, but as yet unknown, artists like Carter, Bradford and Tapscott to appear; in that way, it might plow back a token portion of the extortionate profits it rakes in especially from the black audiences of Los Angeles. Such enlightenment, however, is apparently far beyond anything to which the *Manne-Hole* might aspire. The public is denied an opportunity to hear these new talents, the men themselves are forced to perform their music wherever and however they can (Carter and Bradford have appeared more times at the folk club *The Ash Grove* than they have at the *Manne-Hole!*), so that philistinism and racial exclusivism may reign supreme and profits grow ever more large and secure.

How ironic it is that the same voices which claim to be so concerned for the future of jazz and never lose an opportunity to derogate rock and roll are willfully blind to the antisocial role that "clubs" such as the *Manne-Hole* play in the jazz world. If nothing else, booking policies that insist on prohibiting all the new, exciting black artists and pricing policies that make it almost impossible for young people to visit jazz "clubs" more than once a month are strangling the music and turning it into the exclusive preserve of the white, middle-aged business executive out for the evening on his expense account.

If jazz is unpopular with young people — which is something that I tend to doubt — then a large part of the cause resides in the way in which the typical jazz "club" is conducted. For $6 or $7 a young person can take himself and a companion to an entire evening of rock, in which they may hear as many as three different top-notch bands perform two sets each. The same amount of time spent at a jazz "club" of the *Manne-Hole* stripe would cost, at the bare minimum, around $13 to $15. With comparative prices of that nature, is any more needed to explain "the death of jazz"?

In point of fact, from what I have observed on various college campuses, jazz continues to have a sizable audience among the young — despite all the efforts of the jazz entrepreneurs to destroy it. Jazz concerts on campus, *any* campus, are almost uniformly well attended, if not packed. The audience *is* there; that much is not open to doubt. If that same youthful audience chooses not to patronize the jazz "clubs" — chooses, that is, not to be hustled every five minutes for watered-down "drinks" at exorbitant prices and not to be subjected to outrageous admission prices — who can blame them? The fault lies not with them, but with the business mentality that dominates the jazz "club" situation today. In order for the present generation of young people to develop an abiding interest in jazz, it is more important than ever to expropriate the "jazz-club" expropriators.

Photo by Frank Kofsky

JOHN COLTRANE

Chapter 7
JOHN COLTRANE AND THE
BLACK MUSIC REVOLUTION

Thomas S. Kuhn's *The Structure of Scientific Revolutions* [1] is a work that demands the attention of anyone interested in a *theoretical* approach to the problem of how successive developments in jazz music are brought about. Kuhn, as is implied from the title of his work, is concerned primarily with the abrupt replacement of one scientific theory by another, an event he subsumes under the rubric of "scientific revolution"; but much of what he has to say possesses, within the appropriate limits, immediate applicability to the arts as well.

Kuhn's point of departure is the proposition that science does not — indeed, cannot — develop in a smooth, continuous fashion, science textbooks to the contrary notwithstanding. The day-to-day activities of most scientists, what Kuhn terms "normal science," is possible, he observes, only so long as they have at their fingertips a model ("paradigm") of their particular portion of the universe adequate to explain the phenomena considered of key importance (since no paradigm ever suffices to explain all the phenomena). Sooner or later, however, certain crucial data accumulate which disagree with the predictions of the paradigm. When enough of these significant anomalies have emerged, the authority of the old paradigm becomes undermined and the science enters a phase of crisis. (Though Kuhn does not attempt to deal with the question of what imparts decisive weight to a particular anomaly or set of anomalies, beyond remarking that not all discrepancies are perceived as crucial, it seems a straightforward conclusion that such deficiences of theory are likely to seem acute when they begin to act as the principal obstruction to a society's further economic-technological advancement. This would be why, for example, the long revolution in astronomy

THIS ORIGINALLY APPEARED IN *JAZZ*, JULY AND SEPTEMBER 1965.

beginning with Copernicus and ending with Isaac Newton occurred in the seventeenth century and not, say, in the tenth or the twentieth. [2]

The hallmark of a crisis period in science stems from the fact that the previously accepted paradigm can no longer be looked to for an account of critically important natural phenomena, while there is as yet no single new one which can serve as an adequate replacement. In this fluid situation, numerous theoretical innovations will be propounded, and their various adherents will be in competition with each other in proselytizing to secure the allegiance of the remainder of the scientific community. The crisis is ultimately resolved when one of the new paradigms wins the approval of the majority of practicing scientists and "normal science" once again becomes the order of the day. The rapid and discontinuous shift in paradigm that has eventuated is nothing more or less than a "scientific revolution."

Yet the matter does not end here, for the physical universe — that is, the universe as viewed by the scientist — is never the same after the revolution as before. One result of discarding the old paradigm for the new is that some problems that were held to be legitimate before the revolution are relegated to the status of pseudo-problems after it. (Astrology became scientifically disreputable after Newton; alchemy became so also, following the chemical revolution which overthrew phlogiston theory in the eighteenth century.) But not every scientist is able to make the transition to the new paradigm. Specifically, those older scientists who have done the greater part of their lives' work under the old paradigm will generally have extremely strong emotional connections with it, which some of them may be unable to surrender. They may in consequence be ostracized by their former fellows and hounded out of the community of scientists. But in any event the final outcome is to ensure the triumph of the revolution and the concepts associated with it. Subsequently, the revolutionary origins of these concepts will be quietly effaced by textbook writers in the interest of presenting a roseate picture of uninterrupted and unilinear scientific progress to students beginning their education; and all subsequent orthodox scientific activity will — until the inescapable next revolution — take place within the boundaries implicitly set by the newly ensconced paradigm. (In the wake of Newton's achievement of accounting for planetary motion by countervailing gravitational and centrifugal forces, attention waned from the question of what *caused* gravity —

although this had occupied such of Newton's predecessors as William Gilbert and Johannes Kepler — and refocused on an examination of the *effects* of gravitational attraction. It was only in the twentieth century when the paradigm formulated by Einstein and others overthrew that of Newton that the former problem resumed its pre-Newtonian scientific primacy.)

Now admittedly all of this may *seem* far removed from the world of jazz; but the distance, as I shall endeavor to demonstrate, is more apparent than real. As an illustration, take the concept of an aesthetic revolution as a shift in paradigm: surely there is no more succinct or precise way (once the terminology has been mastered) of describing the momentous changes wrought by Charlie Parker, Dizzy Gillespie, Thelonious Monk (and others) in the early forties in substituting a paradigm, bebop, based on harmonic improvisation with the metrical unit an eighth note, for one based on melodic improvisation with the metrical unit a quarter note (swing). Kuhn's thesis similarly illuminates the events that transpired after the bebop paradigm became established. Younger musicians, who hadn't yet developed profound commitment to swing, were able to abandon it and immerse themselves in the new style with relative ease; but a sizable fraction of the previous artistic generation proved to be incapable of severing their attachment to the older music and remained with it; while the new canons of orthodoxy were then redrawn so as to exclude the veteran practitioners. That there was a subsequent reconciliation between revolutionaries and conservatives does not detract from the essential correctness of this (necessarily oversimplified) account, which draws on the model suggested by Kuhn, of the revolutionary and immediate postrevolutionary period in bebop's history.

There are, of course, rather patent boundaries beyond which the analogy between scientific and aesthetic revolutions, particularly as regards jazz, ought not to be pushed. For one thing, inasmuch as scientific hypotheses are evaluated on the basis of their success in describing objective physical reality (although Professor Kuhn would probably disagree with this statement), science possesses a fixed criterion for choosing between rival paradigms which jazz and every other art lacks. And while perhaps the majority of jazz critics continue to remain in blissful ignorance on this point, the truth of the matter is that there simply is no absolute frame of reference which permits one unequivocally to assert that this artistic idiom is "better" and that one "worse," anymore than one can decide the ancient question of whether it is the landscape which is moving by the train or the train moving by the landscape (or both).

Another notable difference between the two kinds of revolution, especially in the short run, stems from the substantial amount of independence which scientists, in comparison to artists, have come to enjoy in determining the fate of a proposed paradigm, its acceptance or rejection. By virtue of a three-thousand-year history from which to learn, it is beginning to be appreciated that attempts to dictate the contents of scientific theories from without — whether as in the case of Platonic theological astronomy, American eugenics in the early twentieth century, or Lysenkoism in the Soviet Union more recently — have invariably been disastrous for further development. (The amount of scientific independence in any country, however, ought not to be overestimated. Societies have found ways, usually indirect, of making certain that scientific research — as differentiated from scientific theory — be geared in directions acceptable to the politically dominant economic groups.) The jazz musician, on the other hand, enjoys no such privilege. This is especially true in the event of a revolution.

Granted that such intellectual upheavals can be marked by acrimoniousness in the best of circumstances, the scientist is not additionally encumbered by having mutually hostile groups of critics, recording-company executives, promoters, nightclub owners and the like, enter the fray in order to defend their own particularistic economic interests. It is highly unlikely that these extraneous participants alter the outcome of a jazz revolution much one way or another over the long haul, since only acceptance by the community of musicians can assure the viability of a new paradigm; in this repect, the arts and the sciences are similar. Nonetheless, by the very fact that these groups are all to one degree or another parasitic off the jazz musician's art, their eagerness to take sides in a revolutionary situation cannot help but obscure the genuine issues at stake, exacerbate antagonisms, and to that extent obstruct the efforts of the musicians themselves to heal the breach. To see these processes in action, we need look no further than the avant-garde revolution in jazz which is under way as I write these words. *

---

* It must also be understood that, in contrast to the conditions which prevail in the sciences, an older paradigm in the arts can be maintained by a dedicated lay public even after the attention of the most talented members of the artistic community has long since progressed beyond it; *vide* European painting and composed music

It is this same avant-garde revolution which is my present subject and to which I wish to apply the concepts of Kuhn set forth previously. If it was the bebop paradigm in all its variegated manifestations which issued from the successful jazz revolution of the forties, it should by now have become abundantly clear that this paradigm has been seriously crippled — probably beyond recovery. Does this mean, then, that a successor paradigm has already emerged? While it is personally tempting to give a "yes" answer, on balance a more judicious response would almost have to be in the negative. The jazz avant-garde has firmed up its ranks and gained immeasurably in self-confidence, in my estimation, since last I had occasion to express myself publicly on the topic some three years ago; still, one would be compelled to do more than a little violence in order to force its myriad and diverse styles to conform to a single pattern. What we have to deal with instead is the state of affairs which, were it to occur in one of the sciences, would fit nicely into Kuhn's model of the crisis situation: breakdown of the old paradigm, numerous new contenders in various states of perfection being offered to fill the vacuum, but as yet no single idiom dominant.

Supposing this diagnosis to be correct, it sheds some light on recent trends in jazz. Leonard Feather has correctly called attention (in his article in *Down Beat Music '65*) to the ambivalence of musicians and critics alike when faced with the necessity of pronouncing judgment on Ornette Coleman. But despite Feather's strictures, these responses to Coleman are not to be dismissed as mere "fence-sitting" (Feather's term), for they are entirely predictable reactions, *given the fact that the "normal" standards of evaluation have been largely destroyed without a substitute being found.* Lacking any firm criteria for deciding one way or another, the majority of both musicians and critics, not surprisingly, equivocate, vacillate and contradict themselves repeatedly. Far from demonstrating the superiority of musician-critics over their amateur brothers ("the musician," Feather informs us, "is less likely to be fooled into believing a bad perfomance is good" — which might be a valid assumption provided only that the musicians themselves could arrive at a working consensus as to what constituted "good" or "bad" in jazz). Feather's citations tend to indicate that the bulk of musicians and critics alike are wandering over un-

---

as excellent instances in point. The net result is to render aesthetic revolutions more diffuse and less thoroughgoing than those that take place in science, and consequently of greater difficulty to detect.

charted terrain desperately in search of some fixed landmarks. But these landmarks will be discovered only when there emerges a new paradigm that obtains the approval of a significant portion of the community of musicians.

Because it is characterized by no single dominant style, it does not at all follow that we can do nothing whatsoever about the avant-garde. For even if we cannot be exhaustive about what the avant-garde *is*, we need not be so hesitant in proclaiming what it is not. And one of the things which it very definitely is not is: *atonal*. Quite often avant-garde improvisations are *nondiatonic*—i.e., depart from the fixed scales found on a tempered piano—but this is not be confused with atonality, the absence of a tonal center (or centers). Incidentally, the writer most responsible for perpetrating confusion between the two, Martin Williams, appears finally to have been able to draw the distinction between atonality and nondiatonicity. Apropos of Ornette Coleman, whose playing Williams has been in the habit of describing as atonal, he remarks that: "Sometimes he isn't free enough, you know, because *he always plays modally*. People say he's too free—no he's not, *he's always right in that key*." (From a discussion of the jazz avant-garde in *Down Beat Music '65*; emphasis added.) We will return to Williams and some of his more idiosyncratic views momentarily.

As long as misconceptions are being dispelled, it might be worthwhile to make the further observation that, despite the sheer mass of verbiage devoted to him in the jazz press (and not only there), the single most influential figure on (and in) the avant-garde is not Coleman but—John Coltrane. Inasmuch as this notion may come as a revelation to some, the evidence for it—which is more than ample—merits examination in some detail. (A negative confirmation, e. g., might be inferred from the fact that the initial diatribe against "antijazz" had Coltrane's group, which at the time included Eric Dolphy, rather than Coleman as its principal target.) But before following out this theme, I want to focus on certain aspects of Coltrane's career previous to about 1961, a date that marks a rough watershed in his transformation into a member of the avant-garde.

One could hardly find a better example than the contrast between Coltrane's development before and after 1961 to buttress the thesis (inspired by Kuhn) that art *of necessity* proceeds by revolution. Although it has yet to be widely realized, what Coltrane was in actuality involved in up until that time was the attempt to carry jazz improvisation forward by a nonrevolutionary utilization of the basic bebop conventions. Consider: Coltrane's musical apprenticeship was served out under the bebop masters — Dizzy Gillespie, Thelonious Monk, Miles Davis. And if, as maintained by Andre Hodeir (in *Jazz: Its Evolution and Essence*), bebop may be schematically characterized as utilizing the eighth note in place of the quarter-note of swing, harmonic rather than melodic improvisation, and more involved chordal progressions than was standard in the large swing bands, then the inescapable concomitant is that Coltrane was as late as the end of the fifties seeking to push the devices instituted by the bebop revolutionaries to their logical, evolutionary conclusion; he was not striving to subvert these devices — even though that was the ultimate outcome of his experimentation.

Thus the Coltrane "sheets of sound" technique, which seemed to puzzle so many critical auditors in the previous decade, must be viewed in perspective as the direct successor to the improvisations of Charlie Parker (possibly this is what one commentator intended when he called attention to the "general essences of Charlie Parker" in Coltrane's style). Where Parker had used the eighth note, Coltrane employed the sixteenth; and he similarly augmented the melodic complexity by invoking more elaborate chords and a greater quantity of them. Of this stage in his artistic maturation — the analysis of which by Zita Carno in *Jazz Review* still remains unsurpassed Coltrane has been quoted by Ralph J. Gleason as recalling: "When I was with Miles [Davis], I didn't have anything to think about but myself, so I stayed at the piano and chords! chords! chords! chords! I ended up playing them on my horn!"

These two novel departures — the sixteenth notes and the heavier harmonic textures — quite naturally interacted to produce the sheets of sound as the only way of "covering" all of the chords in the alloted number of measures; they also led to an original kind of rhythmic attack and phraseology that was as intricately challenging as anything played by the first generation of bebop musicians. "I found," Coltrane told Don DeMicheal, "that there were a certain number of chord progressions to play in a given time, and sometimes what I played didn't work out in eighth notes, sixteenth notes, or triplets. I had to put the notes in uneven groups like fives and sevens in order to get them all in." A number of critics — most notably, I believe, LeRoi Jones — have recently begun to call attention to the fundamental role which changing conceptions of rhythm have played in the evolution of jazz styles. If for no other reason than the immense advance in rhythmic sophistication which they heralded, Coltrane's sheets of sound belong in the front rank of contributions to the literature of jazz improvisation, notwithstanding their having gone largely unsung in critical annals.

Most jazz musicians — or most scientists — would be more than content to be able to lay claim to a single major innovation in their lifetime; Coltrane's name is rightly associated with several. Having brought the sheets of sound technique to perfection in the latter fifties, he was forced to let them drop very shortly thereafter. To believe that this decision was due merely to capriciousness would be to misunderstand it indeed. Thus far I have avoided mention of what is surely one of the most controversial topics in jazz criticism: the ultimate causal agents which provide the driving force for aesthetic change. Comprehension of the in-progress jazz revolution and Coltrane's position within it requires that a few words be now directed to that unwieldy subject.

Viewed from one aspect, the history of jazz may be treated as the continuous (which is not to say uniform) emancipation of the soloist from the accompanying rhythmic-harmonic framework. Bebop, in this approach, would then be perceived as a set of inventions whose net result was to make the rhythmic pulse more subtle (by removing the steady beat of the bass drum and the pianist's left hand) and to widen the harmonic horizons (through employment of the upper intervals of a chord), giving the soloist additional freedom thereby. Admittedly speculative, my hypothesis is that Coltrane's extension of accepted bebop practice, crystallized in the sheets of sound, had, paradoxically enough, just the opposite effect: the dense harmonic matrix and tremendously rapid speeds of execution demanded to refer to the numerous progressions threatened to smother the soloist beneath their combined weight. Only a supremely gifted creator — only a Coltrane, in short — could hope to negotiate this chordal straitjacket and still emerge with something of value; and in the end presumably even he found the game not worth the candle. Implicit in Coltrane's decision to abandon the sheets was the conclusion that the daring improvisational procedures introduced by the bebop revolutionaries of the preceding decade had by the end of the fifties congealed into an artistic *cul-de-sac*. In that respect, bebop was no different from its predecessors: beyond a certain point, con-

tinued aesthetic progress became possible solely through the
wholesale demolition of the regnant paradigm — and not by
successive evolutionary refinements of it. (The parallel with
the bebop revolution is rendered more striking when one considers that Coltrane, like Parker and Gillespie before him, was
thoroughly grounded in the music that he subsequently did so
much to undermine). Nothing offers us a more direct verifica-
tion of the applicability of Thomas Kuhn's conceptions to
aesthetic revolutions than the sudden and wholly unexpected
mutations in Coltrane's style that arose after he reached what
quite reasonably could have been held to comprise the pinnacle
of his development. *

Turning now to the question of Coltrane's influence on the

---

* Of course I realize that the foregoing impressionistic sketch leaves
unresolved the more precise problems of historical causation in aesthetic revolution. Even if bebop ultimately had to yield to newer forms
offering greater freedom of expression to the soloist, that does not
in itself clarify why the transition began to occur in the late 1950s
instead of half-a-dozen years before or after. I am myself inclined
to accord primacy to a massive constellation of socioeconomic forces
impinging on the urban Negro ghettos during this period: the movement for African independence, increased technological unemployment of Negroes, the consolidation of Negro determination to remove
and white insistence on maintaining the second-class citizenship pattern, and especially the crystallization of overt black nationalist moods
on a widespread basis, etc. To judge by the relevant articles in the
jazz press, such of them as there are, at any rate, the majority of
(white) writers would not agree; their objections strike me as singular-
ly unconvincing. It is universally conceded now that long-term social
processes affecting the ghetto — the Great Depression, the rise of industrial unionism, migration from the rural South to urban centers,
and the integration of the Negro into the industrial economy during
World War II are the ones most commonly mentioned in this connection — were refracted in the drastic changes in jazz and other Afro-
American musics in the forties. Why should this principle be any
more outlandish when applied to the present era? Surely, the fact that
any broad movement, aesthetic or otherwise, is shaped and channeled
by the larger social determinants cannot be said to detract from the
importance assigned to that movement's leadership. To point to the
objective historical trends that find a partial representation in the
current avant-garde revolution, therefore, should in no way interfere
with one's enjoyment of the music, or reduce it to a "purely sociological" phenomenon. On the other hand, there is every possibility that
appreciation and comprehension of an art will be enhanced by some
firm *scientific* knowledge of the historically concrete circumstances out
of which it has sprung.

avant-garde, the evidence with which we have to deal is of three types. Firstly, an enumeration of his recorded appearances with various other members of that movement: Coltrane has been employed on albums recorded under the leadership of George Russell (*New York, New York*) and pianist Cecil Taylor (*Hard-Driving Jazz*); the latter was most explicit in telling a *Down Beat* interviewer: "See what happens when Coltrane and I play together? He and [Eric] Dolphy can hear me." The linking of Coltrane and Dolphy moreover, was not fortuitous, for Coltrane had on several occasions incorporated the late multi-instrument virtuoso into his regular group. Coltrane's remarks to the annotator of *"Live" at the Village Vanguard*, the second of a pair of his albums on which Dolphy appeared (the first was *Ole*, which also featured avant-garde trumpeter Freddie Hubbard), demonstrate that more than a chance collision between the two men was involved. "For a long time," Coltrane related, "Eric Dolphy and I had been talking about all kinds of possibilities with regard to improvising, scale-work, and techniques. *Those discussions helped both of us to keep probing*, and finally I decided that the band was here, . . . and it made sense for Eric to come on in and work. Having him here all the time is a constant stimulus to me" (emphasis added). Finally, the notes to his most recent release, *A Love Supreme*, inform us that Coltrane has recorded some selections with fellow tenor-saxophonist Archie Shepp, one of the outstanding avant-garde luminaries. In all, Coltrane's collaborations with the avant-garde make up an impressive list, taking on even greater significance when one recalls how infinitesimal is the number of major artists who have seen fit to associate their talents with that movement. [3]

There are, however, even more basic, if less tangible, manifestations of Coltrane's influence on the jazz revolution. Naturally enough, this is most apparent in the case of saxophonists, although by no means confined to them. As long ago (as these things are measured in terms of jazz's evolution) as 1961 LeRoi Jones, among the most perspicacious of the non-Establishment critics, wrote that "most of the avant-garde reed men are beholden to John [Coltrane]"; the passing of time has done nothing to lessen the validity of Jones's dictum. Jimmy Woods, Paul Plummer, Charles Lloyd, Prince Lasha, Sonny Simmons, Ken McIntyre, Wayne Shorter, Sam Rivers — these are a few of the musicians who could be cited as paying open deference to Coltrane on their horns. Archie Shepp and

Eric Dolphy, whose careers, as we have seen, Coltrane has assiduously promoted, are also indebted to him for certain elements of their respective styles, but in a fashion more subtle and diffuse than with the other men. The number of saxophonists under the sway of Ornette Coleman to a similar degree is, I would argue, considerably less.

Coltrane's effects on the avant-garde have been felt even beyond the saxophonists' ranks. In *Jazz: Its Evolution and Essence* Andre Hodeir astutely observed that Charlie Parker's genius was illustrated not only in his playing but in his choice of accompanists who shared his revolutionary concepts for reinvigorating the rhythmic-harmonic foundation over which the soloist spins out his creation. The same is true, *pari passu*, of Coltrane. His inventions in rhythm — worked out, according to him, in conjunction with the entire group — have been particularly fertile; even where they have not been adopted whole they have been of overriding importance in accelerating the emancipation of bass and drums from the fetters of a strictly metronomic function. I am at a loss as to why the critics have so generally tended to neglect Coltrane's contributions, when it would seem unexceptionable that they have played a momentous role in this liberation process. Nonetheless, I have still to read the analysis which gives proper weight to Coltrane's use of two basses, for example, as an initial step toward shattering the orthodox timekeeping approach that, until extremely recently, was exclusively dominant. It is impossible to digest the work of such drummers as J. C. Moses and Sonny Murray except as offshoots of Elvin Jones, or an exceptionally "free" bassist like the incessantly iconoclastic Richard Davis without the prior explorations of the Coltrane rhythm section. For that matter, isn't it significant that Elvin Jones himself turns up with increasing frequency on avant-garde recordings these days?

It should not be astonishing that Coltrane's radical revisions of the jazz rhythmic conventions began around the time of his initial forays with the soprano saxophone. Even if Coltrane had not himself provided us with hints to this effect, it would be plausible to assume that the novel difficulties involved in working out a style on an instrument so dissimilar to the tenor, and one for which there was no immediately relevant modern jazz tradition in the bargain, would perforce have impelled him to make substantial alterations in his playing. Fortunately, we have something superior to intuition to go by. Interviewed by Bill Coss for the album commentary

to *My Favorite Things* — his recorded debut on soprano, incidentally — Coltrane remarked apropos that instrument: "It
lets me take another look at improvisation. It's like having
another hand." Very likely the confluence of his soprano experiments and the diminishing returns from the sheets of sound
fixed Coltrane's determination to pursue hitherto untrodden
paths. "I've got to keep experimenting," was the way he expressed it to Coss. "I have part of what I'm looking for in my
grasp, but not all." Patently the existing wellsprings of inspiration had been sucked all but dry. The same note recurs in
all of his conversations on this subject. "I don't know what
I'm looking for," he has elsewhere been quoted, "something
that hasn't been played before. I don't know what it is. I know
I'll have that feeling when I get it and I'll just keep on searching."

Those who have stood so ready to condemn Coltrane for his
relentless probing of the music's nether reaches might do better
to muse for a while on the alternatives. An artistic style that
once was pulsating with vitality may come, through nothing
more than its unconditional acceptance over an extended time
span, to appear incipiently moribund to a later artistic generation. By the end of the last decade, when Coltrane and many
others were embarking on a root-and-branch restructuring of
the improvisatory tradition, such was the case in jazz. It would
have been more convenient, perhaps, if there were a new paradigm to hand as soon as the old one showed itself to be obso-
lete — but life is seldom that beneficent. Hence the only meaningful options that presented themselves were those of a prolonged
period of somewhat random experimentation — itself the certain
indicator of breakdown and crisis — or aesthetic stagnation;
the most creative musicians (including, to a degree, Miles Davis
and Charles Mingus in addition to Coltrane), naturally, took
the former option. Rather than indulging in their endless acerbic
complaints, the jazz public and critics ought more properly to
be grateful that they have these invaluable progress reports
preserved through recordings (which is more than we possess
for the early days of bebop). But that, I imagine, presumes
an amount of enlightenment hardly to be met with in the jazz
milieu.

It goes practically without saying that not everyone would
concur with this diagnosis. The preponderant element in the
critical Establishment, for one, would have us believe that the
enshrined canons which have served jazz for the past two
decades will suffice equally well for the next two. Such a static

outlook is unhistorical in the extreme. It is contradicted by the entire development of jazz up to the present (not to mention being wholly untenable as a philosophy of aesthetic history) and for that reason is really beneath refutation.

Another point of view, advanced primarily by Martin Williams, displays a more subtle form of distortion. It maintains the genuineness of the avant-garde — or, in Williams's terminology, the "new thing" — but insists that Coltrane possesses no rightful niche therein. As I have been at pains to demonstrate, Coltrane is organically connected to the avant-garde by numerous and diverse bonds. Williams's thesis, therefore, is in direct opposition to the existing factual evidence; it has, moreover, inextricably embroiled him in all manner of indefensible logical antinomies. Yet because he is a writer not without influence in certain circles, it may be of some value to provide an abbreviated examination of his treatment of Coltrane vis-a-vis the avant-garde.

Williams's general critical stance derives directly from the fact that he is striving to reconcile a long and uninterrupted history of derogating Coltrane with his own position as an unofficial propagandist for the "new thing." Taking the points in reverse order, Williams was, if not actually the first, one of the first writers to proselytize extensively for Ornette Coleman, beginning around 1959 in the pages of *Jazz Review* (and elsewhere); his 1961 article in *Harper's* likewise represented an initial effort to publicize avant-garde music outside of the jazz world and within the larger "intellectual" community. At the same time, however, his avant-garde predilections implied no sympathy for Coltrane's increasingly unconventional explorations. In the identical article in which he first proclaimed the merits of Ornette Coleman, Williams dismissed Coltrane with an offhand slur to the effect that "Coltrane invites the melodic disorder of running up and down scales." Three years later, in a review of Coltrane's *Africa/Brass* album, the substance of Williams's lament had changed but not its pejorative tone: Coltrane, he alleged, "makes everything into a handful of chords." (In reality, of course, two of the three compositions discussed by Williams were based on *modes* — not chords.) Overall, his verdict on the recording was that "If one looks for melodic development or even for some sort of technical order or logic, he may find none here."

When the teapot tempest over "antijazz" arose in the winter of 1961-1962, Williams, in replying to the antijazz polemicists, took the opportunity to attempt to establish the existence of a separation between Coltrane and the avant-garde. Emphasizing that "my opinion of John Coltrane's current work in no way reflects my opinion of Ornette Coleman," Williams by this tactic aimed at having Coltrane excluded from the "legitimate" (as determined by him) avant-garde. This was not in the least a fortuitous line for Williams to espouse; it was, in fact, the *only* means by which he could save face as an "authority" on the avant-garde, given his continued record of hostility to Coltrane. But inasmuch as it necessitated a rather blatant misrepresentation of the actual relationship of Coltrane to the avant-garde, it unfailingly involved Williams in some monstrous inconsistencies.

When, for example, Eric Dolphy in 1962 became a quondam sideman with Coltrane's group, Williams's problem became that of how to praise Dolphy, as typifying the *creme* of the avant-garde, while still dissociating him from his employer and collaborator, Coltrane. (That Coltrane and Dolphy regarded their music at least in part as a joint product is testified to by the quotation, given earlier, in which Coltrane discussed his reasons for having Dolphy join him.) Williams "resolved" this dilemma in the following terms: "Coltrane plays improvisations based on chord changes [*sic.*]. So does Eric Dolphy, although Dolphy's fleeting departures from harmonic-orientation[?] seem to come more often [?] than Coltrane's." Yet barely six months previous to this, in the *Harper's* article on "The 'New Thing' in Jazz," Williams had reported that Dolphy "has said that he thinks of everything he does as *tonal and harmonic*" (emphasis added). This was the selfsame Dolphy who departed from "harmonic-orientation" with Coltrane — and "more often" than Coltrane, at that!

If for nothing else, one would have to admire Williams for his heroic exertions to have Coltrane denied admission to the avant-garde. In the essay on Dolphy and Coltrane from which I have already excerpted some of his *dicta*, the writer went on in an attempt to give the definitive *coup de grace* to the idea of Coltrane as an avant-gardist by asserting that "Basically, Coltrane's playing is conventional and traditional in its point of departure." Presumably, then, being "basically conventional and traditional" is mutually exclusive with belonging to the avant-garde. But in a subsequent paragraph of the *identical article* from which this quotation is taken, Williams sprang to the defense of Ornette Coleman on the grounds that — of all things — "a legitimate part of the jazz tradition is involved." So beneath all of this bandying about of "tradition," it would appear that the operative principle is: whose ox is gored? To compound the confusion centering around Williams's invocation of the two-edged sword of "tradition," moreover, consider a few of his choices in the *Down Beat* International Jazz Critics' Poll for 1961, held less than a year before his Dolphy-Coltrane article appeared: trumpet: Louis Armstrong, Roy Eldridge; trombone: Jack Teagarden, Benny Morton; alto saxophone: Johnny Hodges, Benny Carter; tenor saxophone: Coleman Hawkins, Ben Webster; baritone saxophone: Harry Carney; clarinet: Pee Wee Russell, Edmond Hall. And this is the self-announced prophet of the "new thing" in jazz! Well might one wonder if it is not a somewhat elastic concept of "tradition" that can be stretched to damn Coltrane and apotheosize Ornette Coleman at one and the same blow. Or further, if it is not more than a little ironic — to refrain from employing a harsher term — that a man who is so ready to disparage Coltrane as "basically conventional and traditional" experiences no qualms in selecting Jack Teagarden or Edmond Hall for inclusion in the Critics' Poll in 1961. Such gross contradictions as occur ubiquitously in the work of Martin Williams can in the long run only serve to disqualify his ideas from any serious consideration.

By this point the reader hopefully has been convinced of Coltrane's central importance with respect to the avant-garde. (Martin Williams's writings illustrate the consequences of affirming the contrary.) Is it to be concluded from this that his style will set the model for the avant-garde revolution? Put another way, will we, after a few years have elapsed, be able to refer to the jazz revolution of the early sixties by his name in the same way that we call the seventeenth-century revolution in astronomy "Newtonian" or the twentieth-century one in physics "Einsteinian"? As I have already indicated, the situation is still too fluid, the trends too mixed and uncertain, to allow one to answer with finality. It may not, however, be totally amiss to inquire into the subject a little more deeply.

It is in no way inconsistent with the tremendously exhilarating and liberating effect that Coltrane has had on jazz to observe that the bulk of the young revolutionaries have diverged from his footsteps in a multitude of directions; nor is this to be taken as signifying that Coltrane is "basically conventional and traditional" in his aesthetic. On the contrary, what we must do here is strive to gain a modicum of insight into the psychology of artistic revolutions. The avant-garde revolution is at the moment still in its infancy: the old restraints are in the process of being summarily tossed off without any new conventions having been found to substitute. In this "glorious dawn" we can hardly be surprised that all manner of weird, and in some instances actually anarchic, notions are being brought forward in the name of art. Doubtless just this sort of thing has occurred in every artistic upheaval of the past—surely in every sociopolitical one. Revolutions, after all, are notorious for releasing immense amounts of previously untapped energies and aspirations. Having just smashed the "dead hand of tradition," the youthful radicals are intent on savoring their freedom to the fullest; and indeed, who can blame them for that? Moreover, the fact that the aesthetic revolution coincides with and partially reflects an incipient *social* revolution lends heightened urgency to the creations of these jazz insurrectionaries. (Don Heckman, himself a participant in the avant-garde, has observed that "Some of today's players conceive of jazz as a symbol of social change—even social revolution.")

When such symptoms of a crisis par excellence obtain, it cannot seriously be anticipated that the aesthetic revolutionaries will settle at once into any single new style, no matter how shockingly different it may appear in contrast to its immediate predecessors. That the avant-gardists are appreciative of Coltrane's monumental achievement in overleaping the stultification that afflicted bebop and its derivates in the latter fifties is scarcely to be disputed; but that they intend to confine themselves to the path he has hewed is, for the time being at any rate, not a necessary corollary. For my own part, I would continue to insist that a good portion of Coltrane's work—his *Chasin' the Trane*, for example—is as "advanced" and perhaps more directly meaningful than anything the avant-garde has produced. But I can also understand that some of the restraints which the artistically mature Coltrane has deliberately imposed on himself (the use of modes as a basis for improvisation, the retention of a piano in his quartet) may rankle the more determinedly rebellious among the avant-garde. By no means is it precluded that the jazz revolution will come to accept the bulk of Coltrane's innovations in the end; along this line, I suspect that many of the seemingly aimless solos of some avant-gardists would benefit immensely were they compelled to develop against the sort of skeletal framework which Coltrane typically employs. Be that as it may, for any individual, whether involved directly or, like the author, merely a spectator, to maintain that this or that is the single road down which the avant-garde revolution *must* proceed impresses me as being the height of both folly and presumption.

   Aside from Albert Ayler, who is discussed in relation to John Coltrane in the next chapter, the most glaring omission from the foregoing analysis is the name of tenor saxophonist Pharoah Sanders. When the essay was first composed, Pharoah had yet to be recorded, and hence was known only to denizens of the New York "underground" jazz scene. His debut album on ESP—recorded in 1964-1965, but released in 1966, showed him as a soloist who had come closer than anyone else (Charles Lloyd, Wayne Shorter, or Joe Farrell, say) to producing a literal re-creation of the Coltrane style of the early 1960s. Pharoah's next significant appearance in the public eye came in 1966, with his amalgamation into the Coltrane unit that included Rasheid Ali (drums) and Alice Coltrane (piano). By this time, though his base in the idiom wrought by Coltrane was still clearly distinguishable, it was equally evident that he had begun to develop into an original and (quite commanding) stylist. In my conversations with both John Coltrane and Pharoah Sanders, I was impressed by the similarity in their thinking, not only musically but in other dimensions as well. It is not fanciful to assert (indeed, Pharoah told me as much) that it was this similarity that drew the two men together. Since Coltrane's death, Pharoah has emerged (with Albert Ayler) as perhaps *the* key figure in the new jazz movement. His ideas, however, continue to bear the stamp left by the master teacher. Thus such recent of Pharoah's recorded works as *Tauhid* and particularly *Karma* strike the listener as an effort at carrying on the line of musical development begun by Coltrane with *A Love Supreme* and extended (with the addition of Pharoah himself) on *Meditations, Ascension, Expression* and *Cosmic Music*. Far from contradicting the thesis of this chapter and that on Albert Ayler, the emergence of Pharoah Sanders as a leading interpreter of the new music only serves, in my opinion, to underscore its correctness in all essentials.

ALBERT AYLER

Chapter 8
JOHN COLTRANE AND ALBERT AYLER

In the previous chapter I set forth the thesis that the innovations of John Coltrane, while neglected by most writers, were
decisive for the thinking of younger jazz revolutionaries. The
purpose of this chapter will be to document that claim for one
particular revolutionary jazz artist, Albert Ayler. Before beginning that task, however, I want to clear up some misconceptions.

First of all, there is the matter of "influences." If we say that
one artist — or one scientist, or one writer — has been influenced
by another, I do not see that this necessarily detracts from
the reputation of the former. It is all very well to state, as
one commentator has done, that the new jazz musicians are
influenced "by their own individuality." But so far as that goes,
what artist is not? More germane is the point that the artist's
individuality is never the only root out of which his art grows.
Every artist lives at a certain time, in a certain place; absorbs
certain social and intellectual conventions, some implicit, some
explicit; undergoes certain formative experiences, artistic and
otherwise, and so on. All of these things, to a greater or lesser
degree, are the "influences" that shape the man's art. [1] It should
be clear from this that there is nothing to be ashamed of in
admitting to these influences; indeed they could be avoided
only if one were to be reared, Crusoe-like, in total isolation
from the rest of the human community.

The question to ask about "influences," therefore, is not whether an artist has them; by the very fact that he has learned
enough from his predecessors to deserve the title of artist, he
most assuredly does. The question is, rather, what *use* he
makes of these influences. The artist of genius transmutes these
raw materials of his craft into artistic gold. The second-rater,

---

THIS ORIGINALLY APPEARED IN *JAZZ*, SEPTEMBER AND OCTOBER 1966.

on the other hand, remains rigidly bound by his "influences" and is unable to rise above the stature of imitator. Both Paul Quinechette and Sonny Rollins have drawn on the ideas of Lester Young; but what a world of difference in the way the two men have employed thêm!

There are countless other instances to be found in jazz of the process whereby a creative artist reworks ideas absorbed from the environment and presents them to us in a brilliant and radically unexpected form. It has frequently been noted, for example, that Charlie Parker was far from the first saxophonist to base his solos on the chord sequence of a song rather than its melody. But what saxophonist before him could duplicate the unflagging inventiveness and harmonic imagination of Parker's inventions? [2]

Similarly for John Coltrane. Many of the devices that we associate with him were in fact initially introduced by other musicians: in the case of utilizing mid-Eastern modes, Yusef Lateef; in the case of playing harmonics on the saxophone, a still-anonymous Philadelphia musician. From this we conclude that there is much more to originality and creativity than mere artistic priority; what Coltrane does with harmonics is of vastly greater interest to us than whether he was the first saxophonist to play them. Still less can creativity be equated with complete freedom from "influences."

A second point concerns the relative importance of John Coltrane in the jazz revolution. It has been argued that in calling attention to Coltrane's role in the jazz revolution, I have slighted the contributions of other artists. [3] If so, my sole defense is that I have been guided by the aural evidence. I have always felt, and continue to do so now, that the practicing artist is the final arbiter of what is valuable and what is not in his art; and that the function of the critic is, accordingly, not to lecture the artist, but to explain what he is doing. Consequently, when I say that Coltrane's impact on the jazz revolution, particularly saxophonists, has been greater than that of, say, Ornette Coleman, I am merely transcribing into print what I detect in the playing of the jazz revolutionaries, not attempting to foist my own ideas off on either the musician or the listener.

To call attention to Coltrane's significance in the jazz revolution, of course, does not mean that other artists have not helped shape the course of that revolution. This disclaimer is especially necessary with regard to Ornette Coleman. I must confess that, with the exception of Coleman's wholly impro-

vised *Free Jazz* album (Atlantic 1364), I do not hear in any of
his recordings developments so earthshaking as to justify some
of the ambitious titles bestowed on this music (*The Shape of
Jazz to Come, Change of the Century, Tomorrow is the Question*). Indeed, if one were to compare the rhythmic freedom of
Coleman's group with that of Coltrane's, the only possible
conclusion would be that Coltrane's approach liberates the
soloist to a much greater degree. That this is so is a consequence of the more flexible rhythmic base of Coltrane's music,
which in turn arises not from the absence of a fixed pulse —
only a few drummers of the jazz revolution, namely Milford
Graves and Sonny Murray, have been able to dispense with
such a pulse — but from the juxtaposition of rhythms based on
a beat of *four* against those based on a beat of *six*. Still, simply by bringing into the open the idea that neither the bass
line nor the pulse have to be maintained unchanged throughout a performance, Coleman has had a profound effect on
young black musicians; and this would be true if he had never
recorded a note of music. For that reason it is impossible to
estimate Coleman's importance to the jazz revolution down to
the last decimal place. Even if we don't find Coleman's phrases
popping up in the work of the new saxophonists with the same
frequency as those of Coltrane, we can nonetheless be certain
that the thinking of the younger men has benefited from his
groundbreaking efforts. For that matter, it is quite possible
that Coleman's ultimate significance for the jazz revolution will
be primarily that of a theoretician, rather than that of a performer. [4]

A final subject remains to be mentioned before passing on
to consider Albert Ayler. My essay on John Coltrane and the
Jazz Revolution was revised and completed in the winter of
1965, shortly before a whole host of new saxophonists burst
upon the scene. If the argument of that essay regarding Coltrane's sway over the jazz revolution is not to be invalidated,
it must now be shown that the more recent arrivals — including,
besides Albert Ayler, Byron Allen, Marion Brown, Giuseppi
Logan, Pharoah Sanders, John Tchicai, and Charles Tyler —
also mirror his influence. Although I will not take space here
to go into great detail, I think it quite clear that Coltrane's
innovations can be heard in the playing of these men, with the
single possible exception of Tchicai. Thus even in a composition
titled *Decision for the Cole-man* (ESP 1005), Byron Allen
inserts phrases that we have learned to recognize from Coltrane; and this is much more the case on the succeeding track,

Today's Blues Tomorrow. For Giuseppi Logan, the imprint of Coltrane's mid-Eastern soprano saxophone ventures is plain in such compositions as *Tabala Suite* and *Dance of Satan* (ESP 1007). As of 1964, Pharoah Sanders's descent from the Coltrane family tree was so marked (for instance, ESP 1003) that any further comment would be superfluous; his current work (e.g., on John Coltrane's *Ascension,* Impulse 95), shows him to be an independent thinker, but still broadly in the Coltrane mold. To the time of this writing (June 1966), I have not been able to purchase a copy of Marion Brown's ESP album — such is the state of the arts in Pittsburgh — but his brief appearance on *Ascension* is sufficient to suggest that he too has integrated Coltrane's concepts into his art. I shall say nothing about Charles Tyler here, because what I have heard of his music (on Albert Ayler's *Bells,* ESP 1010) indicates a strong similarity between his playing on alto and that of Ayler on tenor; hence my analysis of Ayler will stand as well for him.

The single apparent exception to the universality of Coltrane's appeal to the new wave of saxophonists is to be found in the music of John Tchicai. I say *apparent* exception, however, because Tchicai's origins are European rather than American and, in consequence, his ideas have been shaped by different forces than those that have inspired American musicians. Once this is taken into account, it no longer comes as a surprise that Tchicai harks back for a portion of his inspiration to the music of Lee Konitz, for Konitz, like numerous other musicians of the cool period, enjoyed much more sustained popularity in Europe, particularly Scandinavia, than in this country. This only goes to underline what I have above written on the subject of "influences" — that they are as inescapable for the artist as eating, drinking, and breathing are for the rest of us.

It also occurs to me that before launching into the discussion of Albert Ayler and John Coltrane, one additional remark may be in order. The jazz revolution, like life itself, is not a static phenomenon. Efforts to classify musicians according to whether they are or are not revolutionary are bound to err on the side of oversimplification. It was objected to my initial piece on Coltrane that some of the musicians I cited as being indebted to him were, in the words of one correspondent, "still playing bebop, advanced bebop maybe, but bebop nonetheless." Among those mentioned in this connection was Wayne Shorter; yet I think it indisputable that Shorter's latest efforts with Anthony Williams (Blue Note 4216) demonstrate that he has progressed beyond "advanced bebop." What this instance ought to remind us is that art is a matter of infinitely more complexity than can be encompassed by a series of rigid definitions, and that nothing is to be more militantly resisted than the notion that every artist must be thrust into a precisely measured pigeonhole.

Given the paucity of his recordings and the surely minute number of people who have ever seen him perform, the quantity of sheer nonsense that has been written about Albert Ayler is awesome to contemplate. Critics have been eager to read into his music all sorts of metaphysical implications: a manifesto of total freedom (with that entity being left conveniently undefined), a philosophy of anarchic nihilism, and so on. I certainly have no objections to interpreting the music; if anything, my constant lament has been that the Establishment writers are indecently eager to bury its social overtones. And for all I know, the critics who have reviewed Ayler with such virulent negativism really do hear all the unpleasant things in his playing that they claim to find. But at the very least our suspicions should be aroused by the fact that the anti-Ayler polemics have been devoid of any *musical* analysis. If, after all, Ayler is a fraud, shouldn't there be some more persuasive way of demonstrating this than mere name-calling?

My own belief is that the absence of any musical analysis on the part of the saxophonist's opponents is not simply accidental; that, in actuality, the results of an examination lead to conclusions just the opposite of those favored by the anti-Ayler faction. As I hope the following discussion will suggest, Ayler's music is not structureless, anarchic, or any of those things. It is, on the contrary, highly organized and gives every evidence of having been carefully thought out. But to appreciate this fact one needs to have kept abreast of recent developments in jazz — which is just where the critics have failed us. Similar situations in the other arts spring readily to mind. James Joyce was condemned by the literary critics of his day for the same alleged "defects" that permeate Ayler's work, even though, in retrospect, it has become embarrassingly obvious that form and structure was the one thing which Joyce did not lack. What happened with Joyce is the same thing that is happening today with Albert Ayler and the other practitioners of the jazz revolution: the reigning critics who have cut their teeth on other styles, are being outpaced by developments in the arts that are their supposed province.

On the other hand, though few in number, there are some critics who have refused to toe the line in denouncing Albert Ayler; two writers whom I have found particularly helpful in appreciating his music are LeRoi Jones and Frank Smith, whose remarks form the jumping-off point for my own discussion. To begin with, I quote Jones's observation that "Albert Ayler has heard Trane and Ornette Coleman and has still taken the music another way."[5] If Jones is correct — and I have no doubts on this score — it follows that if one hasn't come to grips with Ornette Coleman and John Coltrane, it will be impossible to grasp the mercurial essence of Albert Ayler.

Let us rephrase Jones's statement about Albert Ayler, Coltrane, and Ornette Coleman in a somewhat different way. Supposing that one were to try and devise a symbolic "equation" that expresses the rudiments of Ayler's playing, I think it would appear something like this:

$$Ayler = 50\% \ Coltrane + 20\% \ Coleman + 30\% \ X$$

where X represents Ayler's own unique contributions to the foundations which Coltrane and Coleman have already laid down. Although these contributions have been the source of much controversy, I will have relatively little to say about them in this essay. The reason for this choice is my belief that many listeners — and in any event, most critics — have yet to comprehend the bases on which Ayler's music rests, and that until this elementary comprehension has been attained, it is clearly pointless to attempt to go beyond. Thus my primary focus will be on Ayler as he relates to the music that preceded him, particularly that of Coltrane and Coleman.

In electing this approach, it should be apparent that I mean no slur at Ayler's "originality." I have already tried to explain why I believe that every artist possesses roots in the tradition of his art. If I concentrate on these roots in the case of Ayler, I do so not to belittle his own stature as an innovator — the howls of bewilderment arising from critical circles should be ample evidence for that stature — but to give the listener a bridge to the new music.

Of the saxophonists Ornette Coleman and John Coltrane, the effect of the former on Ayler's thinking is the more ob-

vious, but, in my opinion, the less profound. Echoes of Coleman are heard chiefly in Ayler's writing, much less in his
playing. Ayler's composition *Ghosts* (ESP 1002), for example,
is reminiscent of such Coleman songs as *Ramblin'* (Atlantic
1327) — both evoke a perennial blues-folk vein in jazz stem-
ming from the Southwest. Similarly, the intricate tenor-trumpet
contours of Ayler's *Holy Ghost*, performed with his brother
Donald on trumpet and issued as one track on *The New Wave
in Jazz*, is a direct offshoot from any number of Coleman's
early works recorded by him and Don Cherry.

To anyone who has had more than incidental encounters
with the music of Coleman, his impact on Ayler will more
than likely be apparent at once. This ought equally to be so
in the case of Coltrane, especially if, as I hold, Coltrane's
artistry looms larger in Ayler's playing than that of Coleman. Be that as it may, Coltrane's significance in this connection has gone largely unperceived, aside from the writings
of LeRoi Jones. There are reasons for this, of course, just as
there are for everything else under the sun. The aspects of
Coltrane's work most relevant to Ayler are those first unveiled
to the public on *Chasin' The Trane (Coltrane "Live" at the
Village Vanguard*, Impulse 10). Indeed, it is no exaggeration
to assert that the breathtaking devices which Ayler employs
in such compositions as "Ghosts" — the anguished screams, the
ferocious belches, the electrifying shrieks, the rasping harmonics
— all have their roots in this incomparable performance by
Coltrane. It was here that Coltrane gave us some notion of
the extraordinary range of human passions which the tenor
saxophone could convey; properly conceived, therefore, it forms
a landmark in the history of the jazz revolution.

For all of that, *Chasin' the Trane* was unambiguously damned
by the jazz Establishment when it initially appeared in 1962.
One of the two men to whom *Down Beat*, for instance, assigned this record for review dismissed Coltrane's magnificent
accomplishment as a collection of "yawps, squeaks, and countless repetitive runs. . . . It is monotonous, a treadmill to the
Kingdom of Boredom." The other reviewer, generally more
favorably disposed to the jazz revolution, was more eloquent
but almost equally negative. "In the final analysis," ran his
verdict, the "sputtering inconclusiveness" of *Chasin' the Trane*
made it seem "more properly a piece of musical exorcism than
anything else, a frenzied sort of soul-baring." [6] And this, mind
you, about what posterity will without doubt hail as one of
the high-water marks of this epoch in jazz.

The wave of adverse criticism inspired by *Chasin' the Trane* and Coltrane's successive albums (e. g., *Coltrane,* Impulse 21) largely explains the oblivion in which this period of Coltrane's development has languished so far as the critics are concerned. [7] Whether by his own choice or under the dictates of Impulse records, Coltrane began appearing in a variety of more restrained, even sedate, contexts: first with Duke Ellington (Impulse 30), then in an album of *Ballads* (Impulse 32), and finally in a lovely joint venture with singer Johnny Hartman (Impulse 40). Without casting the slightest aspersion on the value of these performances, it is still clear that they represent something of a retreat for Coltrane from the artistic pinnacle that *Chasin' the Trane* established. [8]

But while *Chasin' the Trane* was being roundly condemned by the critics, this was not at all its fate with the jazz revolutionaries, who, as their music attests, were eager to benefit from the lessons which Coltrane had drawn. There is a certain amount of irony in this situation. Though the jazz situation has finally begun to gain a niche for itself, the artistic sources for that musical upheaval have yet to be completely understood and appreciated; hence one of my aims in this essay is to redress the historical imbalance by pointing to the formative role which Coltrane's music, most notably *Chasin' the Trane*, has played in the jazz revolution.

Inasmuch as Albert Ayler is among the most adventurous of the revolutionaries, I take it that if the argument regarding Coltrane's influence is valid for him, it certainly will be equally applicable to Ayler's less iconoclastic peers. [9]

In a perceptive and enlightening essay on Ayler, Frank Smith notes that, "All of Albert's playing . . . follow[s] the same simple straightforward format: a very lyrical tune with an old-timey feeling is set forth and then the playing gradually gets into something more and more intense and ferocious until the listener is practically overwhelmed." [10] Smith is absolutely correct in this discussion, and it is a continual source of amazement to me that no one before him has been able to discern this gradual heightening of complexity as the basis of Ayler's improvisations.

But there is still another facet of Ayler's approach, one not mentioned by Smith, which complements this technique. Here I am thinking of what Gunther Schuller some years ago christened *thematic improvisation*—the construction of spontaneous variations which reflect the contours of the theme as well as its underlying harmony. This component of his music deserves at least as much stress as Smith has laid on the techniques of increasing complexity, provided we bear in mind that an enormous gulf separates Ayler's thematic improvisation from that which is familiar to us from the work of, say, Thelonious Monk or Sonny Rollins. As for the missing link between Monk and Rollins on the one hand, and Ayler on the other — that is supplied by none other than John Coltrane.

The most direct way to hear the relationship between Coltrane and Ayler is by comparing one of Ayler's recent works with Coltrane's *Chasin' the Trane*; I have for this purpose selected the second version of *Ghosts* from Ayler's *Spiritual Unity* album (ESP 1003). *Chasin' the Trane* is, of course, a blues, whereas *Ghosts* is a sixteen-measure piece with a Midwestern, almost folksong lilt to it; yet in view of the profound similarities that connect the two, these differences are ephemeral. Beginning with the Coltrane selection and following it with the Ayler, the first thing that strikes the listener is the parallel between the two: the identical tonal devices which Coltrane introduces as a means of creating tension are, as I have remarked above, utilized and extended by Ayler. This is not to say that Ayler is a carbon copy of Coltrane, for such a statement is totally false; were it not, Ayler's path would have been much smoother than the obstacle course which the critics have erected for him to run. The point I wish to make by calling attention to his use of certain Coltrane devices is that the supposedly alien sounds emanating from Ayler's saxophone are, in reality, an integral part of the jazz vocabulary — unless, that is, one is prepared to banish Coltrane as well as Ayler beyond the gates of jazz's Garden of Eden.

Once the selections by Coltrane and Ayler have been heard in immediate succession, the similarities in timbre, in the use of the upper and lower register, multiple repetitions, harmonics, shrieks, screams, and so forth, should require no further commentary. [11] But beneath the resemblances of tone and timbre there is an even more basic link between Coltrane and Ayler: *both men base their improvisations throughout the entire solo on the theme.* This is a very significant consideration which much not be lost sight of. Coltrane and Ayler possess a highly developed sense of structure (though as the more mature man, this intuition has been perfected to a higher degree by Coltrane). Contrary to what the critics have maintained in each case, it is anything but true that the music of either is sprawling, formless, chaotic. In point of fact, the pair of compositions at hand indicate that the two saxophonists are capable of devising a solo of several minutes duration based on a single underlying theme, a procedure which imparts an impressive degree of continuity to their improvisations.

Conceivably, the continuity of thematic improvisation may be easier to detect in *Chasin' the Trane*—where the theme includes the first few solo choruses as well as the initial melody —because it is a blues, and as such is familiar to most jazz devotees. An intensive listening to this piece reveals that Coltrane develops his solo using the few basic phrases of the first half-dozen or so choruses as building blocks; and that these building blocks are repeatedly inserted as points of reference as the improvisation gains in complexity and fervor. Exactly the same principle can be used to dissect Ayler's performance on "Ghosts," for *each one of his choruses is shaped as a variation on the theme of the composition.* To appreciate this, all one need do is hum that theme while listening to the solo. As the recognition dawns that Ayler ascends where the theme ascends, descends where it descends, breaks off his phrases where the melody shifts from one sequence to the next, and so on, whatever "mystery" one may have found in his playing should be dispelled.

Although it is always risky to try and plumb the motives of an artist, my guess is that Ayler has adopted the technique of spinning out a solo based on a simple theme because this allows him to create a series of sounds of extraordinary force and effectiveness, all the while keeping the overall work relatively direct and comprehensible. In any case, it should be noted that Ayler's procedure is just the reverse of that of the neobeboppers, who choose to utilize intricate chord sequences but are then forced to pay the price by restricting themselves to comparatively conservative sounds and melodies. Ayler appears to have elected to sacrifice something of the harmonic complexity of bebop in order to gain a greater freedom to evoke certain feelings and emotions in a very immediate fashion. But regardless of whether Ayler's reasoning has actually proceeded along these lines, if one listens to any of his compositions in the way I have suggested, it should be evident that there is a guiding logic to them. Indeed, the claim of some writers to discover nothing but raging anarchy in his work would be merely ludicrous, were it not for the fact that each one of these mistaken verdicts places new barriers between Ayler and his potentially large audience.

To be sure, if I may refer again to Frank Smith, with Ayler "there is even less heed paid to the tempered pitch of the piano keyboard than in Ornette Coleman's playing." Well, and what of it? Let us not forget that this is not 1956. Coltrane and Ornette Coleman have each in his own way shown us that jazz need not be forever chained to the keyboard of a piano. For that matter, one hallmark of the jazz revolution lies in the attempt to dispense with the framework of tempered pitch, which is now perceived by the new black musicians as an unnecessary restriction. It is only a question of time until this viewpoint becomes generally accepted, although it may never be the only one in jazz. Already one can hardly listen to Albert Ayler on *The New Wave in Jazz* album and then immediately turn, as does the record, to traditional styles of improvisation without feeling that there is something terribly constricting, even banal, about these repetitive chords and invariant rhythms of the fifties.

Perhaps an analogy to the present situation in jazz is to be found in the bebop revolution of the nineteen-forties. Many men who had served abroad during World War II were completely disoriented by the startling changes that jazz had undergone in their absence. Much the same sense of dismay and noncomprehension now prevails even within the ranks of those critics convinced of the necessity for aesthetic, not to say social, change. While their good will is not open to question, their preparations seem sadly remiss; and this time there is no World War II on which these deficiencies can be blamed. Good will, in short, is insufficient; it will carry one only a very limited distance. Above all, the music emanating from the jazz revolution must be *listened to*, not only as it appears before us today, but as it evolved in its transitional stages since the late 1950s. Only in this way can we hope to remain in touch with the most vital developments. Faced with a schism between the aspirations of the musicians and the critical response to those aspirations, one must conclude that it is the critics who have fallen behind the times, rather than the musicians who have gotten "ahead" of theirs. When all of the critical bluster has long been buried and forgotten, the musicians will still be there, and it will be their consciousness alone which determines what the jazz lovers of future years will be privileged to hear.

JOHN COLTRANE (L), PHAROAH SANDERS (R)

Chapter 9
A DIFFERENT DRUMMER:
JOHN COLTRANE AND THE
REVOLUTION IN ROCK

Hardly a week goes by that one cannot pick up an "underground" or other music publication and find a proclamation of the imminent death of jazz. One of the things that never fails to astound me about this oft-announced, but as yet unrealized, demise is that the prediction more often than not flows from the pen or lips of someone previously involved in the world of jazz, but now up to his eyeballs in rock.

Since these commentators exert a certain collective weight on the contemporary popular music scene, it may not be entirely amiss to offer some passing comments regarding their repeated prediction of the impending death of jazz, especially as these comments may help throw some light on the most important single feature in the jazz of the 1960s and the subject of this essay, tenor and soprano saxophonist John Coltrane.

Because jazz is by and large black music — dominated by a black mentality, driven to new accomplishments by black innovators — it has always been, and will probably long remain, a minority taste In White America. This being so, the dedicated "jazz fan" (what is the comparable category for rock?), particularly if he is white, needs to be something of a thick-skinned fanatic if he is to continue to insist on the validity of "his" music in the face of all but total contempt which the WASP Cultural Establishment displays toward all forms of serious black music (e. g., the nearly complete neglect of jazz by Establishment publications, from Luce *Timelife* at one extreme to the intellectual journals — *New York Times, Nation, New York Review of Books*, etc. — at the other). Allegiance to jazz is thus something not likely to be proffered by the timid. And conversely, just about the only way in which a onetime "jazz fan"

THIS ARTICLE WAS COMMISSIONED, BUT NOT PRINTED, BY *ROLLING STONE*.

can protect himself from guilt feelings on deserting the True
Faith appears to be via a lengthy, and perhaps not entirely
convincing, process of self-persuasion that his youthful love is
dead, *kaput,* finished. Hence the spectacle of yesterday's jazz
tastemakers as the prophets of its approaching moribundity
today.

If this hints at an explanation of the vehemence with which
these apostate jazz fanciers have turned on their former mistress, it still leaves us with the question of what impelled them
to desert the old girl in the first place — leaves us, that is, with
the music of John Coltrane and a few of his contemporaries
— he had no peers — and many disciples.

One of the things that has always made the jazz scene so
intriguing for sociologically-oriented white onlookers is its propensity to mirror in microcosm all the complexities and convo-
lutions of the turbulent racial stew that bubbles, gurgles and
from time to time like witches' brew, erupts over the side of the
pot in this racist society.

Come to think of it, "mirror" is not precisely the right word;
for developments can often be glimpsed in the hothouse jazz
environment long before they emerge onto the horizon of the
general public. Thus close followers of events in the jazz milieu
were less than wholly surprised when Stokely Carmichael first
raised the cry of "Black Power!" After all, the disputes, debates,
and deluge of literature which Stokely's cry unleashed had for
some time been a permanent fixture in the narrower jazz world.
And with much the same results, it might be added. Just as
white liberals began to defect from the black liberation movement when it swerved from its initial civil rights orientation
toward black nationalism, so did prominent white writers and
disc jockeys react with implacable hostility to all the various
manifestations of black nationalism in jazz. Ultimately, like
their counterparts in the civil rights movement, they turned
their back on jazz and found a niche where they would be
made less uncomfortable by a rising tide of black militancy
in music and/or politics.

The key figure in provoking this split — in weeding out the
musically militant sheep from the liberal lambs, if you will —
was John Coltrane. Not that Coltrane was politically a black
nationalist, though there doubtless were aspects of nationalism
that were attractive to him. He considered his contemporary
Malcolm X, for instance, "a man I had to see"; and having
duly seen him at one of Malcolm's last public appearances,
reported himself "quite impressed." (The admiration may have

been mutual: Malcolm was widely known to be an ardent
follower of jazz.)

For all of that, however, Coltrane never thoroughly immersed
himself in the swirling and turbulent currents of political black
nationalism. In point of fact, the antinationalist forces in jazz
would most likely have had an easier time of it if Coltrane's
relation to nationalism had been political and overt, as has
been that of Charles Mingus, Max Roach, or, later, one of the
first converts to the Coltrane persuasion, Archie Shepp. Just
because these men tend to think — and write and speak to reporters — in unabashedly radical nationalist terms, it has been
relatively easy to isolate them and expose them to endless
ostracism in the cloistered and sometimes fetid world of jazz.
It may, of course, be no more than an accident, but there is
no self-proclaimed black nationalist in jazz who works with
any degree of regularity. Coincidence? Judge for yourself.

But Coltrane's appeal was so widespread and its nature
so elusive as to transcend political nationalism as such. Coltrane, like many in the creative arts, had a philosophy that
was basically cosmic mysticism, albeit of a radical and egali-
tarian sort. In response to a question about his own importance
for the work of many of the younger jazz players, Coltrane
replied with characteristic mysticism — and modesty — "It's a big
reservoir that we all dip out of." Yet his mysticism did have
definite social correlates. "This music is an expression of higher ideals," he said, "so, therefore, brotherhood is there; and I
believe with brotherhood, there would be no poverty. And also,
with brotherhood, there would be no war."

Still, these views are not in themselves intolerably radical,
in view of the time, the place, and the social position of black
people. Certainly they do not take us very far in understanding
why it is that Coltrane, the man and his music, has become
a symbol par excellence of black manhood to all of the young
revolutionary nationalists, outranked in popularity as a subject for the nationalistically inclined poets only by Malcolm X.

If it seems paradoxical that a man not overtly aligned with
nationalism should find such great popularity in nationalist
ranks, the paradox is more apparent than real. For whatever
his relationship to political nationalism, his young black followers discovered in his music — and rightfully so, I should
say — the clearest possible expression of the Afro-American consciousness in midtwentieth century America, the quintessential
distillation of what it means to be black just now.

There were moments, moreover, when Coltrane himself ap-

peared to recognize that his music amounted to a rejection
of the European concert-hall tradition, with its rigidity and
artifice, for an embrace of the more spiritual world of color.
Many of his compositions from the early sixties bore titles such
as *Africa, India, Gold Coast, Dahomey Dance,* and the like.
One of his children carries the name Ravi, token of the mutual
esteem in which Coltrane and India's Ravi Shankar held each
other (an esteem undoubtedly heightened by the similarities
in their musics). A year before his tragic death, he spoke of
"a trip to Africa to gather whatever I can find, particularly
the musical sources." Ornette Coleman, also a significant innovator in his own right, once explained to an interviewer: "I
came up with a music that didn't require European laws applied to it," a "revolutionary breakthrough" for jazz. The same
could be said, with conceivably greater accuracy, for the ideas
of John Coltrane.

It was this counter-European character of Coltrane's music
that, more than anything else, led to the Great Schism that
rent the jazz world as the sixties began. In the course of this
split, many if not most of the New York-based writers who
dominate the jazz press — including even some of Coltrane's
original supporters — turned their withering fire against him
and condemned his music with the contemptuous epithet, "antijazz." When a complete account of the period has been com-
piled, the verdict may well be that this signified the lowest of
many low-water marks in the history of white understanding
of black art.

In retrospect, it becomes clear that the white writers, who had
their roots in the music of the preceding bebop era and had
grown accustomed to their easy predominance as arbiters of
fashion, were decidedly uneasy with the naked emotions, fervid
evangelicalism, and spiritual exaltation — with the nonwhite
nature, in short — of a typical Coltrane performance. To this
day, the bulk of these writers have proven unable to assimilate
their taste to the Coltrane Revolution, and continue to dispense
meaningless twaddle about him (and others) "rehearsing in
public." (In jazz, the new jazz especially, there is little meaningful opportunity to rehearse *except* in public, because the
nature of a performance will depend, among other things, on
the interaction between audience and artists. As Coltrane himself explained, "the audience, in listening, is in an act of participation, you know. And when you know that somebody is
maybe moved the same way you are, to such a degree or approaching the degree, it's just like having another member in

the group.") Or else, as I have already asserted, they have deserted jazz for other, greener pastures.

At the same time, ironically, the rock community is becoming increasingly conscious of the many contributions it has drawn from jazz. This is particularly true as concerns Coltrane, who, with the single possible exception of the late Wes Montgomery, is quite likely the jazz musician best known in rock circles. I have talked, for example, to young rock devotees who, even while they claim to "hate" jazz, make it a point to exclude Coltrane from their blanket judgment. Similarly, in conversation with rock people whom one would not expect to be especially familiar with jazz, the name of Coltrane will frequently crop up. Many will state that they "don't know much about jazz," but they "love" some record by Coltrane (typically, *A Love Supreme*, conceivably because of the pervasive mysticism that caused the Airplane's Marty Balin to refer to it as "Coltrane's acid trip"). Still others will tell you, "Man, I really dig jazz"; and when you question them further, will reveal that by "jazz" they mean — John Coltrane. Whatever their feelings about jazz in general, there is widespread respect and even affection for Coltrane among those members of the rock audience who have anything more than a passing acquaintance with his music.

While Coltrane enjoys a comparatively small but nonetheless dedicated following among rock listeners, his reputation among working rock *musicians* could hardly be higher. This is only to be expected from those groups, such as the various blues bands, the Collectors, Buddy Miles Express, Linn County, Traffic, Chicago Transit Authority, and others, in which there are saxophonists. Thus, to point to just one of many possible illustrations, the *Invocation and Ritual Dance to the Young Pumpkin* on the Mothers' *Absolutely Free* album is best described as a somewhat simplified version of the kind of modal improvisation first unveiled by Coltrane on his Atlantic recording of *My Favorite Things* (also the title of the album). For the *Invocation*, Mothers' multireed man Bunk Gardner, here on soprano saxophone improvised a contrapuntal duet with Frank Zappa (whose formidable talents as a guitar soloist, clearly in evidence on the *Invocation*, have tended to be overshadowed by his other considerable accomplishments). Subsequently, as Coltrane added other horns to his band, he himself began to include extensive passages in which two or more horns improvised simultaneously; one of the outstanding instances is the Coltrane-Pharoah Sanders soprano and tenor saxophone dialogue recorded on a later version of *My Favorite Things* on the *Coltrane Live at the Village Vanguard Again* album (Impulse label).

For all of his influence on reed players, it would be greatly mistaken to conclude that Coltrane's influence in rock ends there. In actuality, keyboard instrumentalists, like saxophonists, have not been slow to discover the applicability of some of Coltrane's ideas to their own instruments. Al Kooper, for one, before leaving Blood, Sweat and Tears for his new role as producer, has explained at some length and on numerous occasions how he has drawn on the Coltrane legacy in learning to play his bastard keyboard instrument, the ondioline. He had, he said, simply gotten his hands on every available recording of a Coltrane soprano solo; by the time he had committed all of Coltrane's improvisations to memory and was able to play them, lo and behold! the ondioline had been mastered. Kooper's solo on that instrument on *Holy Modal Majesty*—the title, like Whiteman's *Two Tranes Running*, can be presumed to be a tribute to the memory of the late saxophonist—on Kooper's *Super Session* LP with Mike Bloomfield, is an uncannily accurate likeness of the Coltrane soprano style.

To judge from their recorded work, other keyboard artists would agree with Al Kooper's estimate of the relevance of Coltrane for their own work. Particularly is this true of organists, perhaps because the stops on that instrument can be arranged to produce a sound approaching the sonority of a soprano saxophone played a la Coltrane. Of these men, Traffic's impressive Stevie Winwood is probably the most famous case in point (as his solo *Cryin' to be Heard*, from the new Traffic LP, amply reveals); but there are as well a number of first-rate soloists with lesser known bands who likewise show the Coltrane influence. Among them, to list but three, are U. S. of Arthur (Resnick) with San Francisco's Salvation; Ralph Shuckett, a talented musician who had the bad fortune to be saddled with a short-lived and somewhat less capable group (Clear Light); and Michael Ratledge of the Soft Machine.

The number of those in rock who have been touched by the Coltrane muse would, moreover, have to be extended still further to include musicians whose concepts have been partially shaped by Coltrane's various sidemen. The most important and influential of these sidemen have been drummer Elvin Jones, pianist McCoy Tyner (who were with Coltrane from 1961 to 1966), and bassist Jimmy Garrison. Being an

inveterate drummer-aspirant, I make it a point of talking with
all of the professional drummers of whatever persuasion whom
I can engage in conversation. I have yet to encounter one
rock drummer who did not place Elvin Jones high on the
list of his major idols and/or influences. The most dramatic
illustration of Elvin's effect on his rock brethren that I know
of was reported in an interview with the members of the Jimi
Hendrix Experience that appeared in the *East Village Other*.
As Experience drummer Mitch Mitchell — certainly among the
most creative in rock — was discussing Elvin Jones, Hendrix
interjected that his response to one of Elvin's records played
for him by Mitchell had been to turn in surprise to his own
drummer and exclaim, "That's you!" Need more be said?

In relating the foregoing, my purpose has been to give some
notion of how extensive the Coltrane influence has been among
rock musicians. Although it was natural to begin with reed
men and keyboard players, it is necessary to move beyond
their ranks if we are to do justice to the subject. Again relying
on my own informal conversations, I would have to estimate
that almost every rock band contains at least one stone Coltrane freak, sometimes more. Phil Lesh of the Grateful Dead,
for instance, can argue authoritatively on why he believes
that Elvin Jones was a more appropriate drummer for the
Coltrane group than his successor Rashied Ali. In 1968, eons
after *Eight Miles High* led the pop charts, and with innumerable personnel shuffles and reshuffles under their belts, the
Byrds still continue to introduce that song as their attempt to
recreate the music of John Coltrane. Spirit, the Southern California group, went the Byrds one better: at one point, they
actually had several of Coltrane's own compositions in their
repertoire. And so it goes.

Since it provides a particularly vivid example of how Coltrane's innovations have been diffused ubiquitously, if unob-
trusively, throughout rock, we might do well to take a look
at Grace Slick's composition *rejoyce* from the Airplane's *After
Bathing at Baxter's* LP. To do that, we have to begin with a
journey backwards in time to San Francisco, 1965, when two
of the most potent underground culture heroes were John Coltrane and Lenny Bruce. Not surprisingly, then, when Grace's
original group, the Great Society, took shape at that moment
as one of the area's indigenous rock bands, it included in its
book one number dedicated to *Father Bruce*, as the Slick dubbed
Lenny (*Grace Slick and the Great Society*, vol. 1), and another called simply *Father*, in which bassist Peter Vandergelder

abandoned his usual instrument to play a long and unmistakably Coltrane-derived (if not notably in tune) soprano saxophone solo (*Grace Slick and the Great Society*, vol. 2). In Vandergelder's defense, it should be noted that the soprano saxophone is an extremely difficult horn to intone properly. Vandergelder also apparently made it a practice to contribute an extended soprano introduction to the Great Society's version of *White Rabbit* (vol. 1); and what is interesting is that some of his *Arabian Nights* figurations lodged themselves deeply enough in Grace's head to turn up again on *rejoyce*, her evocation of Joyce's *Ulysses*, but this time on flute rather than soprano (the flutist was Bob Hardaway, a Hollywood studio musician with a strong jazz background). In the same way, Grace's evident exposure to the music of the Coltrane band of that period, even if only at second hand, makes much more understandable the similarities, also apparent on *rejoyce*, between her piano style and that of Coltrane's McCoy Tyner. None of this, needless to say, is of earthshaking significance, save to collectors of musical marginalia. Still, it does provide additional testimony, if such be needed, about the breadth and persistence of the Coltrane influence in rock.

How are we to account for that extraordinary breadth and persistence? For although it is easy enough to tabulate endless instances of Coltrane's influence on this or that rock musician, it is another matter to comprehend it.

As nearly as I can ascertain—and this must be clearly labeled as my own set of intuitions, nothing more—Coltrane's charisma over his fellow musicians, rock and jazz, can be understood partly in musical terms, partly in extramusical ones.

The musical ones first, because they are more concrete, easier to pinpoint. To venture once more into the past, return to the first years of the 1960s. At that point in time, nearly twenty years since the bebop revolution had shaken jazz in the 1940s, the orthodox procedures of bebop—basically, improvising a solo melody over a fixed set of chords, as is done in blues playing—had turned utterly stale and unexciting for the most creative spirits in the music. And yet, there was still the unanswered question: where to go from here? It was that question that Coltrane faced squarely and, to his immense credit, did more than anyone else to answer. Initially, he himself had thought along traditional, if nonetheless highly advanced, bebop lines: more chords and more complex clusters of chords might serve to make bebop again a challenging music for restless improvisers. But this hope proved false. Coltrane, typically enough, did not shrink from the recognition of the fact; instead, cutting his losses, he began a series of experiments that took him in myriad different directions. Ultimately, after a period of searching that was to be repeated more than once in his career, he hit on what was to become the backbone of his new approach. Drawing on the ideas of Miles Davis, with whose group he had played for several years late in the fifties, fellow saxophonist Ornette Coleman, and even the ragas of Ravi Shankar — Coltrane was always open to an unbelievable variety of stimuli — he decided that the solution to his difficulties lay in abandoning rigid chord sequences altogether, and simply spinning out an improvisation with nothing more than a scale and a tonic note as framework.

Simple in content, but revolutionary in effect! Such would have to be the historical evaluation of Coltrane's innovations as the 1960s began.

It may be that the easiest way to see what Coltrane was about is by comparing his approach to that of raga. Like a raga, a Coltrane improvisation is based, typically, on a scale — one of Coltrane's favorites was the Dorian mode or scale — in some ways similar to a minor blues scale (whence the appeal of Coltrane's playing for many rock guitarists). Underlying the scale is the tonic note, or in raga parlance, the drone. The supporting instruments serve both to establish the scale, drone, and meter and to provide constant rhythmic counterpoint against the main (solo) instrument.

So much, raga and Coltrane's music have in common. What sets them apart to my mind, is the greater diversity that can be obtained with the Western instruments (saxophone, piano, bass, drum kit) and especially the immense *power* that this instrumental combination is capable of generating. Liberated from the tyranny of one cycle of chords endlessly repeated, Coltrane used this new freedom to introduce into music some of the most incredibly moving and incredibly *human* sounds ever played on *any* instrument. The possibilities were virtually unlimited; and Coltrane, it must be said, made the most of them. In this day of electronic amplification, the sensation of being surrounded by and, quite literally, overpowered by pounding waves of music is a familiar, even commonplace, one; but this sensation is not unique to rock. In point of fact, even before the Beatles wanted to hold your hand, Coltrane and his men — Elvin Jones on drums, in particular — were whipping audiences up to crescendos of emotional fervor and leaving them limp, drained, spent at the conclusion of an hour-

long set that seemed as if it must have lasted days at least.
For those who were willing to submerge themselves under
these dense layers of sound, the results were almost always
ecstatic. Others, as we have seen, lacked either the determination or the ability to let themselves be swept away to the heights
with Coltrane; they were the ones who became musically rigid
reactionaries, condemning in bitterest vitriol Coltrane's "antijazz"; or else, incapable of coping with the new black music,
abandoning jazz altogether.

It was at this point that the extramusical aspect of Coltrane's
career began to become more pronounced, as Coltrane increasingly took on the stature of a charismatic culture hero
(the way, say, Mick Jagger has for Rock). It is true that,
initially, his reputation depended on the innovations that re-
vivified jazz music and rescued it from sterile and repetitive
formulas; much of his influence among musicians and listeners
alike will always depend on the improvisational procedures
he devised and the devastating force and logic with which
he presented them. That, however, is only part of the story.
For in the course of developing his ever-changing art, the
saxophonist gradually assumed the proportions of a larger-
than-life symbol. Symbol of what? Of many things. Of the
present-day artist who, after Varese, refuses to die. Of the pri-
mal energy and spiritual exaltation of a suppressed black
community.

But maybe above all else, Coltrane's career could be read
as an object lesson in uncompromising honesty, total devotion
to the creation of beauty as he, the artist, perceived it, regardless of the cost in terms of lost popularity. This facet of the
man is difficult to convey to those who have never heard him
or seen him perform in person. Some of his recordings, though,
especially those made "live," can at least suggest why, even
before his unhappily early end, Coltrane was the object of
veneration by many of his audience. On his first *Live at the
Village Vanguard* album, there is one track, *Chasin' the Trane*
(a name chosen by the recording engineer, incidentally, and
not by the performer), in which Coltrane took a simple blues
riff and reworked it for a steady sixteen minutes, with only
drums and bass by way of support — a *tour de force* that
in intensity of passion and feeling, eclipses almost everything
else in recorded jazz and even manages to make Ravi Shankar's extended raga excursions appear a bit on the anemic
side.

Such a performance—alas, all too infrequently captured on records—was the rule rather than the exception with the man. Coltrane's popularity was great enough to have allowed him to get by easily, as many another has preferred to do, with far less ardor; but the demands he placed on himself were always the highest. He never ceased to be interested in exploring new ideas and instruments; at the time of his death, he was in the habit of keeping a flute in his bedroom, so that after a tiring day of playing, he could "go there . . . and lay down and practice"! That was one index of Coltrane's devotion to art—music—as the supreme value.

Another was his willingness to take under his wing the youngest, most iconoclastic black artists. He interceded with Impulse, for whom he recorded during the last half-dozen years of his life, to secure a recording contract for Archie Shepp (whose first album, appropriately enough, was called *Four for Trane*). On several occasions, he asked to have the group led by Albert Ayler included with his own on concert bills. His generosity even went to the point of having another saxophonist, Pharoah Sanders, incorporated into his band, heedless of the additional expenses that would have to come out of his own pocket, or of the possibility that he might be upstaged in his own group by a man more than ten years his junior. Behavior of this nature would be generosity itself in any area of life; coming in the supercompetitive world of jazz, it was practically unheard of. With his incessant devotion to pushing his music beyond the already perfected and his constant and genuine humility, it was one of the things that made the man into an almost Christlike symbol of personal integrity and the search for truth in an environment that measures success only in terms of box-office receipts and record sales.

Though Coltrane, as I have observed, was not a person who dealt with the world in political terms, there is nonetheless an unmistakable parallel between his career and that of another black man who died only a few years earlier at roughly the same age—Malcolm X. The very fact that both men have become folk heroes to the young radical black nationalists suggests that there are eminently genuine similarities, based on shared experiences, that unite them. Both men perceived the ultimate reality about this country—a reality you could know only if you were black and had worked your way up and through the tangled jungle of jazz clubs, narcotics, alcohol, mobsters. Both men had the inner strength of character (to use an unfashionable word) that prevented their being destroyed by that milieu: instead, they were able to draw on these experiences to show us how to create a world without ghettos of any sort, by using our reason and emotions to reconstruct society. Doubtless Malcolm X would have agreed with Coltrane's desire, expressed in a late interview, "to be a force for real good. In other words, I know that there are bad forces, forces put here that bring suffering to others and misery to the world, but I want to be the force which is truly for good." Both men called upon their followers to break out of accustomed ways of thinking and feeling, and they themselves were willing to lead the way by challenging all the conventional assumptions and discarding those that failed to meet the rigorous test of reality — even if, in doing so, they were forced to sacrifice their own material security. Both men could have assured themselves of lives of relative comfort and well-being merely by making a few seemingly minor compromises; yet both refused to exchange a mess of consumer-goods pottage for the right to seek after and enunciate the truth as best they could.

For this dedication and compulsive honesty, both these giants among men paid with their lives. In the final analysis, it is conceivably less significant that Malcolm was snuffed out by the bullets from assassins' weapons while Coltrane was destroyed from within by illness; it is more significant that this country showed itself unable to create a society in which two of the century's must gifted and creative figures — two men who were attempting to bring the fruits of the black experience to the rest of us — could be permitted to live out their lives to their natural conclusion. For make no mistake about it, Coltrane was destroyed not by himself, as the artist in romantic legends of the previous century supposedly was, he was destroyed by a society that has been, and in the main continues to be, unremittingly hostile to the achievements of the black psyche, unless those achievements are cast in a mold palatable to whites on *their* terms. The lesson of his life, if it is a lesson you are after, is that it is literally suicidal to pour all your heart and soul into art when that art is to be marketed in the dingy rooms and before the half-drunk audiences that figure as the standard setting for the music called "jazz." Had a man of Coltrane's genius been white, more than likely he would have been enabled to end his days as a much revered elder statesman of the art world, after the fashion of Picasso and

Pablo Casals, who have become near-sacred institutions. Having instead been born black, Coltrane was dead before his forty-first birthday. Ultimately, the tragedy of this country is as simple and stark as that.

PART III

THE ANATOMY OF
THE COLTRANE QUARTET

The John Coltrane band (1967): Jimmy Garrett and Jimmy Garrison
(bass); Pharoah Sanders; Rashied Ali (not shown—behind Sanders,
on drums); John Coltrane; miscellaneous percussionists.

Photo by Frank Kofsky

ELVIN JONES

Chapter 10
ELVIN JONES: POLYRHYTHMIC INNOVATOR

Every revolution in jazz is fundamentally a revolution in the mode of sensing jazz rhythm; and that is of course as true of the jazz revolution of today as it was of the bebop revolution of some two decades past.

I wish that my technical limitations were not so great, so that I could present a precise description of the nature of the present jazz revolution. But if wishes were horses. . . . For the most part, the people who have the musicological competence to offer a formal analysis of the changes taking place do not seem in the least interested in clarifying our understanding of the new music. Quite the contrary—their primary interest appears to be that of aborting, or at the least retarding, these changes. Consequently, it falls to the lot of musical semiamateurs like myself to attempt the task of illuminating the aesthetic logic underlying the new music. I console myself with the thought that, crude as my account might be, it may perhaps provoke others who possess the requisite skills to go beyond my efforts.

The first thing that one does in striving to grasp the essence of a revolution—social or aesthetic—is to compare the new synthesis with the one it replaced; the before-and-after bit, if you will. With respect to jazz rhythm, the transition is that from the unvarying 4/4 pulse (granting occasional insignificant exceptions) of bebop to a fragmented and polyrhythmic fabric which juxtaposes patterns of three beats, four beats, and beats of other bases against one another.

To be more detailed: the bebop drummer generally kept time with his right hand and left foot. The right hand played a modified 4/4 on the cymbals (*one* . . . two-and *three* . . . four-and *one*, etc.), while the left foot squished the hi-hat cymbal closed on every even beat. The drummer could also, if he

THIS ORIGINALLY APPEARED IN *JAZZ*, JANUARY 1967.

chose, use his right foot on the bass drum on every beat; but since the bass ordinarily played a steady 4 quarter-notes per measure, most bebop drummers preferred to leave the bass drum free for irregular accents (the function of the left hand as well).

For the bebop audience (including members of the group who happened not to be playing at the moment) there were thus two basic methods for keeping time. One could tap one's foot on every beat, in synchrony with the drummer's right hand and the bass, or one could snap one's fingers (or clap one's hands) on the even beats, in time with the hi-hat cymbal. (If particularly energetic, it was possible to do both.)

But as audiences and musicians became more skilled in responding to this basic pulse, the pulse itself became more monotonous and even obtrusive, until the logical question finally dawned: since everyone can now sense 4/4, why is it necessary to be stating it continually? The answer was just as obvious: it isn't.

As art, and jazz in particular, is preeminently a social phenomenon, it was inevitable that numerous musicians would begin asking this question and arriving at the same answer simultaneously. Yet merely to discard the old rhythmic framework amounts to but half a revolution. For then the questing musicians must immediately go on to stub his toe on the unavoidable problem of what is to be put in its place.

The most effective solution, if not necessarily the first in time, was that arrived at early in the 1960s by John Coltrane and his then drummer Elvin Jones; subsequently, the Coltrane-Jones approach was extended by a group of young percussionists — Sonny Murray, Milford Graves, Rashied Ali, Andrew Cyrille — largely trained by the other major strategists of the jazz revolution, Cecil Taylor and Bill Dixon.

The essence of the Coltrane-Jones innovation was to shatter the hegemony of the single quarter-note beat and supplant it with two different but complementary kinds of rhythmic organization. On the one hand, Elvin Jones, while still maintaining the basic 4/4 pulse on his cymbal, introduced a counter-rhythm by playing patterns based on eighth-note triplets on his drums. At once this invention served to heighten the interest of the music of the Coltrane quartet, since the listener could respond not only to the four-based meter or the three-based (or six-based) meter, but to the creative tension produced by their interaction (a fact which seemed to confuse some writers of the time, who make the mistake of thinking that Coltrane's accompanists were just unsure of whether they were in 4/4 or 6/4!). At one point, Coltrane seemed to feel that two basses, each in a different meter, were necessary to create this rhythmic tension (e.g., *Africa Brass*, Impulse 6). Later, as Elvin demonstrated the polyrhythmic potentialities of the drums, a second bass became an expensive and super-fluous luxury.

As if the added complexity from Elvin Jones were not enough, Coltrane was broadening the rhythmic palette in a different direction by changing the phraseology of the jazz horn player. This he accomplished by shaping the bulk of his phrases to fall within a space of four, eight, etc., beats, establishing yet a third pulse, besides the two projected by drummer Jones. The hesitant beginnings of this post-bebop approach to rhythm were initiated by Coltrane on soprano saxophone — notably on his Atlantic *My Favorite Things* album — as he was perfecting his aesthetic on that instrument; but they were soon extended to Coltrane's tenor horn even before he cut his first releases for Impulse (*Africa/Brass, Live at the Village Vanguard, Coltrane, Impressions*), and they still form the foundation for his more recent improvisations on that label (*A Love Supreme, Ascension, Meditations*). (For early versions of this stylistic departure, hear Coltrane's extended coda on *Summertime* and his second solo on *But Not for Me*, both on the *My Favorite Things* LP.)

Despite the fact that Ornette Coleman is usually cited as the father of the jazz revolution, it has actually been the combination of Coltrane and Jones — along with Cecil Taylor, Bill Dixon and the drummers whose latent promise they polished into maturity — that provided the innovations which eventually undermined the rigid bebop approach to rhythm. And inasmuch as rhythm is *the* fundamental component of all jazz music, it follows that these innovations were the decisive ones, regardless of the furor that swirled about the head of Coleman.

If one can be so foolhardy as to speak of any set of practices as having become "standard" among the jazz revolutionaries, then it is certain that those introduced by Elvin Jones and John Coltrane must be referred to by that term. Several drummers have, in fact, taken Elvin's ideas one or more steps beyond where he left them. That remarkable Pittsburgh product Beaver Harris, for example, has dispensed almost entirely with the cymbals as time-keeping instruments. In his playing with Archie Shepp's quartet, Harris, who is clearly inspired by Elvin's work even as he transcends it, lays down a steady fusillade of drum beats that always implies but never directly states the underlying 4/4 meter. Andrew Cyrille, Sonny Murray, Milford Graves, Rashied Ali, Bob Pozar, and Bobby Kapp are, as I have already mentioned, other leading percussion figures to have taken advantage of the greater musical opportunities inherent in replacing a steady cymbal beat with an asymmetric and polyrhythmic approach.

How has the jazz listener been able to keep pace with the new rhythmic developments? Even though jazz has not been played primarily as dance music for over 25 years, it nonetheless retains a heavily kinesthetic aspect. Indeed, I suspect that if this were not so, the music would lose much of its appeal. Thus the jazz audience has been challenged to find an appropriate means of responding on a physical level; and it has not been unequal to the challenge. While some die-hard spirits still attempt to maintain a regular 1-2-3-4 beat by tapping their feet, the furious tempos favored in the new music and the limited stamina of the onlookers has made this impractical for most. Instead, what promises to become the conventional response consists in moving the upper half of the body forward and back in periods of four beats (or multiples thereof). As the horn players, particularly the saxophonists, tend, following Coltrane, to develop their phrases in units of this length, such a body movement jibes perfectly with the music. The hornmen themselves, moreover, often sway in precisely this manner, so there in a certain empathetic quality manifested when the audience gets moving in phase with the soloist(s). On a good night at a concert or club, a man just in off the street might be forgiven for thinking he had mistakenly barged into a *shul* full of *davining* orthodox Jews!

Such, I believe, are the rudiments of the rhythm of the new jazz. I hope that it will not be too long before some bright young musicologist takes it upon himself to fill in the gaping holes that this summary sketch has necessarily left, and presents us with a detailed picture of all the rhythmic elements that go to make up the music of the jazz revolution.

As long as I have broached the subject of rhythm, a few paragraphs more on Elvin Jones are in place. I have tried in the foregoing to suggest that Elvin's ideas have been crucial to the success of the jazz revolution in its ascendant phase; I think that many of the young drummers whose names I have mentioned would confirm this (certainly Beaver Harris, for one).

Nonetheless, there has been a fair amount of rather peevish criticism about Elvin bruited about in the jazz underground recently.

The basis for these complaints has usually centered around Elvin's alleged "sell-out." As evidence, his decision to leave the John Coltrane group and his record with an Episcopalian priest who dabbles on the piano (Father Tom Vaughn) have been cited. While these things are incontestable, it is possible to differ with Elvin's critics in interpretation.

There are two essential elements about Elvin that should be kept in mind — his total devotion to the music and his character as a transitional figure midway between bebop and the jazz revolution.

Although my own acquaintance with Elvin is, to my own regret, relatively slight, I would nevertheless stake my "reputation" on the belief that the man's love for his work, as manifested in his playing (even on records), is so great as to preclude absolutely the chance that he would ever do anything that he conceived as unworthy of the music. That he recorded an admittedly execrable album with Father Vaughn must, if I am correct, be explained by other considerations. My own guess — and it is only that — is that bonds of friendship with the priest, and not Elvin's personal greed, dictated the choice (the same probably applies to Elvin's selection of painter Larry Rivers [!] as a sideman). While I can hardly give my approval on aesthetic grounds to the musical syrup that has resulted, I still maintain that it is decidedly premature to be reading Elvin out of the lists of creative artists (especially when Allen Ginsberg is such a devotee of his drumming).

What about Elvin's departure from the Coltrane brood? As a transitional musician, Elvin has roots that extend in many directions. He could not be happy playing the kind of music that would content Milford Graves, say, as his sole fare. Nor is he alone. There are quite a few musicians who straddle the jazz revolution, with a foot in each camp; McCoy Tyner, Tony Williams, Bobby Hutcherson, Joe Chambers, Richard Davis, Joe Henderson — these are a few names that come quickly to mind. While all of these men can be spoken of as belonging to the jazz revolution, evidently they are as yet reluctant to identify themselves with it completely. Which simply goes to illustrate that aesthetic definitions, which we introduce to bring a measure of clarity into our discussions, will never be adequate as an exhaustive definition of a more complex and contradictory reality.

Seen in this light, Elvin's decision to split from Coltrane may become more intelligible. Suppose the circumstances had been reversed and Elvin were the leader of the group; no one would have condemned Coltrane for leaving to seek after his own musical personality. Why should it be different in this case? Doesn't Elvin have the same obligation to be true to himself as Coltrane did when he left Miles Davis? They why the eagerness to disparage? Why the hasty accusations of "sell-out"?

It's ludicrous to think that Elvin needs or can in any way benefit from a defense by me. Still, as a man whose music has given me innumerable hours of superlative pleasure — and as a man who has befriended me though he knows my radical views and dissents from them entirely — I regard it as an elementary debt of conscience to make this effort to set matters straight.

Chapter 11
McCOY TYNER: AN INTERVIEW

The following interview with McCoy Tyner was obtained August
16, 1966, in New York, as part of a series seeking to relate
new styles in "jazz" to the resurgent currents of black nationalism in the nation's ghettos. As such, the questions put to Mc-
Coy were as standardized as was possible under the circumstances.

The name McCoy Tyner will probably be familiar to many,
if not most, followers of contemporary American music. For
upwards of five years his piano was a mainstay in the quartet
of the late saxophonist John Coltrane, a period during which
his approach to the instrument became nearly as influential
and pervasive with the younger musicians as was that of Coltrane himself. Though primarily, of course, a "jazz" musician,
traces of McCoy's characteristic way of playing can nevertheless be heard in rock groups ranging from the Jefferson Airplane (whose Grace Slick feeds chords quite in the Tyner manner) to Spirit, to any number of others.

It will be noted that McCoy was guarded, if not downright
reluctant, in expressing himself on controversial questions pertaining to black nationalism, radical politics, etc., during the
early part of this interview. Such reluctance has to be seen as
the product of bitter experience. Now that most of the barriers
have been broken down by Bob Dylan and the Beatles, white
rock musicians are free to write and sing about virtually any
subject in language of their own choosing, with no penalties
attached (thus the Airplane can intone "bullshit" on the *House
at Poohneil Corners, Crown of Creation*). Black "jazz" musicians
enjoy no such license. There are some outspoken and radical
critics of the status quo in jazz circles: Max Roach, Charles
Mingus, Archie Shepp, and others. Significantly, none of them

work with any regularity; neither Roach nor Mingus have had a record in years; and such records as Mingus is able to make are released only through his own label. Most jazz musicians, finding survival difficult enough In White America with two strikes against them — their color and their art (for this country has never been hospitable to its serious artists) — are not so suicidal as to wish to add a third in the form of explicit radical politics. Until one has shared their experience, it hardly behooves one to criticize this decision. Typically, the black "jazz" musician can expect to sweat his too-brief life out in a series of underpaid "gigs" in incredibly sordid "clubs." Until we are able to alter these circumstances, how can we have the temerity to ask him to add to the already formidable obstacles he will inevitably encounter?

Kofsky: Do you think the phrase "new black music" is an accurate title for some of the newer styles that are being played today in jazz?

Tyner: That's a very difficult question. I guess maybe to some this may be an accurate description of what they're doing. But I don't know whether you could . . . I really couldn't speak for them on that particular —

Kofsky: I think you should speak for yourself.

Tyner: It's not an accurate title. It's really hard to say; still, I can't be specific on that point, because some individuals feel that what they're doing is . . . that this title is more appropriate to what they're doing, because of the fact that they are more or less nationalistically geared.

Kofsky: What about for what you're doing? Do you see it as accurate for yourself?

Tyner: Not necessarily. No, not necessarily. Number one, I don't like to categorize myself or my music in any respect, because I feel that music, number one, is universal; and that, at least the way I feel, is that I'm motivated by different aspects of life. I'm not motivated mainly by —

Kofsky: Political considerations?

Tyner: Yes, necessarily politically motivated.

Kofsky: When we spoke of this earlier, you said that it was true that society did influence the music, but that you didn't want to concentrate exclusively on that. Do you still think that it is true that there is a relationship between the society and the music?

Tyner: I think there is an indirect relationship, yes.

Kofsky: Would you talk about the relationship?

Tyner: Well, I feel it's like anything else. I mean that if you're living in a society . . . that this music has been influenced by the environment, by the things that people have gone through. To me this is how this music, one of the reasons why the music emerged, because of the fact that the society had imposed certain things upon people and this was an outlet.

Kofsky: Restrictions?

Tyner: Restrictions or certain pressures, and people — the black people in particular — used it as a form of expressing themselves. So I believe that society does have an effect on the music.

Kofsky: Do you ever find that the response of an audience to your music is different according to the race of the audience? That is, that a black audience might respond differently than a white audience? Have you ever noticed that about your own music?

Tyner: That's a very difficult question to answer. It all depends on where you're playing; and it's really hard, because sometimes you find . . . you can't really categorize audiences, because sometimes you get a good audience one place one set. It varies from set to set . . . you can't really tell.

Kofsky: So there's no generalization that would apply, say, 60 percent of the time?

Tyner: Right, right — It's really difficult —

Kofsky: Malcolm X's autobiography reveals that he was a jazz lover and a close friend of many jazz musicians. Do you think that this is just an accident, or that there is some deeper significance about this — that this says something about the nature of jazz and the nature of Malcolm X?

Tyner: Well, I believe that there is something related there, because Malcolm came out of the ghetto, was a product of the ghetto, as I feel the *music* is a product of the ghetto. So I feel that it is only natural that he would have a close feeling, you know, to the music, because it is something that was just part of him, because it's a part of the ghetto. I believe that both of them . . . that they're one and the same.

Kofsky: And his ideas also came out of the ghetto then, would you say?

Tyner: Yes, basically, I think they did.

Kofsky: Would you ever consider dedicating a composition to Malcolm?

Tyner: I might consider that.

Kofsky: Would you ever consider dedicating a composition

to *anyone?* Political, musical, social — any public figure that would be known by everybody?

Tyner: Possibly, yes; possibly.

Kofsky: But you can't think of anyone right off hand?

Tyner: No, not right off hand, no.

Kofsky: So your reluctance to talk about jazz and the social questions doesn't come about because you see these social questions as unrelated, but simply because you would rather focus on the music?

Tyner: I feel that for me, as a musician, this is the primary thing — the music. If you want to, let's say, dedicate some time to discussing social problems, I feel that it's a different category, even though it's all related, but it's still a different category, it's a different subject.

Kofsky: Do musicians spend time discussing such social questions?

Tyner: I don't think they spend any more time than anybody else who's involved in the social problems.

Kofsky: Well, it's been said that they don't spend any time *at all.*

Tyner: [Laughter.] Well, I don't think they do specifically. I mean just like if you're socializing, or if you're playing together, occasionally something pops up in the news, you might discuss it. It's only natural, it's like anybody else. But to just set aside an appointed time to discuss —

Kofsky: No, I don't mean —

Tyner: It's just haphazardly, like any other general subject.

Kofsky: What I'm trying to establish is whether or not musicians are *interested* in these questions.

Tyner: Well, I think they *are.* I think they're interested, just like any other citizen would be interested in social problems.

Kofsky: In general, do they see the music as related to these problems?

Tyner: I feel that, being that the problem is directly related to them, that they may feel an inner urge or inner feeling to maybe write or express themselves, express this problem through their music, sometimes. Occasionally, a person may dedicate a number to something that has happened. I think that this type approach has been incorporated years ago. Guys used to write about social problems, what happened in society; so it's really nothing new.

Kofsky: You don't disapprove?

Tyner: No, I don't disapprove of that, no.

Kofsky: Some musicians have said that jazz comes out of

conditions of poverty and oppression and is opposed to those conditions of poverty and oppression. Would you agree?

Tyner: I think it has a lot to do with it, I think that has a lot to do with it. I think that has a great deal to do with it. I really do. But I think also, I think it probably would have happened maybe naturally. I think that it happened to be a vehicle to express the suffering that the black man had incurred in this country; but I think that maybe . . . that being that the uniting of the two cultures, I think if it had just taken place under any other circumstance, maybe it might have happened. Maybe with not as much meaning — I don't know, it's really hard to say. But I think that it's really an amalgamation of the two cultures — the African and the European culture.

Kofsky: What is your general opinion of working conditions for jazz musicians? Do you feel that jazz musicians are treated, on the whole, as artists deserve to be treated?

Tyner: No, they're not.

Kofsky: Why?

Tyner: That's a very difficult question. I think that jazz music, if you want to use that term, jazz — I don't particularly care for it, but it's an accepted word and I use it because I have so much respect for the music, that I feel that the word really . . . but, getting off that, I think that jazz is really not given the proper exposure, and it's really not exposed in the true light of what it really is. This is the way I look at it; and consequently I think that we suffer, because people get the wrong idea about what it's all about. And I think that sometimes deliberately it seems as though the music doesn't get the proper exposure — it's not being exposed right or properly. It gets sort of a minimum amount of exposure — not enough, I don't feel.

Kofsky: Could this be connected with the fact that many of the musicians are themselves black?

Tyner: Possibly, possibly. I believe that, to a degree, I really do. Because I mean that's like in any other field, any other thing, especially. I believe that being that black musicians seemingly have been the innovators in this particular field, that's another thing that I think keeps it at a certain level.

Kofsky: You mean white people find it difficult to accept the fact that black people could make valid artistic innovations?

Tyner: I wouldn't say as a whole, white people; but I think that there is a good majority, probably because of the way society points to the black as inferior, in many, many ways. So I guess it's very difficult for white people to accept that.

Kofsky: Just as in the history textbooks you don't read that there were three black men who crossed the Delaware with Washington.

Tyner: Right, right. That's what I'm saying.

Kofsky: Do you think in jazz white musicians get better treatment than blacks, on the whole?

Tyner: In jazz? Well, to tell you the truth, I really couldn't be conclusive on that; but one thing I do feel: that being that society is the way it is, and white supremacy seems to be a dominant thing, it's only natural that a white musician, under certain circumstances, would get better treatment.

Kofsky: So when you have a fellowship to give, you give it to Don Ellis instead of Cecil Taylor?

Tyner: Maybe in some cases that would happen.

Kofsky: It has happened.

Tyner: In most cases, that would happen.

Kofsky: What I'm interested in is the general rule.

Tyner: Yeah, in most cases, right.

Kofsky: Do you have any idea about how conditions could be improved for jazz musicians?

Tyner: Like I said, exposure has a lot to do with it — the right kind of exposure. But like I say, jazz doesn't get the exposure that rock and roll gets, and I really can't understand it, in a sense — in a way I can and in a way I can't. I think it's unjust, because we don't get the same amount of exposure that the other art forms get, as far as the radio medium is concerned and television medium. And the image that's being painted of the jazz musicians is a very degrading one. So we can go back to the old reason, if you want.

Kofsky: It all comes back to slavery.

Tyner: Yes, and keeping the black man at a certain level.

Kofsky: Because how else could you keep them a slave? And how else could you convince the white people that it was a good idea to keep them that way?

Tyner: That's right.

Kofsky: What do you think about attempts like that of the Jazz Composers Guild to organize jazz musicians to better their circumstances?

Tyner: I think that it's a very good, I think it's very good.

Kofsky: What about Cecil Taylor's idea of a boycott of all recording companies, night clubs, promoters?

Tyner: I think that would be very difficult. Especially if you want to survive. It's very hard as it is you know. But I think that jazz musicians can do a little more to better their condition by doing some things together, it's only natural. But I don't think they should completely boycott—

Kofsky: Well, just as a technique for getting better wages?

Tyner: Well that might . . . Well, when I mean boycott, I mean boycott completely, or indefinitely. But I think maybe if that was tried, it might be successful.

Kofsky: Do the musicians who play in some of the newer styles look to Africa and Asia for their musical inspiration?

Tyner: I know I do, I do.

Kofsky: Is there any particular reason why you do?

Tyner: I have a lot of personal reasons. I think mainly because of my religious convictions — I'm orthodox Muslim. But I think that has a lot to do with my leaning. And not just because of that, I think because a lot of musicians are realizing that this is where the roots of the music really come from, as far as this music is concerned.

Kofsky: Rather than Europe?

Tyner: Yea, yeah, know what I mean? But I think that mostly black musicians feel that they can better relate to Africa.

Kofsky: Can I quote you on that?

Tyner: That's all right. I'm not speaking for all, but I mean there's a great number of them.

Kofsky: Do you think that group improvisation is becoming more important in the newer styles?

Tyner: I think so.

Kofsky: Can you think of any reason why it should be becoming more important at this particular time?

Tyner: All I can say is that there's something that is a different approach. I think anything different . . . I think a lot of musicians are seeking to explore new areas and I think that this is a new area, a different style of playing. Now years ago, I think they used to play like that; it's nothing new.

Kofsky: Yes, several generations ago.

Tyner: It's a different concept now — it's a sort of conglomeration of what has happened before and what's happening now. I believe that all of it is related, the whole scope.

Kofsky: Another kind of new music that started a while back and never caught on was Third Stream Music, as an attempted fusion between the jazz and European traditions. Why do you think it didn't win more of a following among the musicians?

Tyner: I really couldn't say for sure why it didn't catch on, but I found out from my observation over the last years — at least my participation in the art form — that seemingly if there isn't enough of the roots there to really identify the music for what it is, it seemed very difficult to reach the average person, the average listener to the music. I feel that this element definitely has to be present in order to even approach the majority of the listeners, anyway, to jazz. Not that one should compromise; but I think that this element is very important and distinguishes jazz from other forms of music.

Kofsky: When we were talking earlier about African and Asian music being important, it seems as though this might have some bearing on the case, too. Because if musicians are going to look to Africa and Asia for their musical inspiration, perhaps they're not going to be as interested in Third Stream Music, which really is going in another direction.

Tyner: Yeah, I guess so. But quite naturally you're going to find musicians who are going to delve into areas similar to the Third Stream area. I couldn't say what they're going to come up with; but this is the way I feel — I feel that's the way I'm looking towards, in the direction of Africa.

Kofsky: But the young black musicians, most of them seem not to be very interested in Third Stream. They seem to be much more interested in Africa and Asia.

Tyner: Right, right, sure; that's true.

Kofsky: Here's another question on musical developments that maybe you can help me solve: I notice that many of the newer groups are pianoless; and even in cases where there is a piano, oftentimes the piano lays out when the horn is playing. I noticed, for example, that when you were with John Coltrane, he had you lay out in some parts of his solos. Why do you think that is? Why do you think this tendency to de-emphasize the piano, or to give it another role in the music, is developing?

Tyner: Well, one thing is the practical end of it. I used to try to play the length of his [Coltrane's] solo. He brought it to my attention first; but after I thought about it, I realized that it didn't make sense to play the length of the solo, because after all the horn player is familiar with the structure of the tune, whatever you're playing. And it's not really important for the piano to play the entire length of a person's solo. I feel that it's there purely for color and support; but I feel that a musician, a soloist, shouldn't have to depend upon the piano being there. You see what I mean? Not only that, it gives him more of an area harmonically, melodically, to work. It doesn't restrict him, in other words.

Kofsky: That's what I was thinking.

Tyner: In some areas, when a person reaches a peak in their solo, they might want to move into different areas, and there may come a time when I'm moving maybe into the area that may not be simultaneous to the area that they're moving into.

Kofsky: Particularly so if he's going to play notes that aren't really on the piano, or overtones, or shrieks, or squeals. How are you going to reconcile that with what the piano is playing?

Tyner: Yeah, that's true. And then at times it may, at times. . . well actually it's reallv left up to . . . to what's happening at the time. Maybe a piano would sound good at that particular point, but it all depends on what's happening at the time.

Kofsky: How was that determined in John's group? Was it just he asked you to lay out or you just decided to lay out?

Tyner: No, it was just decided at a certain point.

Kofsky: Certain writers and critics have charged that the new music in jazz lacks form, lacks structure, and so on and so forth. What do you think about those charges?

Tyner: I really can't say that they're valid altogether, although I can say this: that at times it's very hard to comprehend the structure of most of the newer attempts by some of the groups. Of course my way of doing it wouldn't be quite as . . . well, it would be sort of different from a lot of other groups. You know, I have a way of approaching a thing — free form, or whatever you want to call it — and it wouldn't be quite as "free" as some of the other groups, if you want to use that term.

Kofsky: Is this inherent in the nature of the piano, or just something of your own choice?

Tyner: What do you mean, my approach?

Kofsky: Yes. I mean, do you see it being dictated by the piano, or do you see it being simply as a matter of your own choice?

Tyner: I think it's a matter of my own choice, I don't think it's dictated by the piano necessarily, no.

Kofsky: Why do you think so much of the new music has met with hostility on the part of many critics?

Tyner: I really couldn't say.

Kofsky: Remember, there was a time when John's group especially was given a roasting, back in 1961-62?

Tyner: I think mainly because, in the function of being a critic, one doesn't like to feel that he's misinformed or . . . Well, that's just like anything else, anything new that comes along quite naturally is going to meet some sort of rivalry from certain elements. I guess that's like anything else . . . a change. And some people might accept it, some might reject it; but in this particular position, where they have to speak with some sort of authority, they don't want to be at a disadvantage if something new comes along.

Kofsky: Do you think there's anything social here, in the sense that most of these critics are white and many of them are middle-aged, and many of the musicians are young and black, and in some cases have radical ideas, radical political ideas?

Tyner: I think in most of the cases — I mean, I can't speak for all, because I know that there are some probably that are men of integrity — but I believe that there is an element of dishonesty among the critics. I couldn't say that with proof, but there's certain things that seem to point in that direction. They seem to be biased biased in points.

Kofsky: Well, if you want some proof, here are two quick examples. First of all, Ira Gitler, two years in a row, voted for albums in the *Down Beat* Critics Poll that he wrote the liner notes for.

Tyner: [Laughter.] Yeah, I know what you mean. You see, that's the problem — it becomes a job.

Kofsky: It is a job.

Tyner: The guy has a position; his interest in the art might be minimal; it might not be that much.

Kofsky: At some point he becomes more interested in keeping himself alive.

Tyner: Right.

Kofsky: And he may have to do that by something that isn't criticism at all, such as writing liner notes, which isn't in the least criticism.

Tyner: No, it isn't. And not only that, sometimes I think that it can do harm at certain points.

Kofsky: Another example is that Leonard Feather, who wrote the liner notes for Eric Dolphy's memorial album on Vee Jay after giving Eric such unfavorable mention when he was with John Coltrane.

Tyner: Yeah, that's the thing. See, that's what I'm talking about. That's something . . . I can't accept that. And I mean, after the man dies, put him in the [*Down Beat*] Hall of Fame — that's ridiculous!

Kofsky: The same people who put him in poverty —

Tyner: That's what I mean, see, he couldn't work, he couldn't work in this country.

Kofsky: One other example. Speaking of working, I don't know if you read *Down Beat* some time ago, but there was a very laudatory review by Dan Morgenstern of Cecil Taylor, which finished up by saying that this man Taylor was a genuis and needed many more opportunities to play his music for an audience. But what he didn't say was that he, Dan Morgenstern, as New York editor of *Down Beat*, had been responsible for drawing up the list of artists who participated in the Jazz in the Garden series at the Museum of Modern Art. [Laughter.] And he *didn't* have Cecil Taylor in that list. So that's what really gripes me — that's why I don't even like to call myself a critic, because when you say "critic," one thinks of those people.

Tyner: Not only that, it's very hard, you see, in an art form to really set yourself up as an authority.

Kofsky: The only genuine authorities are the musicians.

Tyner: Yes, you really can't do that. You have to accept whatever is here for whatever it's worth. You can only speak from a personal point.

Kofsky: Ultimately, it comes down to whether or not other musicians are going to pay attention to what you're doing.

Tyner: Yeah, that's about it.

Kofsky: As an artist, do you feel that you have any responsibility to educate your audience, besides in the music?

Tyner: Not necessarily. I feel that, really, the only way that I can communicate with them — besides now and then talking — is musically. That's about the only way I can do. Because I don't believe that if you explain the thing to a person, that doesn't mean that they're going to better their musical taste. They have to be exposed to it, listen to it, and see what they can absorb; that's about all that I can say.

Kofsky: To you, who are the most influential artists playing the music? And how did you arrive at your decision?

Tyner: Well, I don't know. That's another difficult question, although I feel that Ornette Coleman and John Coltrane have been tremendous influences.

Kofsky: Four quick biographical questions. Where were you born and where were you raised; and how old are you; and what's your educational background?

Tyner: I was born in Philadelphia, Pennsylvania, was raised there, and I'm twenty-seven years old, and, well, I had elementary, you know, I had a little harmony theory at Granoff Music School, and I studied privately, first of all, at the age of thirteen I started, and I studied privately for a while with a teacher. I had about two or three teachers during that time, and I studied about four years. After that I went on my own from what I learned. That's about the size of that. I think that most of the things I learned really was through practical experience, applying myself. I think that's the best.

Kofsky: That's the end of my list of prepared questions, do you have anything else that you'd like to put down on the tape?

Tyner: Well, all I can say is that I hope that people will at least listen more closely to us musically and not be so conclusive on certain things, musically, without remaining open-minded. I feel that, not that everything that happens is valid, because everything that a person does, doesn't mean that it's right. But it has some purpose . . .

I was just saying, like about the black power thing, I feel that a lot of people have gotten a wrong concept about that. I'm pretty sure that all that the black Americans want is the same thing as the whites. They seized this phrase as a means to convey emotionally what they mean—what they mean by what they've been demanding, actually.

Kofsky: Whites never had to talk about white power, because they had it all the time.

Tyner: Yeah, that's true. So I believe it's very significant in this situation.

Kofsky: You know, in the forties what happened was that a tremendous gap opened up between the new musicians of that day and the public. And the critics didn't really do anything to help; in many cases they made it worse.

Tyner: Here is what I can't understand: why, when I spoke to you earlier about labels, I realize that things have to be identified, as a means just to identify. But at times these labels can hamper an individual or they can be very harmful, in a sense. It all depends on how they are being used and what they mean, you know what I mean?

Kofsky: Like the "new black music"?

Tyner: Yes. Well, I was saying, like they used it when Bird was alive, they had certain words for them, "antisocial," and what have you.

Kofsky: That's right. In the case of the "new black music," I think one can use it in a very simple descriptive sense, just the way you did, to mean that the *innovators* almost always are black.

Tyner: Yeah, right.

Kofsky: If you just say *that*, I don't see how anybody can take offense. But then the thing gets distorted, it gets out of perspective, it becomes another "black power" thing. People start screaming that you're a racist and you're talking about black supremacy.

Tyner: Yeah, that's the way it's defined, that's true.

Kofsky: There's a lot of distortion going around [Laughter] and nobody is very happy about it except the distorters.

Tyner: Yeah, that's true.

Photo by Frank Kofsky

McCOY TYNER

Photo by Frank Kofsky

JOHN COLTRANE

Chapter 12
JOHN COLTRANE: AN INTERVIEW

I am not a religious person, but John Coltrane was the one man whom I worshipped as a saint or even a god. I could never have written that when he was alive — if nothing else, it would have been too embarrassing for him had he read it. But since he is gone, no cause remains for denying it; and I feel that that tribute is the smallest gesture I can make toward acknowledging how much beauty and happiness he has brought into my life.

My veneration of John began, I think in the winter of 1958, when I first heard him on Miles Davis's *Round About Midnight* LP. I was immediately hypnotized and entranced by his sound. If familiarity is supposed to lead to contempt, the process worked just the opposite way in my love affair with Coltrane's music: the more I heard, the heavier was I hooked. Especially so with his later, post-1961 periods. Indeed, there have been times recently when one of the few things I could consistently rely on to convince me that life was worth the effort was the indomitably affirmative spirit that could be heard even in Coltrane's recordings. I'm sorry if that sentence reads like something by Nat Hentoff, but that is the way I felt, and Nat and everyone else will just have to bear with me for the resemblance.

Meeting John in the flesh not only did not tarnish his appeal for me, it enhanced it. I do not pretend I knew him well. I met him shortly after he formed his own quartet in 1961 to the best of my recollection, when he played his first West Coast engagement at San Francisco's *Jazz Workshop*. It had been arranged that he would do a benefit concert sponsored by the Students for Racial Equality at the University of California, the proceeds to go to the Student Nonviolent Coordinating

THIS ORIGINALLY APPEARED IN *JAZZ AND POP*, SEPTEMBER 1967.

Committee. The concert itself was never held — the then Chancellor Clark Kerr would not allow us to raise funds on campus for the use of organizations like SNCC, which meant that there was no point putting on the concert. (Later, the Free Speech Movement was able to mobilize the Berkeley campus around this issue; but in 1961 there was not that much concern.) Nonetheless, it had been a very real thrill for me (as liaison with Coltrane) to carry on even those few fragmentary and truncated conversations we had in the cubbyhole that passed for a dressing room in the *Workshop.*

I did my best to keep up the acquaintanceship in the years that followed. I moved to Los Angeles later in 1961, and whenever Coltrane played there — which wasn't often, due to the backwardness of the Los Angeles jazz audience — I made it a point to seek him out and exchange a few words with him. Poor man! How I now regret robbing him of those precious minutes that he liked to use for cat-napping between sets. But then I thought only of how I could manage to bask for a few extra moments in the presence of the Great Man himself.

In the summer of 1966 I was able to arrange for a two-week stay in New York to interview the leading musicians of the Jazz Revolution. The name that topped my list, of course, was that of John Coltrane. In spite of his crowded schedule, I was able to persuade John to allow me to question him, a triumph that left me glowing. The circumstances of that interview may help explain the affection I felt for John and why the closer one got to the man, the more one loved and respected him.

There was no earthly reason why he should have consented to be interviewed, especially since it involved a certain amount of inconvenience for him. First off, he had to drive thirty or forty minutes from his house to pick me up at the Deer Park station of the Long Island Railroad. Then, since there wasn't time for us to return to his home if I were to be on the afternoon train returning to New York, he sat with me in his station wagon for over an hour, sweltering in the August heat and humidity while we tape-recorded an interview in the parking lot of a local supermarket (part of our conversation is inaudible on the tape, owing to the rattling of the shopping carts). After the interview was over and John had returned me to the station, he insisted on waiting with me on the sunny platform until the next train back arrived. As we waited, he asked me about my political philosophy (we had talked during the interview about changing the world for the better).

He was thoughtful and attentive, when I told him I was a socialist and tried as best I could, given my nervous state, to explain the reason why. And then the train came.

That, however, was not the last of John's kindnesses to me. The next day I received a telephone call from Pharoah Sanders, saying that John had told him I was searching for him (as indeed I had been, fruitlessly, ever since my arrival in New York) to interview. And so an appointment with Pharoah was thus set up through the agency of John Coltrane.

I have never understood to this day why John went so far out of his way to assist a complete nonentity like myself. I can only surmise that, however much he may have had reservations about or outright disagreements with some of my ideas, he was convinced of my sincerity in working for a radical improvement in the human condition; and for that reason, if I am not mistaken, he put himself at my disposal. To say that his actions touched me would be the greatest understatement imaginable. But by then I appreciated that John Coltrane was unlike other men: his humility seemed to grow in proportion to his greatness, and I believe him the most *genuinely* modest man I have ever met. (Those younger followers who are so anxious to try and fill his shoes with their own considerably lesser talents would do well to emulate the master in this regard.) It was the combination of modesty and human warmth that overwhelmed me in talking to John and lent another whole dimension to my understanding of what he was saying in his music.

In the 1964 election, I wrote in the names of Malcolm X and John Coltrane for President and Vice-president. I mention this now only because I have been musing about it frequently in the days since John's passing. Then, I made that choice because those were the two greatest Americans I could think of. But now, I've begun to wonder if there isn't some hidden but nonetheless real connection between them. I think that there is. Both men perceived the ultimate reality about this country — the reality that you could know only if you were black and you were exposed at close quarters to the jazz club-narcotics-alcohol-mobster-ghetto milieu. Both men escaped being trapped in that milieu; both sought to use the lessons they had learned from it to show us not just the necessity for creating a society without ghettos of any sort, but also how to go about it; both, that is, exhorted us to make maximum use of our *human* potentialities, our reason and emotions. Neither was ever content with a static description of reality. Instead, both continually

brought their most treasured concepts, assumptions, and definitions under relentless scrutiny. When these proved inadequate
or outmoded, so much the worse for them: once their shortcomings became apparent, they were discarded like yesterday's
newspapers. Such was the compulsive honesty of these two
giants, the total dedication to truth at any cost, that made Malcolm X and John Coltrane the charismatic figures they were
and won for them their large following of young people, black
and white alike. Though cut down in the prime of life with
their work far from finished and their best years perhaps still
in front of them, it is surely safe to say that their influence
is just beginning to be felt.

    I was not close enough to John Coltrane to expound on
"what he would have liked us to do"; it would be a cheap
trick unworthy of the reverence in which I hold him were I
even to try. Possibly there are others who have this knowledge, I cannot say. What I can do is to tell you what he stands
for in my mind and how I feel we can make use of his life
to guide us, now that he is gone. More than anything else,
I think of John as a man who could never sacrifice what he
perceived as truth for mere expediency, no matter how ad-
vantageous this might have proved. He refused to accept a
single set of ideas as final for all time; for him there was no
orthodoxy or dogma that could not be challenged. He was
ever trying to probe deeper inside himself, convinced that if
he could reveal the essence of himself to his listeners, they
would be moved to do the same, thus developing their creative
faculties to the maximum. He therefore required absolute and
total honesty of himself at all times; and though he sometimes
worried about the unfavorable consequences that such a course
would inevitably bring in its wake, the hesitations were momentary, the decision to push ahead, unalterable. If we are to be
worthy of the music that he has left us, I do not see how we
can do less than try to be as skeptical of what we are indoctrinated with as Truth and as demanding of ourselves as he
was while he lived.

Kofsky: The first thing I want to ask you about is a story
that somebody told me. The first night I came here, the people I was staying with have a friend, a young lady, and she
was downtown at one of Malcolm X's speeches — and lo and
behold, who should pop in on the seat next to her, but John
Coltrane. [Laughter.] Right away, that whetted my curiosity,

and I wanted to know how many times you have seen him, what you thought of him, and so forth.

Coltrane: That was the only time.

Kofsky: Were you impressed by him?

Coltrane: Definitely. That was the only time. I thought I had to see the man, you know. I was living downtown, I was in the hotel, I saw the posters, and I realized that he was going to be over there so I said, well, I'm going over there and see this cat, because I had never seen him. I was quite impressed.

Kofsky: That was one of his last speeches, wasn't it?

Coltrane: Well, it was toward the end of his career.

Kofsky: Some musicians have said that there's a relationship between some of Malcolm's ideas and the music, especially the new music. Do you think there's anything in that?

Coltrane: Well, I think that music, being an expression of the human heart, or of the human being itself, does express just what *is* happening. I feel it expresses the whole thing — the whole of human experience at the particular time that it is being expressed.

Kofsky: What do you think about the phrase, *the new black music*, as a description of some of the newer styles in jazz?

Coltrane: Phrases, I don't know. They don't mean much to me, because usually I don't make the phrases, so I don't react too much. It makes no difference to me one way or the other what it's called.

Kofsky: If you did make the phrases, could you think of one?

Coltrane: I don't think there's a phrase for it, that I could make.

Kofsky: The people who use *that* phrase argue that jazz is particularly closely related to the black community and it's an expression of what's happening there. That's why I asked you about your reaction to Malcolm X.

Coltrane: Well, I think it's up to the individual musician, call it what you may, for any reason you may. Myself, I recognize the artist. I recognize an individual when I see his contribution; and when I know a man's sound, well, to me that's him, that's this man. That's the way I look at it. Labels, I don't bother with.

Kofsky: But it does seem to be a fact that most of the *changes* in the music — the innovations — have come from black musicians.

Coltrane: Yes, well this is how it is.

Kofsky: Have you ever noticed — since you've played all over the United States and in all kinds of circumstances—have you ever noticed that the reaction of an audience varies or changes if it's a black audience or a white audience or a mixed audience? Have you ever noticed that the racial composition of the audience seems to determine how the people respond?

Coltrane: Well, sometimes, yes, and sometimes, no.

Kofsky: Any examples?

Coltrane: Sometimes it might appear to be one; you might say . . . it's hard to say, man. Sometimes people like it or don't like it, no matter what color they are.

Kofsky: You don't have any preferences yourself about what kind of an audience you play for?

Coltrane: Well, to me, it doesn't matter. I only hope that whoever is out there listening, they enjoy it; and if they're not enjoying it, I'd rather not hear.

Kofsky: If people do enjoy the music, how would you like them to demonstrate it? Do you like an audience that's perfectly still and unresponsive, or do you like an audience that reacts more visibly to the music?

Coltrane: Well, I guess I like an audience that does show what they feel; to respond.

Kofsky: I remember when you played at the *Jazz Workshop* in San Francisco, you sometimes got that kind of an audience, which you didn't get when you played at *Shelly's Manne-Hole* in Los Angeles; and it seemed to me that that had some effect on the music.

Coltrane: Yes, because it seems to me that the audience, in listening, is in an act of participation, you know. And when you know that somebody is maybe moved the same way you are, to such a degree or approaching the degree, it's just like having another member in the group.

Kofsky: Is that what happened at the *Ascension* date? The people that were there—did they get that involved?

Coltrane: I don't know. I was so doggone busy; I was worried to death. I couldn't really enjoy the date. If it hadn't been a date, then, I would have really enjoyed it. You know, I was trying to get the time and everything, and I was busy. I hope they felt something. To hear the record, I enjoyed it; I enjoyed all of the individual contributions.

Kofsky: What do you think, then, about playing concerts? Does that seem to inhibit the interaction between yourself, your group, and the audience?

Coltrane: Well, on concerts, the only thing that bugs me might be a hall with poor acoustics, where we can't quite get the unit sound. But as far as the audience goes, it's about the same.

Kofsky: Another reason I asked you about Malcolm was because I've interviewed a number of musicians and the consensus seems to be that the younger musicians talk about the political issues and social issues that Malcolm talked about, when they're with each other. And some of them say that they try to express this in the music. Do you find in your own groups or among musicians you're friendly with that these issues are important and that you do talk about them?

Coltrane: Oh, they're definitely important; and as I said, the issues are part of what *is* at this time. So naturally, as musicians, we express whatever is.

Kofsky: Do you make a *conscious* attempt to express these things?

Coltrane: Well, I tell you for myself, I make a conscious attempt, I think I can truthfully say that in music I make or I have tried to make a conscious attempt to change what I've found, in music. In other words, I've tried to say, "Well, *this* I feel, could be better, in my opinion, so I will try to do this to make it better." This is what I feel that we feel in any situation that we find in our lives, when there's something we think could be better, we must make an effort to try and make it better. So it's the same socially, musically, politically, and in any department of our lives.

Kofsky: Most of the musicians I have talked to are very concerned about changing society and they do see their music as an instrument by which society can be changed.

Coltrane: Well, I think so. I think music is an instrument. It can create the initial thought patterns that can change the thinking of the people.

Kofsky: In particular, some of the people have said that jazz is opposed to poverty, to suffering, and to oppression; and therefore, that jazz is opposed to what the United States is doing in Vietnam. Do you have any comments on that subject?

Coltrane: On the Vietnam situation?

Kofsky: Well, you can divide it into two parts. The first part was whether you think jazz is opposed to poverty and suffering and oppression; and the second part is whether you think, if so, jazz is therefore opposed to the United States' involvement in Vietnam?

Coltrane: In my opinion I would say yes, because jazz — if you want to call it that; we'll talk about that later — to me, it is an expression of music; and this music is an expression of higher ideals, to me. So therefore, brotherhood is there;

and I believe with brotherhood, there would be no poverty. And also, with brotherhood, there would be no war.

Kofsky: That also seems to be what most of the musicians feel. David Izenson for example, said almost the same thing when I talked with him. He said, well, we're saying in our music we want a society without classes, without these frictions, without the wastes, and without the warfare.

Would you care to comment on working conditions for "jazz" musicians? Do you think that jazz artists are treated as they deserve to be treated; and if not, can you see any reason why they wouldn't be?

Coltrane: I don't know. It's according to the individual. Well, you find many times that a man may feel that the situation is all right with him, where another man might say, that situation is no good for you. So it's a matter of a man knowing himself, just what he wants, and that way, it's according to his value. If he doesn't mind a certain sort of treatment, I'm sure he can find it elsewhere. If he does mind it, then he doesn't have to put up with it. In my opinion, at this stage of the game, I don't care too much for playing clubs, particularly. Now there was a time when it felt all right to play clubs, because with my music, I felt I had to play a lot to work it out, you see. But now I don't think that that was absolutely where it was at; but I had to find it out myself. It is a matter of being able to be at home and be able to go into yourself. In other words, I don't feel the situation in clubs is ideal for me.

Kofsky: What is it about clubs that you don't like?

Coltrane: Well, actually, we don't play the set forty-minute kind of thing anymore, and it's difficult to always do this kind of thing now. The music, changing as it is, there are a lot of times when it doesn't make sense, man, to have somebody drop a glass, or somebody ask for some money right in the middle of Jimmy Garrison's solo. Do you know what I mean?

Kofsky: I know *exactly.*

Coltrane: And these kind of things are calling for some other kind of presentation.

Kofsky: In other words, these really are artists who are playing, yet they're really not being treated as artists, but as part of the cash register.

Coltrane: Yes, I think the music is rising, in my estimation, it's rising into something else, and so we'll have to find this kind of place to be played in.

Kofsky: Why do you think conditions have been so bad for

producing art by the musicians? What do you think causes these poor conditions that you've spoken of?

Coltrane: Well, I don't know; I don't really know how it came about. Because I do know there was one time when the musicians played more dances, and they used to play theatres and all; and this took away one element, you know, but still it was hard work. I remember some of those one-nighters, it was pretty difficult.

But it just seems that the music has been directed by businessmen, I would suppose, who know how to arrange the making of a dollar, and so forth. And maybe often the artist hasn't really taken the time himself to figure out just what he wants. Or if he does feel it should be in some other way. I think these are the things which are being thought about more now.

Kofsky: Do you think the fact that almost all of the original jazz musicians were black men and have continued to be throughout the generations, do you think this has encouraged the businessmen to take advantage of them and to treat their art with this contempt—ringing up of the cash register in the middle of a bass solo?

Coltrane: Well, I don't know.

Kofsky: Most of the owners, I've noticed, are white.

Coltrane: Well, it could be, Frank, it could be.

Kofsky: How do you think conditions are going to be improved for the musicians?

Coltrane: There has to be a lot of self-help, I believe. They have to work out their own problems in this area.

Kofsky: You mean, for example, what the Jazz Composers Guild was trying to do?

Coltrane: Yes, I *do* think that was a good idea, I really do; and I don't think it's dead. It was just something that couldn't be born at that time, but I still think it's a good idea.

Kofsky: This is true in the history of all kinds of organizations in this country—they're not always successful the first time. But I think it's inevitable that musicians are going to try and organize to protect themselves.

Coltrane: Yes.

Kofsky: For example, I was at the *Five Spot* Monday night, and I figure that there are about a hundred tables in there; and with two people at a table, it comes to about $7.50 a set, at three drinks a set. That means the owner's making $750, say, a set and he has five sets. And I know the musicians for that night aren't getting anywhere *near* five times $750, or even two times $750. So actually it turns out that these businessmen are not only damaging the art, but they're even keeping people away.

Coltrane: Yes, it's putting them up tight, lots of people, man. I feel so *bad* sometimes about people coming to the club and I can't play long enough for them, because, you know, they're hustling you. They come to hear you play and you get up, you have to play a little bit, then split. Something has to be done about it.

Kofsky: Do the musicians who play in these newer styles look to Africa and Asia for some of their musical inspiration?

Coltrane: I think so; I think they look all over. And inside.

Kofsky: Do they look some places more than others? I heard you, for example, talking about making a trip to Africa, to gather musical sources. Is that the idea?

Coltrane: Well, I intend to make a trip to Africa to gather whatever I can find, particularly the musical sources.

Kofsky: Do you think that the musicians are more interested in Africa and Asia than in Europe, as far as the music goes?

Coltrane: Well, the musicians have been exposed to Europe, you see. So it's the other parts that they haven't been exposed to. Speaking for myself, at least, I'm trying to have a rounded education.

Kofsky: Is that the significance of those rhythmic instruments that you've incorporated into your group — to give it a sort of Middle Eastern or African flavor?

Coltrane: Maybe so, it's just something I feel.

Kofsky: Why do you think that the interest in Africa and Asia is growing at this particular time?

Coltrane: Well, it's just time for this to come about, that's all. It's a thing of the times.

Kofsky: Bill Dixon suggested to me that it might have something to do with the fact that many African nations became independent in the 1950s and changed the way Negroes in this country looked at themselves; it made them more aware of the African heritage and made them more interested in going back and looking for it. Do you think there's anything to that line of thought?

Coltrane: Yes, yes, that's part of it.

Kofsky: Another question along the same lines is: it seems that group improvisation is growing in importance — for example, what you do with Pharoah [Sanders] when you're playing simultaneously. And also, of course, *Ascension.* Do you

think that this is a new trend now, or not a new trend, but do
you think this is growing in importance now?

Coltrane: Well, maybe. It seems to be happening at this time;
I don't know how long it's going to last.

Kofsky: Why do you think that's taking place now?

Coltrane: I don't know *why*; it just *is*, that's all.

Kofsky: But it is there — I'm not making something up when
I say that?

Coltrane: No, no, I feel it, it's there, but I don't know why.

Kofsky: And another question about the new music: I've
noticed that a lot of the new groups are pianoless; or even
in your case, where you have a piano, sometimes you'll have
the piano lay out during a solo, or during parts of a solo.
Why is this coming about at this particular time? Why the
desire to deemphasize the piano or to give it another kind of
role in the group?

Coltrane: I still use the piano, and I haven't reached the
point where I feel I don't need it. I might, but . . . maybe
it's because . . . well, when you're not playing on a given
progression, you don't really need it to state these things.
And it would get in your way to have somebody going in
another direction and you trying to go in another, there it
would be better for you not to have it.

Kofsky: It seems that the direction the horns are going in,
too, is to get away from the twelve-tone scale — to play notes that
really aren't on the piano: the high-pitched notes, the shrieks
and screams. I don't know what words you use to describe
those sounds, but I think you know what I mean. Sounds
that were considered "wrong" — well, still are considered wrong
by some people.

Now, if you play those notes that really aren't on the piano,
and you have the piano there stating notes, do you feel that
this gives some kind of a clash that you'd rather avoid?

Coltrane: I suppose that's the way some men feel about it.
As I say, I still use the piano. I haven't reached the point
yet, where the piano is a drag to me. The only thing is, I
don't, we don't *follow* what the piano does any more, because
we all move in our own directions. I like it for a backdrop,
you know, for its sound.

Kofsky: You do have the piano, though, lay out for a fairly
large part of the time.

Coltrane: Well, I always instruct the piano players that whenever they wish they can just lay out and let it go on as it

is. Because after a while, lots of times, the pianists, well, they get tired. If you can't think of anything else to play — stroll!

Kofsky: When I talked to you a couple of years ago in Los Angeles and I asked you if you would ever consider adding another horn to the group, you said probably the thing you would do is, if you added anything you would add drums. [Laughter.] Did you have in mind then these kind of things that . . .?

Coltrane: I don't even know, man, but I guess so. I still feel so strongly about drums, I really do. I feel very strongly about these drums. I experimented in it, but we didn't have too much success. I believe it would have worked, but, Elvin and McCoy [unintelligible].

Kofsky: It doesn't necessarily have to be two drums. It could be drums and another rhythm instrument. That's what I was really referring to.

Coltrane: I think so too. It could come in different forms, shapes; I just don't know how to do it, though.

Kofsky: After all, the things that you're using in the group now — shakers, bells, maracas — are rhythm instruments too. Not all rhythm instruments are drums.

Coltrane: Oh, that's true.

Kofsky: That's what I meant, when I asked you if that's what you had in mind.

Coltrane: Yes.

Kofsky: Speaking of Elvin and McCoy reminds me of something Sun Ra said, and I'll repeat it. I'll make it clear that I don't put any faith in it, but since he said it, and he told me to tell you, I'll pass it along.

He says that you hired Rasheid Ali as a means of driving Elvin and McCoy out of the band, because you didn't want them in the band in the first place, and that was your way of doing it. Do you want to answer that?

Coltrane: No, I don't. I was trying to do something. . . . There was a thing I wanted to do in music, see, and I figured I could do *two* things: I could have a band that played like the way we used to play, and a band that was going in the direction that the one I have now is going in — I could combine these two, with these two concepts going. And it could have been done.

Kofsky: Yes. Sun Ra is quite bitter, and claims that you've stolen all of your ideas from him, and in fact that everybody has stolen all of their ideas from him. [Laughter.]

Coltrane: There may be something to that. I've heard him

and I know that he's doing some of the things that I've wanted to do.

Kofsky: How do you feel about having another horn in the group, another saxophone? Do you feel that it in any way competes with you or that it enhances what you're doing?

Coltrane: Well, it helps me. It helps me stay alive sometimes, because physically, man, the pace I've been leading has been so hard and I've gained so much weight, that sometimes it's been a little hard physically. I feel that I like to have somebody there in case I can't get that strength. I like to have that strength in that band, somewhere. And Pharoah is very strong in spirit and will, see, and these are the things that I like to have up there.

Kofsky: Do you feel that spurs you on, the presence especially of a man as powerful as Pharoah?

Coltrane: Yes, all the time, there's always got to be somebody with a lot of power. In the old band, Elvin had this power. I always have to have somebody there, with it, you know?

Rasheid has it, but it hasn't quite unfolded completely; all he needs to do is play.

Kofsky: That was my impression, too, that he really was feeling his way ahead in the music and didn't have the confidence Elvin had. But then, of course, look how long Elvin was with you before —

Coltrane: He was there, Elvin was there for a couple of years — although Elvin was ready from the first time I heard him, you know, I could hear the genius there — but he had to start playing steadily, steadily, every night . . . With Miles [Davis] it took me around two and a half years, I think, before it started developing, taking the shape that it was going to take.

Kofsky: That's what's so tragic about the situation of the younger musicians now: they don't have that opportunity to play together.

Coltrane: Yes, it certainly needs to be done. It should be happening all the time and the men would develop sooner.

Kofsky: Don Cherry has a record out, *Complete Communion.* I think it's a beautiful record, and one of the reasons I think it's so good is because here he has a group that's worked together for a few months.

Coltrane: Yeah!

Kofsky: And so he knows how to put something together for all the men — it isn't just a "date."

Have you listened to many of the other younger saxophonists besides Pharoah?

Coltrane: Yes, Albert Ayler first. I've listened very closely to him. He's something else.

Kofsky: Could you see any relationship between what you were doing and what he was doing? In other words, do you think he has developed out of some of your ideas?

Coltrane: Not necessarily; I think what he's doing, it seems to be moving music into even higher frequencies. Maybe where I left off, maybe where he started, or something.

Kofsky: Well, in a sense, that's what I meant.

Coltrane: Yes. Not to say that he would copy bits and that, but just that he filled an area that it seems I hadn't gotten to.

Kofsky: It seems to me, that your solo on *Chasin' the Trane*, that Albert developed some of the ideas that you had put out there and he had expressed some of them in his own ways, and that this was one of the points from which he had begun. Had you ever thought of it in that light?

Coltrane: No. I hadn't.

Kofsky: Did you ever listen to that selection much?

Coltrane: Only at the time it came out, I used to listen to it and wonder what happened to me.

Kofsky: What do you mean?

Coltrane: Well, it's a sort of surprising thing to hear this back, because — I don't know, it came back another way.

It was a little longer than I thought it was and it had a fairly good amount of intensity in it, which I hadn't quite gotten into a recording before.

Kofsky: You were pleased with it?

Coltrane: To a degree, not that I could sit there with it and love it forever.

Kofsky: Well, no, you'd never be pleased with anything that you did for longer than a week!

Coltrane: I realized that I'd have to do that or better, you see, and then I —

Kofsky: I think it's a remarkable record and I also think you ought to go back and listen to it.

Coltrane: Maybe so.

Kofsky: Because I don't see any saxophonist now who isn't playing something that you haven't at least sketched out before. But maybe you would rather not think about that.

Coltrane: No, because like it's a big reservoir, that we all dip out of. And a lot of times, you'll find that a lot of those things . . . I listened to John Gilmore kind of closely before I made *Chasin' the Trane*, too. So some of those things on there are really direct influences of listening to this cat, you see. But then I don't know who he'd been listening to, so . . .

Kofsky: After *Chasin' The Trane* and then *Impressions* came out, you did a sort of change of pace. You remember; you did the album with Duke Ellington and *Ballads*, and the Johnny Hartman album. Whose idea were these albums? Were they yours, or Bob Thiele's?

Coltrane: Well, I tell you, I had some trouble at that time. I did a foolish thing. I got dissatisfied with my mouthpiece and I had some work done on this thing, and instead of making it better, it ruined it. It really discouraged me a little bit, because there were certain aspects of playing — that certain fast thing that I was reaching for — that I couldn't get because I had damaged this thing, so I just had to curtail it. Actually, I never found another [mouthpiece], but after so much of this laying around and making these kind of things, I said, well what the hell, I might as well go ahead and do the best I can. But at that moment, it was so vivid in my mind — the difference in what I was getting on the horn — it was so vivid that I couldn't do it. Because as soon as I did, I'd hear it; and it just discouraged me. But after a year or so passed, well, I'd forgotten.

Kofsky: That's funny, because I think I know your music as thoroughly as any nonmusician, yet that wouldn't have been apparent to me.

Coltrane: That's a funny thing. That's one of the mysteries. And to me, as soon as I put that horn in my mouth, I could hear it. It feels, you know. . . I just stopped and went into other things.

Kofsky: The reason I asked that was because I recall that was the time you had Eric [Dolphy] in and out of the band.

Coltrane: Yes.

Kofsky: And there was a whole wave of really hostile criticism.

Coltrane: Yes, and all of this was at the same time, so you see how it was. I needed all the strength I could have at that time; and maybe some of these things might have caused me to feel, "Well, man, I can't get what I want out of this mouthpiece, so I'll work on it."

Kofsky: You think this might have undermined your self-confidence?

Coltrane: It could have, it certainly could have.

Kofsky: Why do you think there's been all this hostility to the new music, especially in your case?

Coltrane: Oh, man, I never could figure it out! I couldn't even venture to answer it now. Because as I told them then, I just felt that they didn't understand.

Kofsky: Do you think they were making as conscientious and thorough an attempt to understand as they could have?

Coltrane: At the time I didn't feel they were, because I did offer them, in an article in *Down Beat*, that if any of you men were interested in trying to understand, let's get together and let's talk about it, you know? I thought if they were really genuinely interested or felt there was something here, that instead of just condemning what you don't know about, if you want to discuss it, let's talk about it. But no one ever came forth, so I don't think they wanted to know what I had to say about it. [Laughter.]

Kofsky: I think it frightened them. Bill Dixon and I talked about this at great length; and he said: "Well, these guys, it's taken them years to pick out *I Got Rhythm* on the piano." and now the new music comes along and undermines their entire career, which is built around understanding things based on those patterns.

Coltrane: Yes, I dug it like that too. I said, "Well, this could be a real drag to a cat if he figures this is something that he won't be able to cope with and he won't be able to write about." If he can't write about it he can't make a living at this; and then I realized that, so I quieted down. I wouldn't allow myself to become too hostile in return. Although there was a time I kind of froze up on those people at *Down Beat*. I felt that there was something there that wasn't — I felt that that they were letting their weakness direct their actions, which I didn't feel they should have. The test, was for me. They could do what they wanted to do. The thing was for me to remain firm in what I was doing. That was a funny period in my life, because I went through quite a few changes, you know, like home life — everything, man, I just went through so many . . . everything I was doing.

Kofsky: The perfect wrong time to hit you!

Coltrane: Everything I was doing was like that, it was a hell of a test for me, and it was coming out of it, it was just like I always said, man: when you go through these crises and you come out of them, you're definitely stronger, in a great sense.

Kofsky: Did the reaction of Impulse to these adverse criticisms have anything to do with those records that we talked about?

Coltrane: The ballads and that?

Kofsky: Yes.

Coltrane: Well, I don't know. I think Impulse was interested in having what they might call a balanced sort of thing, a diversified sort of catalog, and I find nothing wrong with this myself. You see, I like — in fact most of the songs that I even write now, the ones that I even consider songs, are ballads. So there's something there, that I mean I really love these things.

And these ballads that came out were definitely ones which I felt at this time. I chose them; it seemed to be something that was laying around in my mind — from my youth, or somewhere — and I just had to do them. They came at this time, when the confidence in what I was doing on the horn had flagged, it seemed to be the time to clean that out. And Johnny Hartman — a man that I had stuck up in my mind somewhere — I just felt something about him, I don't know what it was. I liked his sound, I thought there was something there I had to hear, so I looked him up and did that album. Really, I don't regret doing those things at all.

The only thing I regret was not having kept that same attitude, which was: I'm going to do, no matter what. That was the attitude in the beginning, but as I say, there were a whole lot of reasons why these things happened.

Kofsky: Do you think that learning how to play the soprano changed your style?

Coltrane: Definitely, definitely. It certainly did.

Kofsky: How so? Could you spell it out?

Coltrane: Well, the soprano, by being this small instrument, I found that playing the lowest note on it was like playing one of the middle notes on the tenor — so therefore, after I got so that my embouchure would allow me to make the upper notes, I found that I would play *all over* this instrument. On tenor, I hadn't always played all over it, because I was playing certain ideas which just went in certain ranges, octaves. But by playing on the soprano and becoming accustomed to playing on tenor from that low B-flat on up, it soon got so that when I went to tenor, I found myself doing the same thing. It caused the change or the willingness to change and just try to play as much of the instrument as possible.

Kofsky: Did it give you a new rhythmic conception too?

Coltrane: I think so, I think so. A new shape came out of this thing and patterns — the way the patterns — would fall.

Kofsky: It seemed to me that after you started playing soprano, and particularly after *My Favorite Things*, then you started feeling that same kind of a pulse on the tenor that hadn't been there in your work before.

Coltrane: I think that's quite possible. In fact, the patterns started — the patterns were one of the things I started getting dissatisfied with on the tenor mouthpiece, because the sound of the soprano was actually so much closer to me in my ear. There's something about the presence of that sound, that to me — I didn't want to admit it — but to me it would seem like it was better than the tenor — I liked it more. I didn't want to admit this damn thing, because I said the tenor's my horn, it is my favorite. But this soprano, maybe it's just the fact that it's a higher instrument, it started pulling my conception.

Kofsky: How do you feel about the two horns now?

Coltrane: Well, the tenor is the power horn, definitely; but soprano, there's still something there in just the voice of it that's really beautiful, something that I really like.

Kofsky: Do you regard the soprano as an extension of the tenor?

Coltrane: Well, at first I did, but now, it's another voice, it's another sound.

Kofsky: Did you ever use the two horns on the same piece, as you did on *Spiritual*?[1]

Coltrane: I think that's the only time I've done that. Sometimes in clubs, if I feel good, I might do something like this — start on one and end on another — but I think that's the only one on record.

Kofsky: What prompted Pharoah to take up the alto? Was that to get away from — two tenors?

Coltrane: I don't know. This is something he wanted to do, and about the same time I decided I wanted to get one, so we both got one.

Kofsky: I haven't heard you play the alto. Do you play it much?

Coltrane: I played it in Japan. I played it in Frisco a little bit, but I've had a little trouble with the intonation of it. It's a Japanese make, it's a new thing they're trying out, so they gave us these horns to try, and mine has to be adjusted at certain points where it's not quite in tune, so I don't play it, but I like it.

Kofsky: I saw a picture of you with a *flute!* Are you playing that too now?

Coltrane: I'm learning.

Kofsky: You're always learning, aren't you?

Coltrane: I hope so. Always trying to learn.

Kofsky: I looked at the *Down Beat* and *Jazz* Critics Polls two years in a row, and both years, this and last year, I noticed that European critics are much more in favor of the new music than the Americans. Almost 50 percent or 60 percent of them would vote for new musicians, whereas, say only about a quarter of the Americans. Is this what you found in Europe? — or in general, have you found outside the United States that your music is more favorably received by the critics, the power structure, shall we say, than in the U. S.?

Coltrane: I'd say in the new music — and when I say new music, I mean most of the younger musicians that are starting out — I know that they definitely have found a quicker acceptance in Europe than they have here. When I started, it was a little different, because I started through Miles Davis, who was an accepted musician, and they got used to me here in the States. Now when they first heard me with Miles here, they did not like it.

Kofsky: I remember.

Coltrane: So it's just one of those things: everything that they haven't heard yet and that's a little different, they are going to reject it at first. But the time will roll around, the time when they will like it. Now, by being here with Miles and running around the country with him, they heard more of me here, and consequently they began to accept it before they did in Europe, because they hadn't heard me in Europe. When we went to Europe the first time, it was a shock to them there. They booed me and everything in Paris, because they just weren't with it. But now I find, the last time I was in Europe, it seems that the new music — they've really opened up. They can hear it there better than they do here.

Kofsky: I think that part of this is because what's happening in the new music is analogous to what's happened in painting, say, and sculpture and literature; and the people who appreciate jazz in Europe, are much more aware of this. What do you think of this?

Coltrane: Well, I don't know.

Kofsky: In Europe, jazz is regarded as a serious art, whereas here, it's regarded as, well . . .

Coltrane: Whatever it is.

Kofsky: As part of the nightclub business. Otherwise, you couldn't have a magazine like *Down Beat.*

I know Albert [Ayler] is going back to Europe, and I know that there are many of the younger musicians who want to get away from the States because they just don't feel there's any hope for them here.

Do you remember Third Stream Music, what was called Third Stream Music?

Coltrane: Yes.

Kofsky: Did you ever feel much of an inner urge to play that kind of music?

Coltrane: No.

Kofsky: Why do you think it didn't catch on with the musicians? Was there anything about it that suggests why it was never popular with them?

Coltrane: I think it was an attempt to create something, I think, more with labels, you see than true evolution.

Kofsky: You mean, it didn't evolve naturally out of the desires of the musicians?

Coltrane: Maybe it did; I can't say that. It was an attempt to do something, and evolution is about trying too. But there's something in evolution — it just happens when it's ready, but this thing wasn't really where it was coming from. What was it — an attempt to blend, to wed two musics? That's what it really was.

Kofsky: You said, talking about saxophone players, that there was a common pool that everybody dipped into. Maybe here, there wasn't enough of that pool for the musicians to dip in to.

Coltrane: Well, I just think it wasn't time. It was an attempt to do something at a time when it wasn't time for this to happen, and therefore it wasn't lasting. But there may have been some things that came out of this that have been beneficial in promoting the final change, which is coming. So nothing is really wasted, although it might appear to fail or not succeed the way that men would have desired it to.

Kofsky: Even the mistakes can be instructive if you try to use them.

Do you make any attempt, or do you feel that you should make any attempt, to educate your audience in ways that aren't strictly musical. That is, it's obvious that you want your audience to understand what you're doing *musically.* But do you feel that you want them to understand other things, too, and that you have some kind of responsibility for it?

Coltrane: Sure, I feel this, and this is one of the things I am concerned about now. I just don't know how to go about this. I want to find out just how I should do it. I think it's going to have to be very subtle; you can't ram philosophies down anybody's throat, and the music is enough! That's philosophy. I think the best thing I can do at this time is to try to get myself in shape and know myself. If I can do that, then I'll just play, you see, and leave it at that. I believe that will do it, if I really can get to myself and be just as I feel I should be and play it. And I think they'll get it, because music goes a long way — it can influence.

Kofsky: That's how I got interested in those things I was talking about earlier, Malcolm X. I might not have come to it, or come to it as fast, if it hadn't been for the music. That was my first introduction to something beyond my own horizons, that would make me think about the world I was living in.

Coltrane: Yes. That's what I'm sure of, man, I'm really sure of this thing. As I say, there are things which as far as spirituality is concerned, which is very important to me at this time, I've got to grow through certain phases of this to other understanding and more consciousness and awareness of just what it is that I'm supposed to understand about it; and I'm sure others will be part of the music. To me, you know, I feel I want to be a force for good.

Kofsky: And the music too?

Coltrane: Everywhere. You know, I want to be a force for real good. In other words, I know that there are bad forces, forces put here that bring suffering to others and misery to the world, but I want to be the force which is truly for good.

Kofsky: I don't have any more of my prepared questions to ask you — or my improvised questions to ask you. [Laughter.] I had a lot of questions here that were related just to you. Many of those questions about music I don't ask of the other musicians; but I've always had a very special interest in your work, so I took this opportunity, since I don't know when I'll ever get the chance to get you down on tape again.

Do you have anything else that you'd like to get on here?

Coltrane: I think we just about covered it, I believe, just about covered it.

[As John drove me back to the station, the tape recorder was left on and we continued to talk. After some humorous exchanges, the conversation turned to the proper function of a jazz writer or critic.]

Kofsky: If you can't play the music, and if you're going to write about it, you have, I think, an obligation to do it as conscientiously as possible.

Coltrane: Yes, I believe it, man.

Kofsky: And always when it's a question of your opinion versus the musician's opinion, to give the benefit of the doubt to the musician, because he knows the music far better than you'll ever know it. In other words, you have to be humble. A lot of writers aren't humble; they get arrogant because they think they have some kind of power.

Coltrane: Well, that's one of the main causes of this arrogance — the idea of power. Then you lose your true power, which is to be part of all, and the only way you can be part of all is to understand it. And when there's something you don't understand, you have to go humbly to it. You don't go to school and sit down and say, "I know what you're getting ready to teach me." You sit there and you learn. You open your mind. You absorb. But you have to be quiet, you have to be still to do all of this.

Kofsky: That's what so annoyed me about all of that stuff they were saying about you in '61.

Coltrane: Oh, that was terrible. I couldn't believe it, you know, it just seemed so preposterous. It was so ridiculous, man, that's what bugs me. It was absolutely ridiculous, because they made it appear that we didn't even know the first thing about music — the first thing. And there we were really trying to push things off.

Kofsky: Because they never stand still.

Coltrane: Eric [Dolphy], man, as sweet as this cat was and the musician that he was — it hurt me to see him get hurt in this thing.

Kofsky: Do you think that this possibly contributed to the fact that he died so young?

Coltrane: I don't know, but Eric was a strong cat. Nobody knows what caused it. The way he passed, there was a mystery about it.

Kofsky: I didn't mean that it was directly the cause, but —

Coltrane: Indirectly?

Kofsky: Yes.

Coltrane: Yes. The whole scene, man. He couldn't work . . .

Kofsky: That's what I meant, really.

Coltrane: He always seemed to be a very cheerful young man, so I don't *think* that would put him . . . I don't think so, because he had an outlook on life which was very, very good — optimistic, and he had this sort of thing, friendliness, you know, a real friend to everyone. He was the type of man who could be as much a friend to a guy he'd just met today as he was to one he'd known for ten years. This kind of person, I don't think it would really hurt him to the point where he would do something to hurt himself consciously or unconsciously.

Kofsky: Yes. That friendliness was one of the things that has impressed me about the musicians here. I really didn't expect to be greeted with open arms, because I am an outsider, after all. And yet I have been amazed constantly at how eager the musicians were to cooperate when they decided that I was sincere and that this wasn't a joke or a con or something of that nature.

Coltrane: I think all we need is sincerity, empathy. . . .

I think I want to get closer to town. Maybe there's something I can do in music. Get a place, a little room to play in. I don't want a loft, but maybe there's something I can get to play in, just some place to be able to work in.

Kofsky: Where do you play at home?

Coltrane: Anywhere. There's a room over the garage that I'm getting fixed now and I think it's going to be my practice room. You never know. Sometimes you build a little room and it ends up you're still going in the toilet. I hope I like it, but . . . I keep a horn on the piano and I have a horn in my bedroom — a flute usually back there, because when I go there I'm tired and I lay down and practice.

Kofsky: About how many hours a day do you play?

Coltrane: Not too much at this time. I find that it's only when something is trying to come through that I really practice. And then I don't even know how many hours — it's all day, on and off. But at this time there's nothing coming out now.

Kofsky: I was very surprised to hear you practicing at all, because I just couldn't conceive of what you could find to practice! But I know it isn't like that.

Coltrane: I *need* to practice. It's just that I want something to practice, and I'm trying to find out what it is that I want, an area that I want to get into.

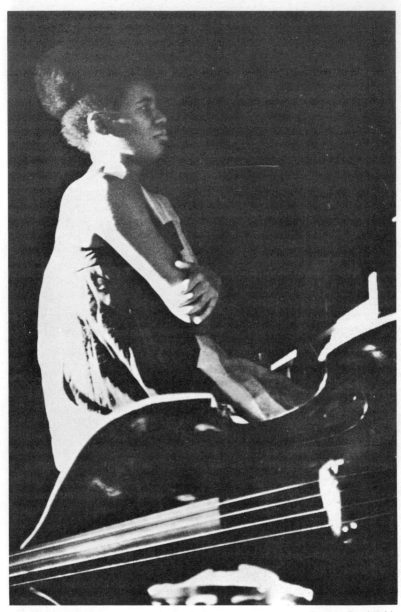

Photo by Frank Kofsky

ALICE COLTRANE

Photo by Frank Kofsky

PHAROAH SANDERS

Photo by Frank Kofsky

ROSWELL RUDD (L), ARCHIE SHEPP (R)

Photo by Frank Kofsky

BENNY MAUPIN (L), MARION BROWN (R)

PART IV

MALCOLM X

MALCOLM X

Chapter 13
BLACK REVOLUTION AND BLACK MUSIC:
THE CAREER OF MALCOLM X

It is now more than a year since Malcolm X was gunned down in cold blood in Harlem — a crime whose origins have yet to be uncovered and perhaps never will be.

Already in death if not in life, Malcolm's figure has become larger than life itself. Even among those whites friendly to Malcolm, his biography is being subtly rewritten and rearranged to symbolize the archetypical odyssey of a latter-day black nationalist Ulysses. From these stylized treatments of Malcolm's history we thus learn of the death of his father, an unyielding disciple of Marcus Garvey, at the hands of a group of white racist assassins; later, institutionalized white bigotry destroys the young Malcolm's family and, in the person of a cruel and boorish grammar school teacher, frustrates the boy's hopes for a legal career. The Little family (Malcolm's original surname) is in this fashion shattered on the altar of white supremacy — the mother goes into a mental institution, the children are disposed of in various ways — and the nationalist pedigree is transmitted intact from father to son. The latter, it is implied, then vows vengeance on white society for its crimes against black humanity.

This is the stereotype. Undoubtedly, a considerable amount of it *is* true. Yet there is still an irritating distortion in the picture: we recognize the subject, but the likeness is not entirely convincing.

That matter of hatred of whites, for example. The New Mythology (which one can find in any number of *favorable* appraisals of the *Autobiography*) depicts the antipathy of Malcolm toward whites as having been forged out of the crucible of his boyhood experiences. The truth of the matter, however, is nowhere near that simple. Though many of Malcolm's earliest

THIS ORIGINALLY APPEARED IN *MONTHLY REVIEW*, SEPTEMBER 1966, AS A REVIEW OF *THE AUTOBIOGRAPHY OF MALCOLM X* (GROVE PRESS, 1964) AND *MALCOLM X SPEAKS* (MERIT PUBLISHERS, 1965).

contacts with whites were unpleasant, this was, by his own account, far from being universally the case. The white family who ran the reform school where he was sent as a boy he described as "good people" who "probably meant well" (though their attitude toward him was one of "kindly condescension"). [1] Significantly, his first mistress was not black but white — ample evidence of the young Malcolm's underlying ambivalence regarding the other race. "Now at that time," Malcolm later recalled, "in any black ghetto in America, to have a white woman who wasn't a known, common whore was — for the average black man, at least — a status symbol of the first order."[2] To the sixteen-year-old Malcolm, the lure of that "status symbol" was overwhelming.

That whatever youthful resentments and hostilities Malcolm harbored remained particular and were not translated into a universal animus needs to be emphasized for a variety of reasons. For one thing, it sheds considerable light on Malcolm's intellectual development. Of even greater significance, it illustrates that antiwhite sensibilities among black nationalists operate to supply a unifying *ideology* which transcends the experience of any single individual. Hence to read Malcolm's evolution, as some reviewers have, as the inevitable consequence of his boyhood rebuffs is profoundly in error — otherwise, there would be 22 million proclaimed black nationalists in this country. In point of fact, however, black nationalism is much more than a response to white outrages (although it is of course that, too). In the hands of such a gifted exponent as Malcolm, black nationalism is a sophisticated and pervasive political ideology based on a generalized understanding of the history of the black man in the United States. As such, therefore, the "hatred" of whites which is one of its central tenets is of primarily symbolic importance and has very little to do with attitudes toward any particular white individual. Marxists especially should have little difficulty in comprehending this notion; from their own practice it should be familiar to them as the very closely analogous sentiment of class solidarity.

Malcolm himself left no room for debate on this question. "When we Muslims had talked about 'the devil white man,'" he explains at one point, "he had been relatively abstract, someone we Muslims rarely came into contact with . . ."[3] A standard passage in many of his speeches dealt with the issue in the same vein:

> Unless we call one white man, by name, a "devil,"
> we are not speaking of any *individual* white man. We
> are speaking of the *collective* white man's *historical*
> record. We are speaking of the collective white man's
> cruelties, and evils, and greeds, that have seen him
> *act* like a devil toward the non-white man. Any intel-
> ligent, honest, objective person cannot fail to realize
> that this white man's slave trade, and his subsequent
> devilish actions, are directly *responsible* for not only
> the *presence* of this black man in America, but also
> for the *condition* in which we find this black man
> here. . . .[4]

Indeed, it is a reasonable presumption that had Malcolm's
characterization of the white man as a devil been personal
rather than ideological, his repudiation of racist dogmas would
never have taken place following the open rupture with Elijah
Muhammad. But even before that schism he had given evidence
of the ideological nature of his "hatred" for whites. Alex Haley,
who transcribed and organized the *Autobiography*, observed
that "I saw Malcolm X too many times exhilarated in after-
lecture give-and-take with predominantly white student bodies
at colleges and universities to ever believe that he nurtured at
his core any blanket white-hatred. 'The young whites, and
blacks, too, are the only hope that America has,' he said to
me once."[5] This point has to be hammered on repeatedly.
There have been all too many whites of good will — including,
regrettably, not a few ostensible radicals — inclined to condemn
black nationalist teachings on the white man as some sort of
"reverse" fascism or racism.* Such a simplistic interpretation
is no more tenable than the romanticized New Mythology,
which postulates a direct and inexorable progression from

---

* In line with the foregoing, this reviewer recalls being one of about
fifty whites out of a total audience of about 1,200 in attendance
at a speech by Malcolm in Los Angeles in 1963, shortly after the
March on Washington. Although I cannot pretend that my com-
panions and I were received with open arms — and, indeed, why should
we have been? — there was never the slightest danger to our precious
white skins. Let all those inclined tò easy equations of black nationalism with genuine "hate groups" such as the Ku Klux Klan and
the American Nazi Party speculate on the probable results had we
been a similar number of blacks who dared to attend a gathering
of one of these organizations.

oppressed black youth to militant nationalist spokesman. Would that the growth of revolutionary black nationalism were that automatic!

As long as misconceptions are being corrected, moreover, something should be said concerning Malcolm's decision to become a follower of Elijah Muhammad. With a certain unimaginative uniformity, the reviewers, confronted with this problem, have tended to throw up their hands and rush to consult William James's *Varieties of Religious Experience*. It is not to be denied that the insights of James can be suggestive on Malcolm's "conversion" to the Nation of Islam (Black Muslims). But to concede this leaves much unsaid. The dicta of James which the reviewers have adduced are all decidedly ahistorical; they fail to elucidaté why this particular black man, Malcolm, in this particular time and place, chose the faith he did (not to mention the reasons why he later quarreled with his spiritual mentor). For if, as has been maintained, Malcolm was psychologically prepared for his conversion by the events of his first year in prison, it is a striking fact that he was altogether beyond the reach of the orthodox Christian faiths — so much so that his fervent cursing of God and the Bible, his "favorite targets," won him the sobriquet of "Satan" from his clearly awed fellow inmates. Obviously, something more was at work within Malcolm than a previously frustrated religious impulse.

At bottom, the cause for Malcolm's conversion was not esoteric: his insatiable curiosity and desire to improve himself simply could not be repressed. While still on "the street," he had rapidly distinguished himself by his ability as a hustler; imprisoned, he turned — even prior to his exposure to the doctrines of Elijah Muhammad — to correspondence courses in English and Latin (the latter because of a desire to learn about word derivations). James, in discussing the conversion phenomenon, cites the maxim, "Man's extremity is God's opportunity." But Malcolm had already reached and overcome his extremity without any assistance from Allah; by the time of his first encounter with Elijah Muhammad, he was moving ahead on the road to recovery.

What Elijah *did* do for Malcolm was to provide him with three things that hastened the recovery process and guaranteed its success. The first of these was the promise of early release (the brother who was closest to him had written: "Malcolm, don't eat any more pork, and don't smoke any more cigarettes. I'll show you how to get out of prison.")[6] It was this which secured Malcolm's allegiance in the crucial first phase of conversion. The second of Elijah's gifts to Malcolm was renewed self-esteem. By adhering to Muhammad's injunctions, particularly the prohibition on pork, Malcolm at once drew attention to himself as a convict, and a Negro, who was somehow different from the rest. The psychological dividends from this were as therapeutic as they were gratifying. "It made me feel good to see that my not eating [pork] had especially startled the white convicts."[7]

But probably the most important thing which Elijah Muhammad accomplished was to inspire Malcolm to impose a systematic discipline on himself, both with respect to his intellectual life and his overt behavior. The gravity of this decision can hardly be overestimated; it restructured and reordered Malcolm's entire existence. The nationalistic doctrines of Muhammad not only furnished Malcolm with a coherent world view that put his entire previous life in perspective; it also enabled the prisoner to pursue his studies with a fixed end constantly in mind: to discover the truth about the black man and his enslavement by the whites. "Once I heard [from Muhammad] of the 'glorious history of the black man,'" Malcolm told Alex Haley, "I took special pains to hunt in the [prison] library for books that would inform me on details about black history."[8] Related to this program of study was Malcolm's desire to become more literate, so as to hold up his end of the correspondence with Muhammad. At the time of his conversion, Malcolm "couldn't even write in a straight line."[9] Without a formal guide, Malcolm was at first at a loss how to proceed. Finally, he began by transcribing a dictionary: "In my slow, painstaking, ragged handwriting, I copied into my tablet everything printed on that first page, down to the punctuation marks."[10]

Like many other prison inmates who became celebrated after their release, Malcolm used his confinement to broaden his political education. (One thinks especially of another notable agitator, Eugene Debs. Where Debs had gone to prison a trade unionist and emerged a socialist, Malcolm went in a hustler and came out a nationalist.) From the time his reading comprehension began to improve "until I left that prison, in every free moment I had, if I was not reading in the library, I was reading on my bunk. You couldn't have gotten me out of books with a wedge."[11] In this way Malcolm familiarized himself with the storehouse of the world's knowledge, from Socrates to W. E. B. Du Bois, from Gregor Mendel to Mahatma Gandhi, from Herodotus to the anthropologist Louis

S. B. Leakey, from Spinoza and Kant to Schopenhauer and Nietzsche. Curiously enough, by imprisoning him, white society performed one of its few services for Malcolm; his own conclusion was that "up to then, I never had been so truly free in my life." [12] Malcolm walked out of the prison gates not only a free man, but an educated and (by virtue of frequent prison debates) a frighteningly articulate one.

The remaining events in Malcolm's biography—his rapid rise within the Muslim hierarchy, the simultaneous catapulting to international fame as a result of his frequent television appearances, the silencing by Muhammad following Malcolm's "chickens coming home to roost" comment on the Kennedy assassination, the subsequent break with Muhammad, and the formation of a rival black nationalist organization—are too well known to call for reiteration here. Interpretation of these facts, on the other hand, is still a matter for some dispute. Can we, for example, really accept the verdict of Truman Nelson, who, writing in *The Nation*, contended that Muslim recruiting efforts "came to a halt" when Malcolm first started appearing in television debates, and that Muhammad's subsequent censure of his chief lieutenant took place solely because Malcolm had been neglecting his organizational responsibilities to concentrate on "explaining [the Muslims] to people who didn't give a damn about them, but only wanted to assess how deeply they should be feared"? I think not.

Although a judgment like the foregoing sounds plausible (and perhaps to some even militant), there are a number of considerations, inconvenient for the writer but essential for our assessment, which it omits.

To begin with, while it is quite likely that Muhammad was envious of the reputation which Malcolm had achieved from his frequent public appearances—*and* from his organizing prowess within the black ghettos—this resentment should not be construed as valid evidence that Malcolm gave short shrift to his Muslim duties. For although some of Malcolm's speaking engagements were in front of predominantly white audiences, the bulk of his radio and television commitments—as the Black Establishment wistfully acknowledged in retrospect [13] —aided the Muslims in disseminating their doctrines in a way that their own limited activities could never have done. Nor did Malcolm slacken his organizing efforts in order to maintain his speaking schedule. On the contrary, as he himself related (in testimony yet to be contravened):

> I couldn't have asked Allah to bless my efforts any more
> than he had. Islam in New York City [Malcolm's juris-
> diction] was growing faster than anywhere in America.
> From the one tiny mosque to which Mr. Muhammad
> had originally sent me, I had now built three of the
> nation's most powerful and aggressive mosques. . . .
> And on a national basis, I had either directly estab-
> lished, or I had helped to establish, most of the one
> hundred or more mosques in the fifty states. I was
> crisscrossing North America sometimes as often as four
> times a week. Often, what sleep I got was caught in
> the jet planes. [14]

Everything points to a conclusion just the opposite of what
Mr. Nelson has alleged: when Muhammad lost Malcolm, he
lost the most capable executive, as well as the most commanding public spokesman, the Muslims possessed — a man who
personally had overseen the meteoric rise of the Nation of
Islam from an obscure sect to a domestic organization perhaps more to be dreaded than any other, in the eyes of the
United States ruling class.

Secondly, the notion that the parting of the ways between
prophet and disciple occurred because of the disciple's mal-
feasance takes no note of Malcolm's own version of the events;
in particular, it writes off as unimportant or irrelevant Malcolm's mounting dissatisfaction with Muhammad's policy of
having the Muslims abstain from all concrete activities aimed
at strengthening the Afro-American liberation movement. Yet
far more than Muhammad's supposed unhappiness with Malcolm's ministerial performance, the real issues pivoted about
Malcolm's personal conviction that "our Nation of Islam could
be an even greater force in the American black man's overall
struggle — if we engaged in more *action.* By that I mean I
thought privately that we should have amended or relaxed
our general non-engagement policy. I felt that, wherever black
people committed themselves, in the Little Rocks and Birming-
hams . . . militantly disciplined Muslims should also be there —
for all the world to see, and respect, and discuss.

"It could be heard increasingly in the Negro communities:
'Those Muslims talk tough, but they never do anything. . .'" [15]
It was this desire of Malcolm to give the Nation of Islam
an actual, as opposed to a merely rhetorical, involvement
in the day-to-day battles of black people which, when com-

bined with his pronounced distaste for the limousine-and-mansion opulence in which Muhammad's plentiful brood had begun to loll, made the schism unavoidable.

After all of this has been said about Malcolm X, we are still left with the question of the larger significance of his life, especially with regard to the whirlwind chain of events that filled his last fifteen months following the attempted silencing by Muhammad. I am afraid that on this question the *Autobiography*, generally invaluable for the insight it affords into Malcolm and the environment from which he sprang,* is of only limited assistance. In saying this I am not at all disparaging the work. At a time when such confections as *Manchild in the Promised Land* and Sammy Davis's *Yes I Can* are offered to the reading public as presumably serious fare, the virtues of Malcolm's *Autobiography* cannot be too highly praised; it is to the previous pair of narratives as reality is to wishful thinking; no one who claims to be a radical can afford to go without reading it. At the same time, its deficiencies as well as its assets must be recognized, and one sizable shortcoming is that, almost of necessity, the *Autobiography* concentrates on the private rather than the public Malcolm. The likeness which peers forth from its pages is, consequently, in some respects two-dimensional; an integral aspect of Malcolm's personality and career has been truncated.

Such an omission might not have proven serious had Malcolm lived to work out and enunciate his vision for the fu-

---

* Although to my knowledge it has not been remarked upon by any reviewer, the same milieu which gave rise to Malcolm had also generated the most vital forms of contemporaneous jazz; Malcolm's *Autobiography* reveals him to have been an intimate friend of many of Harlem's leading jazz figures of the forties and fifties.

There has, incidentally, been a good deal of nonsense written about black nationalism and jazz. Thus, I. F. Stone, reviewing the two Malcolm books in the *New York Review*, followed the lead of E. U. Essien-Udom's *Black Nationalism* in claiming that the Muslims — and by inference all black nationalists — turned up their noses at jazz, from which he inferred that they were involuntarily manifesting their self-hatred. The real situation is nowhere near that clear-cut. In the program which I mentioned in the preceding note, Malcolm's appearance was preceded by 45 minutes of jazz from the organ trio of Groove Holmes. Malcolm himself, moreover, made explicit reference to the music in his opening remarks, saying that he had been in the back of the auditorium patting his foot while Holmes was on stage. Does this sound like the repudiation of Negro culture which Stone would have us believe exists among the nationalists?

ture of black nationalism. As it is, however, the assassin's guns denied him the necessary time, with the result that conclusions about the direction of Malcolm's politics at the moment of his death must always remain a bit tentative.

Be that as it may, thanks to the admirably edited collection of speeches recently released by Merit Publishers, from a watershed period in Malcolm's life, we have something much more substantial to go on than mere speculation. Not that every detail of Malcolm's political philosophy has been elaborated with absolute clarity in his speeches, for such is not the case. Given the workhorse schedule of Malcolm's final months and the absence of any opportunity for sustained reflection, one must expect that here and there an occasional solecism, murky generalization, or even self-contradiction will crop up. But these minor lapses are to be found in the rhetoric of any one who speaks extemporaneously with the frequency that Malcolm did during those hectic days; they are entirely inconsequential in comparison with the overall tendency of Malcolm's thinking, which must impinge on even the most casual reader of these addresses with unmistakable force.

The simplest way to describe this tendency is with the phrase *revolutionary socialist internationalism.* For some it may come as a shock that Malcolm was, or was becoming, an international socialist; these skeptics can best be advised to obtain a copy of the speeches and judge for themselves. To any informed and reasonably openminded person, however, the conclusion will be obvious — even if, for the writers of the popular (and liberal) press, it is a mystery hidden behind the legendary seven veils. At any rate I, for one, am thoroughly persuaded that, barring the intervention of some totally unforseen circumstance, Malcolm's open proclamation of socialist beliefs was imminent at the moment of his untimely and much-lamented slaying.

In the space remaining it is possible to offer only a few representative excerpts from his speeches — they are indicative of the general tenor — illustrating his revolutionary socialist internationalism. First of all, the question of revolution. Prior even to his break with the Nation of Islam, Malcolm had expressed his conviction that no solution for the oppression and subjugation of black peoples in this country could be found short of social revolution. Indeed, social revolution was, for Malcolm, the quintessence of black nationalism. In an address to the Northern Negro Leadership Conference held in Detroit in November 1963, he put the matter succinctly: "If you're afraid of black nationalism, you're afraid of revolu-

tion. And if you love revolution, you love black nationalism." [16]
When Malcolm referred to revolution, furthermore, he did not
invoke the word in the current deplorable Madison Avenue
usage, in which the addition or subtraction of tailfins on some
chrome-plated automotive monstrosity is portrayed as "revolutionary." But here — in his own words, let him tell it like
it is:

> The white man knows what a revolution is. He knows
> that the black revolution is world-wide in scope and in
> nature. The black revolution is sweeping Asia, is sweep-
> ing Africa, is rearing its head in Latin America. The
> Cuban Revolution — that's a revolution. They over-
> turned the system. . . .
> Revolution is bloody, revolution is hostile, revolution
> knows no compromise, revolution overturns and de-
> stroys everything that gets in its way. . . . Whoever
> heard of a revolution where they lock arms . . . sing-
> ing "We Shall Overcome"? You don't do any singing,
> you're too busy swinging. . . . [17]

Similar passages leap to one's eye on virtually every page
of this book. But was Malcolm calling for *socialist* revolution?
Although this continues for the most part to be a well-kept
secret, I do not see how it is possible to give any but an affirmative answer. Replying to a question at the Militant Labor
Forum, for example, Malcolm stated his own view that "all
of the countries that are emerging today from under the
shackles of colonialism are turning toward socialism. I don't
think it's an accident. Most of the countries that were colonial
powers were capitalist countries, and the last bulwark of capitalism today is [the United States]. . . . You can't have capitalism without racism." [18]

That was in May 1964. By the end of the year Malcolm
had become less guarded in his endorsement of the socialist
road: socialism was no longer a topic to be debated in front
of white radicals *downtown;* now it demanded discussion in
front of all-black audiences *uptown* as well. "You don't find
any capitalist countries [in Asia] too much nowadays," Malcolm explained to a meeting of his followers at Harlem's Au-
dubon Ballroom:

> Almost every one of the countries that has gotten in-
> dependence has devised some kind of socialist system,

and this is no accident. This is another reason why I say that you and I here in America . . . before [we] start trying to be incorporated, or integrated, or disintegrated, into this capitalistic system, should look over there and find out what are the people who have gotten their freedom adopting to provide themselves with better housing and better education and better food and better clothing.

None of them are adopting the capitalistic system because they realize they can't. You can't operate a capitalistic system unless you are vulturistic; you have to have someone else's blood to suck to be a capitalist. . . . So, when we look at the African continent, when we look at the trouble that's going on between East and West, we find that the nations in Africa are developing socialist systems to solve their problems. [19]

That Malcolm's commitment to socialism had become an open and avowed one in the six months between May and December, 1964, was due to the observations he made during his pilgrimage to Mecca and subsequent travels throughout Africa. Although it has been claimed (again by Truman Nelson) that Malcolm's pilgrimage was "a tragic diversion" having "no real relevance to the streets of Harlem," just the opposite would seem to be true: the experiences of his travels broadened his political perspective, causing him to view Afro-American liberation in a strikingly different light than had been the case prior to the rift with the Muslims. Besides impelling him to study and, finally to adopt the goals of socialism, the African tour imparted to Malcolm a clear understanding of modern imperialism. In the same address from which I have already excerpted his remarks on socialism, Malcolm offered his black audience a cogent exposition on the workings of the imperialist system. Stressing the need of the capitalist economies for the cheap raw materials and the markets of the underdeveloped world "in order to survive," he assured his listeners that without these things, capitalism in Europe and the United States "wouldn't be worth two cents." It followed, therefore, that in order to preserve "free access" to the vital markets and raw materials of the preindustrial countries, "European nations in the past have kept the nations in Latin America and in Africa and in Asia from becoming industrial powers. They keep the machinery and the ability to produce and manufacture limited to Europe and limited to America. Then this puts America and the Europeans in a position to control the economy of all other nations and keep them living at a low standard." The solution of this dilemma, from the vantage point of the under-developed areas, was to destroy all forms of imperialism and neocolonialism and embark on a program of planned socialist industrialization, such as was exemplified by Egypt's Aswan Dam project. "The people," Malcolm continued in his typically vivid imagery,

> are beginning to see that. The Africans see it, the Latin Americans see it, the Asians see it. So when you hear them talking about freedom, they're not talking about a cup of coffee with a cracker. No, they're talking about getting in a position to feed themselves and clothe them-selves and make these other things that, when you have them, make life worth living. So this is the way you and I have to understand the world revolution that's taking place right now.[20]

Could one ask for a more compact and luminous summary of contemporary imperialism and the way to overcome the disabilities it imposes on mankind?

From what has already been written, the reader will antici-pate that Malcolm's revolutionary socialism was predicated on united action of all the wretched of the earth to destroy the same imperialist foe that threatened them all. Like the conversion to socialism, this idea had been elaborated un-der the stimulus of his contact with the forces of revolution in the underdeveloped countries (again one is struck by the shortsightedness of the view that holds Malcolm's travel in Africa to have been "a tragic diversion"). As was usually the case with Malcolm, he couched his idea in a variety of meta-phors and images. At his most blunt he might laconically state: "If your power base is only here, you can forget it."[21] The same notion, solidarity of the world's revolutionary forces, was also at the bottom of his attempt to utilize the United Nations as a forum for embarrassing the man (Charlie) at home. But regardless of the specific formulation, his premise was always that "you can't understand what is going on in Mississippi if you don't understand what is going on in the Congo. . . . They're both the same. The same interests are at stake. The same sides are drawn up, the same schemes are at work in the Congo that are at work in Mississippi."[22]

But perhaps the most striking versions of this thesis were

the ones Malcolm pronounced in the month immediately preceding his death. In January, 1965, for instance, questioned
by a television interviewer about the possibility of an "Arma-
geddon in the United States by 1984," Malcolm replied:

> I believe that there will ultimately be a clash between
> the oppressed and those that do the oppressing. I believe
> that there will be a clash between those who want free-
> dom, justice, and equality for everyone and those who
> want to continue the systems of exploitation. I believe
> that there will be that kind of clash, but I don't think
> that it will be based upon the color of the skin, as
> Elijah Muhammad had taught it. 23

Three short days before his tragic murder, during an address
at Columbia on "The Black Revolution and its Effect Upon
the Negroes of the Western Hemisphere," Malcolm returned
to the same theme:

> We are living in an era of revolution, and the revolt
> of the American Negro is part of the rebellion against
> the oppression and colonialism which has characterized
> this era. . . .
> It is incorrect to classify the revolt of the Negro as
> simply a racial conflict of black against white, or as
> a purely American problem. Rather, we are today see-
> ing a global rebellion of the oppressed against the
> oppressor, the exploited against the exploiter. 24

It was this global rebellion which convinced Malcolm that
the only realistic approach for the Afro-American liberation
movement to adopt was to merge with like-minded anti-
imperialist and revolutionary movements in Africa, Asia, and
Latin America in a joint campaign against their common
enemy. Once Afro-Americans in this country came to the realization that they were actually part of a revolutionary *majority*, and not an isolated minority, the struggle for freedom
could be joined with renewed intensity and with confidence
of ultimate victory. Alas for his followers and ourselves, he
was cut down almost before the words themselves had ceased
to ring in the air. Who is to say that it was not these very
views which made his continued existence unbearable to the
U. S. ruling class or one of its agencies?
At the moment of his death, Malcolm X was, in the opinion

of this writer, the outstanding American political figure of our time and about to become the foremost spokesman for revolutionary socialism that this country has yet produced. Although our grief at his slaying is rightfully unbounded, we must recall that Malcolm's voice never sounded for himself alone; it cried out as well for the mute millions whose aspirations and goals, resentments and frustrations, would otherwise have gone unarticulated. Malcolm, that is, was, in a very precise sense, the vanguard of his people. Though his death cannot be too much mourned, it is still no meager comfort to know that where the vanguard leads, there too shall the remainder of the columns march.

Photo by Frank Kofsky

JIMMY GARRISON

Appendix
A SELECTED DISCOGRAPHY OF THE
RECORDED WORKS OF JOHN COLTRANE

By all odds, the most representative and enthralling recorded performances are those that Coltrane cut as a series of "live" LPs for Impulse: *Live at the Village Vanguard, Live at the Village Vanguard Again, Live at Birdland, Impressions, Selflessness.* Though not always "easy" to digest in one sitting — as what great music could be? — these should be the first albums in any Coltrane collection.*

The main elements of a style that later became synonymous with his name were first exposed on a very lovely album that Coltrane did for Atlantic, *My Favorite Things,* which also marked his recorded debut with the soprano saxophone. The title song was incorporated as a staple into the repertoire of Coltrane's various groups. There is a thrilling rendition of it by Coltrane (on soprano) and Pharoah Sanders (on flute and tenor saxophone) on the second *Village Vanguard* album — a version that preserves some of the most exciting moments in music ever heard by this writer. Another, intermediate in complexity between the first recording and that on the second *Vanguard* LP, has been released as Side 1 of *Selflessness.* This performance, as well as the material included with it, dates from a mid-1960s set recorded at the Newport Jazz Festival. Overall, the album, like the other "live" sessions, is a mandatory item for serious followers of Coltrane.

There are several albums which illustrate Coltrane's mystical bent. Of these, my own favorite is the very popular *A Love Supreme.* There are those, however, who prefer the somewhat more turbulent *Meditations,* which features Pharoah Sanders as well as Coltrane. The saxophonist's interest in Eastern religions is amply illustrated on *Om* (also with Sanders, whose album under his own name, *Tauhid,* likewise on Im-

---

* Except where specified otherwise, all Coltrane albums are on the Impulse label.

pulse, ought to be heard as a companion piece to *Om*). In this group of records should likewise be placed one of the most recent Coltrane albums, *Cosmic Music*, recorded with Coltrane's wife, pianist Alice Coltrane; and also the one that contains his last recorded work, *Expression*. (Both albums were issued posthumously.)

Occasionally, Coltrane departed from the small-group format. His first release on Impulse, *Africa/Brass*, juxtaposed his saxophones against a brass choir that contributed relatively simple background figures. Far more complex ànd demanding is a later work, *Ascension* (two versions of which have been issued, with the first being a relatively scarce collector's item). Here, passages of collective improvisation by seven horns (three tenors, two altos, two trumpets) and a rhythm section alternate with solos by the individual musicians. A heady brew!

Coltrane's readily evident musical vitality should not be allowed to obscure his complementary lyrical side, well illustrated by a pair of albums, *Ballads* and *John Coltrane with Johnny Hartman*. Now that interest in individual singers, as distinct from groups, is beginning to revive among white youth, the Coltrane-Hartman LP merits special attention; the combination of songs and musicianship fuse with much the same haunting impact as, say, any Billie Holiday performance (or, if that reference means nothing to you, Judy Collins's *Wildflowers*).

In no particular category are two perennial friends: *Coltrane* and *Crescent*, each of which, in its own unique way, presents a fusion of the Coltrane fury with the gentle and warmly loving Coltrane lyricism.

Finally, mention must be made of at least some of the high points of Coltrane's career on recordings prior to the first *My Favorite Things*, even though material from this earlier period has often been neglected since it does not compare with the raw power of his later works. Besides appearing on almost every recording of the various small groups led by Miles Davis between 1955 and 1961 (a subject that merits a separate discography in itself), Coltrane left behind a series of albums under his own name that indicated the furthest limits to which orthodox bebop could be pushed. Outstanding small-group efforts (trios, quartets, quintets) can be heard, generally though not always with members of the Miles Davis rhythm section in support, on the Prestige label: *John Coltrane with the Red Garland Trio (Traneing In); Soultrane; Lush Life.*

In addition, Coltrane also led multihorn groups on two separate occasions, *Coltrane* (Prestige) and *Blue Train* (Blue Note). Toward the end of this period, four quartet albums on Atlantic, in which Coltrane was supported by a variety of rhythm sections, were also highly influential for their numerous innovations, though less so than the post *My Favorite Things* releases: *Giant Steps, Coltrane Jazz, Coltrane Sound, Coltrane Plays the Blues.* Coltrane also functioned on occasion as a co-leader (e.g., with Kenny Burrell and Cecil Taylor) and even sideman (with Thelonious Monk, Art Blakey, George Russell and others). The interested reader is referred to the complete (through 1967) discography published by the Canadian magazine *Coda* (vol. VIII, no. 7, May, 1968).

Photo by Frank Kofsky

JOHN COLTRANE

NOTES

Introduction

1. Karl Marx and Frederick Engels. *The German Ideology*, International Publishers, New York, 1947, p. 14.

2. Ibid., pp. 39-40.

3. Thomas S. Kuhn, *The Structure of Scientific Revolutions*, University of Chicago Press, Chicago, 1962.

4. Karl Marx, *A Contribution to the Critiaue of Political Economy*, Charles H. Kerr & Co., Chicago, 1904, pp. 11-12.

5. Harold R. Isaacs, *The New World of Negro Americans*, The Viking Press, Inc., New York, 1964.

6. For the historically minded, it should be noted that the economy as of 1914 was, as Paul Birdsall's essay in vol. II of *The Shaping of American Diplomacy* (William A. Williams, ed.) has pointed out, in a prolonged crisis from which only Allied orders were able to pull it out, as a corollary committing the United States to enter World War I on the Allied side. Ditto for World War II, with the added consideration of the rivalry of Japanese imperialism. As remarked above, the timing of the Korean War was most fortunate from the standpoint of the performance of the postwar U. S. economy. Ditto the Vietnam War, though other, more strategic factors (related to the preservation of the Empire intact) are surely involved in both of these counterrevolutionary wars. Lastly, there is the contradiction of a permanent war economy in what is ostensibly a time of peace. On World War II, see Howard Zinn (ed.), *New Deal Thought*; Lloyd Gardner, *Economic Aspects of New Deal Diplomacy*; Gar Alperovitz, *Atomic Diplomacy*; William A. Williams, *The Tragedy of American Diplomacy*; on the postwar political economy, see Williams, *op. cit.*; G. W. Domhoff, *Who Rules America?*; Paul Baran and Paul Sweezy, *Monopoly Capital*; Harry Magdoff, *The Age of Imperialism*; I. F. Stone, *The Hidden History of the Korean War*; and on Vietnam in particular, the editorials in *Monthly Review* from 1965 on.

7. On this see A. Kardiner and L. Ovesey, *The Mark of Oppression*, and more recently, P. M. Cobbs and W. H. Grier, *Black Rage*.

8. "Where Is America Going?" *Mayday*, no. 34, June 2-9, 1969.

9. *Down Beat Jazz Record Review*, Jack Tracy (ed.), Maher Publications, Chicago, 1958, vol. II, p. 51.

10. Herbert Marcuse, *Reason and Revolution*, The Beacon Press, Inc., Boston, 1960.

11. The quotation is from John Hope Franklin, *From Slavery to Freedom: A History of American Negroes*, Alfred A. Knopf, New York, 1956, p. 574. See also his entire Chapter 19, "Fighting for the Four Freedoms."

12. Gitler to the editor of *Jazz*, November, 1965. My original letter that provoked Gitler's wrath was in the September, 1965, issue of the same publication; then my rejoinder, December, 1965, and his again in the February, 1966, issue.

13. Francis Newton, *The Jazz Scene*, Penguin Books, Ltd., Harmondsworth, Middlesex, 1961, pp. 203-205. Newton is a pen name of E. J. Hobsbawm.

14. Quoted by Newton in *The Jazz Scene*, p. 205 (from J. E. Berendt, *Das Jazzbuch*, Frankfurt and Hamburg, 1953, pp. 93-95).
Note that Hobsbawm (Newton) and Berendt are European, rather than white North American writers. It is consequently no mere coincidence that they are more perceptive regarding the social origins of jazz.

Note also Hobsbawm's point apropos bebop, that "an even more obvious form of revolt against inferiority, which a leading group of the new [bebop] players shared with other Northern big-city Negroes, was mass conversion to Mohammedanism. The new music was played, among others, by Abdullah ibn Buhaina (Art Blakey, the drummer), Sahib Shabab (Edmund Gregory, alto [saxophone]), Abdul Hamid (McKinley [Kenny] Dorham, trumpet . . .), Liaquat Ali Salaam (Kenny Clarke [the first bop drummer]), Ibrahim ibn Ismail (Walter Bishop, Jr., piano) and other sons of the Prophet . . ." (Ibid., p. 207).

The late Langston Hughes had Simple explain bop as follows:

"Re-Bop certainly sounds like scat to me," I insisted.

"No," said Simple, "Daddy-o, you are wrong. Besides, it was not *Re*-Bop. It is *Be*-Bop."

"What's the difference," I asked, "between *Re* and *Be?*"

"A lot," said Simple. "Re-Bop was an imitation like most of the white boys play. Be-Bop is the real thing like the colored boys play." . . .

"You must not know where Bop comes from," said Simple, astonished at my ignorance.

"I do not know," I said. "Where?"

"From the police," said Simple.

"What do you mean, from the police?"

"From the police beating Negroes' heads," said Simple. "Every time a cop hits a Negro with his billy club, that old club says, 'BOP! BOP! . . . BE-BOP! . . . MOP! . . . BOP!"

"That Negro hollers, 'Ooool-ya-koo! Ou-o-o!'"

"Old Cop just keeps on, 'MOP! MOP!. . . BE-BOP! . . . MOP!' That's where Be-Bop came from, beaten right out of some Negro's head into them horns and saxophones and piano keys that plays it. . . ." (From *The Best of Simple*, Hill & Wang, Inc., New York, pp. 117-118. Copyright © 1961 by Langston Hughes. Reprinted by permission of Hill & Wang, Inc.)

15. Interview by the author, Los Angeles, February, 1968.
16. This and the preceding quotations in the paragraph are from Prof. Leslie B. Rout, Jr., "Reflections on the Evolution of Post-War Jazz," *Negro Digest*, XVIII:4, February, 1969, pp. 92-93.
17. As, for example, when Charlie Parker chose to title his blues *Now's the Time* instead of *Double-V*, or Sonny Rollins decided that his composition would bear the name *Airegin* rather than *Nigeria*.

It should also be kept in mind that the forces of racial oppression are both so immense as to render insignificant any isolated individual attempts to resist them and completely irrational in their workings. That being true, it would be quite foolish and much too simplistic to expect that all protest against these forces would be rational, explicit, political (especially so when protest movements among whites, such as contemporary Protestant fundamentalist movements against sex education and the teaching of evolution, are anything but strictly rational). Indeed, the history of black literature in the United States ought to remind us (or, if we are white jazz critics, teach us) that protest against racism can at times assume forms so diverse or even bizarre, that it requires considerable psychological insight to comprehend the fact that it is protest we are witnessing. Richard Wright's Bigger Thomas in *Native Son*, for instance, kills a white girl, who seeks to aid him, out of his frustration at seeing himself forever trapped in the neoslavery of the ghetto.

More recently, Eldridge Cleaver tells us in *Soul on Ice* of his career as a rapist of white women — a career that, born from a similar motivation, took him perilously close to recapitulating the fate of Bigger Thomas. James Baldwin in his fiction and especially his essays, and Ralph Ellison in *The Invisible Man*, have recounted some of the other ways in which efforts at coping with and overcoming white racism have resulted in various kinds of neuroses (or even psychoses) among blacks. And the psychological literature, of course, is filled with examples (such as *Mark of Oppression* and *Black Rage* for the United States; the works of Frantz Fanon for the colonized in Africa). Resistance to racism, therefore, cannot be understood in any narrow, mechanistic fashion. The Garveyite slogan of "Back to Africa" was probably as much a repudiation of a racist United States as it was an affirmation of Africa.

In like manner, the widespread use of addictive narcotics by musicians of the bebop generation can probably best be interpreted as yet another kind of antiracist protest, the flight from an unbearably hell-

272 Black Nationalism and the Revolution in Music

ish reality into an anxiety-free and nonracist, drug-produced nirvana. One wonders if this point has ever occurred to the critics who are so eager to divorce the music from its social matrix and to deny the existence of a history of protest within jazz.

18. Even at that, it isn't always so easy to speak out. Bill Dixon, who is about *twice* as literate as most of the professors I know (as are Archie Shepp and Cecil Taylor), states that "both *Down Beat* and the old *Metronome* [a defunct jazz magazine] rejected articles that I'd written" (*Sounds and Fury*, July-August 1965, p. 39). Small wonder, given Dixon's politics and ability to articulate them. Robert Levin, who later interviewed Dixon for a *Down Beat* article, has told me that many of the quotes from Dixon that he had included were censored out, a point that Dixon himself confirmed in a subsequent interview. Archie Shepp has related a similar tale of his experiences at that magazine, and hints explicitly at the pressures brought to bear in a panel discussion with the ghastly title, "Heretics' Brew — The Jazz Avant Garde," in *Down Beat's Music '66* (Chicago, 1965, p. 110).

19. *Down Beat Music '66*, p. 20.

Chapter 1

1. "Race Prejudice in Jazz; It Works Both Ways," *Down Beat*, March 15 and 29, 1962.

2. This blanket condemnation must be somewhat modified by taking note of the panel discussion on "Jazz and Revolutionary Black Nationalism" held in December, 1965, under the sponsorship of *Jazz* magazine. Participants in the discussion were Nat Hentoff, LeRoi Jones, Steve Kuhn, Archie Shepp, Robert F. Thompson, George Wein, and this writer; Father Norman O'Connor was the moderator. A transcript of the discussion was serialized in *Jazz*, beginning with the April, 1966, issue.

3. I trust I need not emphasize that I have been dealing in generalizations to which there are patent exceptions; but the thing about generalizations which makes them useful is — their very generality.

4. "Few jazz critics are truly professional. The art or industry cannot support them at a professional level. Few can make a living writing jazz criticism only." Stanley Dance, "Please Take It Seriously," *Down Beat Music '65*, p. 40. Mr. Dance's views, both musical and social, are, it should be added, in diametric opposition to this writer's.

5. "Feather's Nest," *Down Beat*, February 15, 1962.

6. See Feather's notes for the Eric Dolphy Memorial Album on Vee Jay, a now defunct label.

7. I know of only one instance in which a critic refused such an offer, which was especially lucrative as these things go. As is consistent with our hypothesis, he had an independent livelihood that permitted him the privilege of rejecting those assignments which he felt he could fulfill without violating his integrity.

8. For Britain, English critic Francis Newton estimates that the cost of producing the cover of an LP, assuming a press run of 1500, is a bit less than 10 percent of the retail selling price. Translated into American terms—taking $3.50 as the average price and a sale of 2000 as the break-even point—an album jacket costs its manufacturer roughly $700; but that figure includes the front as well as the rear cover. Elaborate double covers, such as those put out by Impulse, may be more expensive yet. In any event, it should be clear that a considerable sum is invested in each album jacket, including the notes.

9. For example, on Andrew Hill, *Judgment* (Blue Note 4159).

10. Robert Levin, who was writing such notes when this article first appeared in 1965, has told me that I have here described the situation exactly. Levin subsequently resigned and found another position.

11. A note cannot explore this point fully but it should be mentioned that the system of art-as-a-commodity also bears the blame for the frantic competition to "discover" a previously unknown artist who shows some signs of developing into a major talent. For the recording company, the anticipated returns are obvious; but for the critic who can lay claim to having "discovered," say, the "new thing," the returns are likewise not to be sneezed at, including as they do a temporary monopoly on the liner notes of "new thing" artists and the opportunity to sell articles to the magazines patronized by the liberal intelligentsia. That these "discoveries" would inevitably have come to light sooner or later in any case, and that the requirement of having to champion one artist or group of artists against all challengers cannot but distort one's views, goes as a matter of course, though the bulk of the jazz critics seem to be oblivious of the point.

Chapter 2

1. LeRoi Jones, *Blues People*, William Morrow & Co., Inc., New York, 1963.

2. "The only Negroes who found themselves in a *position* to pursue some art, especially the art of literature, have been members of the Negro middle class. Only Negro music, because, perhaps, it drew its strength and beauty out of the depths of the black man's soul, and because to a large extent its traditions could be carried on by the 'lowest classes' of Negroes, has been able to survive the constant and willful dilutions of the black middle class and the persistent calls to oblivion made by the mainstream of the society." (*Blues People*, p. 31.)

3. To this it must regretfully be added that Jones has been done an immeasurable disservice by the publisher's incredibly lax job of editing. Elementary errors of grammar abound, and there are some passages that suggest that they have not even been proofread. With little effort one can find puzzling parenthetical phrases which begin

but, due to the absence of a closing parenthesis, never end, apposi-
tions lacking commas to set them off, and a whole series of other
misconstructions that would be absolutely unacceptable in any fresh-
man English class.

4. Jones relates the following amusing anecdote apropos the early
days of bebop: "'You can't dance to it,' was the constant harassment
[directed against the new music]—which is, no matter the irrelevancy,
a lie. My friends and I as youths used only to emphasize the pro-
noun more, saying, '*You* can't dance to it,' and whispered, 'or anything else, for that matter.'" (*Blues People*, pp. 199-200.)

5. For a sample of critical-reactionary literature, see John Tynan,
"Take Five," *Down Beat*, November 23, 1961, p. 40; Leonard Feather, "Feather's Nest," ibid., February 15, 1962, p. 40. Perhaps the
most fitting reply to all of this nonsense about antijazz has come
from A. B. Spellman: "What does anti-jazz mean and who are those
ofays who've appointed themselves guardians of last year's blues?"
(Quoted in *Blues People*, p. 235.) The consummate irony of this
tempest in a very minuscule teapot is that among the ideologists leading the holy crusade against "antijazz" is at least one major critical
figure who was instrumental in urging the music of the beboppers
on a skeptical and at times incredulous (white) public. "Hegel remarks somewhere that all great, world-historical facts and person-
ages occur, as it were, twice. He has forgotten to add: the first time
as tragedy, the second as farce" (Marx, *Eighteenth Brumaire of Louis
Bonaparte*).

6. I am reminded of an experience of an evening not long ago.
For some unexplained reason, two white fifteen-year-olds were on
one of Los Angeles's all-jazz FM stations interviewing the disc jockey
(Negro). When the latter asked the youths to identify their favorite
musicians, they replied, "Miles Davis and John Coltrane." My God!
Coltrane—and at fifteen! And white!! Ten years ago such a thing
would have been unimaginable. To get some idea of how astounding
this development is, imagine the same conversation but on a different
subject: "Who d'ya like in political economy?" (Slight pause.) "Oh,
Karl Marx and Frederick Engels."

Chapter 3

1. Kwame Nkrumah, *Neo-Colonialism: The Last Stage of Imperialism*, International Publishers Co., Inc., New York, 1966, pp.
249-250.

2. Quoted by David Wise and Thomas B. Ross in *The Invisible
Government*, Bantam Books, Inc., New York, 1965, p. 251n.

3. Ibid., p. 345.

4. See, for example, "The Regents" by Marvin Garson in Hal Draper,
Berkeley: The New Student Revolt, Grove Press, New York, 1965,
pp. 215-221.

5. *Down Beat*, August 12, 1965.

6. Quoted by Francis Newton in *The Jazz Scene*, Penguin Books, Harmondsworth, Middlesex, 1961. See note 14 to the Introduction.

7. Archie Shepp, "An Artist Speaks Bluntly," *Down Beat*, December 16, 1965, p. 11.

Chapter 4

1. In Edward Parone (ed.), *New Theatre in America*, Dell Publishing Co., Inc., New York, 1965, p. 211; first ellipsis in the original.

2. The racist cruelty of white America to the antebellum free Negro is surveyed with admirable restraint by Leon F. Litwack, *North of Slavery*, University of Chicago Press, Chicago, 1965.

3. See also in this connection C. Vann Woodward, "Equality: the Deferred Commitment," *The Burden of Southern History*, Random House, Inc., New York, 1960, chapter 4.

4. One not-at-all-astonishing manifestation of this is the fact that Negro children learn self-hatred at a remarkably early age, especially in an "integrated" situation. On this point consult Mary Ellen Goodman, *Race Awareness in Young Children*, The Macmillan Co., New York, revised edition, 1964. This volume possesses the inestimable merit of demonstrating conclusively that it is white social institutions, rather than the Black Muslims or any other Negro nationalist organization that, as the phrase has it, "teach hate."

5. *The Strange Career of Jim Crow*, Oxford University Press, Inc., New York, 1957, pp. 120-121, 148-149. The Court's leisurely pace of enforcing desegregation should be compared with the urgency with which it insists on, say, legislative redistricting.

6. See the penetrating discussion by Wilson, "The Myth of Negro Progress," *Liberator*, January, 1964, pp. 3-6, 19.

7. Louis Harris and William Brink, *The Negro Revolution in America*, Simon & Schuster, Inc., New York, 1964, p. 149.

8. See the moving account by Robert Vernon of a street meeting addressed by Malcolm X, "At a Black Muslim Rally," in *The Black Ghetto*, Merit Publishers, New York, 1964, pp. 9-11.

9. The best discussion of this novel consciousness of the African heritage among American Negroes is probably that in Harold R. Isaacs's *The New World of Negro Americans*, John Day Company, New York, chapter 3.

10. This point has not been lost on musicians; consider for example the comment of composer Bill Dixon that "what they *really* mean when they call the Chinese atom bomb 'primitive' is that yellow men created it." Quoted by Robert Levin, "The Jazz Composers Guild: An Association of Dignity," *Down Beat*, May 6, 1965, p. 12.

11. The subject is discussed at length by Hugh Thomas, *The Spanish Civil War*, Harper & Row, Publishers, New York, 1963, *passim.* Cf. *Newsweek*, May 24, 1965, p. 47: ". . . though U. S. officials are understandably sensitive to comparisons between Vietnam and the Spanish Civil War as a 'laboratory for war,' the parallel nonetheless

exists." The article goes on to provide a detailed inventory of the numerous death-dealing gadgets being "tested" on the hapless Vietnamese.

12. See Ossie Sykes, "A 'Final Solution' for the USA?" *Liberator,* November, 1964, p. 6; and C. E. Wilson, "No 'Final Solution' Yet," ibid.

13. In *Moral Indignation and Middle Class Psychology,* Schocken Books, Inc., New York, 1964, second edition, p. 4.

14. I limit the discussion to saxophonists because my impression is that their influence in the avant-garde is the paramount one; and I have omitted mention of Ornette Coleman in the previous inventory because his musical origins are to be found in the Southwest rather than in the Northern ghetto.

15. Taking as my source the *New Encyclopedia of Jazz,* I estimate that as late as the 1930s fewer than half the men in the Ellington band had undergone any formal musical instruction; some of the biographical entires in the *Encyclopedia* are very brief, however, and may for that reason be incomplete.

16. Again, Ornette Coleman provides the exception to the rule: a self-educated performer, he is both an anomaly and an anachronism. Perhaps Cecil Taylor, with his four-year internship at the New England Conservatory, is more typical of jazz's younger generation.

Chapter 5

1. To do simple justice to the subject, it should be mentioned that two other orchestra leaders, Bill Dixon and Sun Ra, have a much greater significance for the Jazz Revolution that the limited recognition of their work would indicate. In point of fact, it has been largely through the groups maintained by these two and Cecil Taylor that many of the younger men — including John Gilmore, Ronnie Boykins, Marshall Allen with Sun Ra; Albert Ayler, Archie Shepp, Sonny Murray, Jimmy Lyons with Taylor; Rasheid Ali, David Izenson, Howard Johnson, Marc Levin with Dixon — received their early training and grounding in the fundamentals of the new styles.

2. For aural evidence, hear any of the following recordings: Coltrane, *Ascension* (Impulse 95); Coleman, *Free Jazz* (Atlantic 1364); Taylor, *The World of Cecil Taylor* (Candid 8006, out of print); Sun Ra, *The Heliocentric Worlds of Sun Ra* (ESP 1014); Archie Shepp, *On This Night* (Impulse 97); Roswell Rudd-John Tchicai, *New York Art Quartet* (ESP 1004); Bobby Hutcherson, *Dialogue* (Blue Note 4198); Albert Ayler, *Bells* (ESP 1010).

3. It is typical of this generation of jazz artists that their accomplishments extend in a multitude of directions. Shepp, besides his poetry and musicianship, is a professional actor — he appeared in the original production of Jack Gelber's *The Connection* — and has had one of his own plays staged in New York City. Bill Dixon is reputed to be a talented oil painter. Cecil Taylor, who holds a degree

from the New England Conservatory, is a balletomane as well as a poet. And so on.

4. *Sounds and Fury,* July-August, 1965.

5. An interesting sidelight to Coltrane's triumph is the fact that his achievements have been appreciated more readily by European critics than by American; this can be demonstrated by a computation based on any of the various "polls" in which writers from both continents participate. In the 1965 International Critics Poll (*Down Beat,* August 12, 1965), for example, only nine of the twenty-nine American-Canadian writers, or 32 percent, voted for Coltrane in the tenor saxophone category; whereas the proportion of Europeans voting for him, seven of eleven (64 percent), was exactly twice as large. The same two-to-one ratio between Europeans and Americans was also found in the voting for Jazz Album of the Year sponsored by *Jazz* (February, 1966).

These results bear witness to the ever-widening gulf between the innovators of the jazz revolution and the hostile white critical Establishment. The distance between the two groups, moreover, is social rather than aesthetic. Robert Levin reports in *Down Beat* that one white critic turned to him following a performance by Albert Ayler, among the most outstanding and adventurous of the jazz revolutionaries, with the remark, "I'm getting tired of Negroes" (August 12, 1965, p. 42).

6. According to LeRoi Jones, who annotated the album in question, "the Impulse record called *The New Wave in Jazz* was supposed to be called *New Black Music*" (*Down Beat,* February 10, 1966, p. 48). But clearly the latter name is much less salable to a "mixed" public — hence much less profitable — than the former.

7. For example, the Selmer advertisement on the outside rear cover of *Jazz* for February 1966. Shepp's name had suddenly taken on a new significance for Selmer because he had won a first prize in one division of the 1965 International Jazz Critics Poll. What irony! Good enough for the critics (at least the Europeans) and good enough for Selmer, but not good enough for a two-week job in one of New York's many jazz nightclubs.

Chapter 7

1. Thomas S. Kuhn, *The Structure of Scientific Revolutions,* University of Chicago Press, Chicago, 1964.

2. For a more thorough discussion, see Herbert Butterfield, *The Origins of Modern Science,* The Macmillan Company, New York, 1962.

3. Coltrane's use of such avowed jazz revolutionaries as Marion Brown, Archie Shepp, John Tchicai, Pharoah Sanders, and Dewey Johnson on his *Ascension* album should obviate the need for any further debate on this point.

Chapter 8

1. "They tell us that a writer begins where individuality begins and that therefore the source of his creativeness is his unique soul and not his class. It is true, without individuality there can be no writer. But if the poet's individuality and only his individuality is disclosed in his work, then to what purpose is the interpretation of art? To what purpose, let us ask, is literary criticism? In any case, the artist, if he is a true artist, will tell us about his unique individuality better than his babbling critic. But the truth is that even if individuality is unique, it does not mean that it cannot be analyzed. Individuality is a welding together of tribal, national, class, temporary and institutional elements and, in fact, it is in the uniqueness of this welding together, in the proportions of this psychochemical mixture, that individuality is expressed. One of the most important tasks of criticism is to analyze the individuality of the artist (that is, his art) into its component elements, and to show their correlations. In this way, criticism brings the artist closer to the reader, who also has more or less of a 'unique soul', 'artistically' unexpressed, 'unchosen', but nonetheless representing a union of the same elements as does the soul of a poet. So it can be seen that what serves as a bridge from soul to soul is not the unique, but the common. Only through the common is the unique known; the common is determined in man by the deepest and most persistent conditions which make up his 'soul', by the social conditions of education, of existence, of work, and of associations. The social conditions in historic human society are, first of all, the conditions of class affiliation. That is why a class standard is so fruitful in all fields of ideology, including art, and especially in art, because the latter often expresses the deepest and most hidden social aspirations. Moreover, a social standard not only does not exclude, but goes hand in hand with formal criticism, that is, with the standard of technical workmanship. This, as a matter of fact, also tests the particular by a common measure, because if one did not reduce the particular to the general there would be no contacts among people, no thoughts, and no poetry." (Leon Trotsky, *Literature and Revolution*, University of Michigan Press, Ann Arbor, 1960, pp. 59-60.)

2. What made Parker unique was not merely the ability to derive a solo from the chords of a piece; numerous swing-era musicians could do as much. Rather, Parker differentiated himself from his predecessors by employing the upper intervals of the chord as a basis for his solo and by executing the most demanding passages at phenomenal speeds — in sixteenths and thirty-seconds, where others were restricted to eighth-notes — with no loss in swing. Thus simply by extending the accepted procedures of the day one or two steps further than they had previously been taken, Parker emerged with a wholly new style of music, different in kind from anything heard earlier. This is one more illustration of the validity of Hegel's mode

of dialectical reasoning: beyond a certain point, a *quantitative* change (e. g., the use of the eleventh and thirteenth intervals of a chord instead of the seventh and ninth) produces a change in *quality* (the transition from swing to bebop).

3. See, for instance, the letter by Frank Smith in *Jazz*, November, 1965.

4. The above was written before I was able to obtain Coleman's most recent recordings (Blue Note 4224-4225), but there is nothing in them that would lead me to alter a single word. Both of Coleman's drummers, Charles Moffett and Edward Blackwell (the latter now to be heard with Don Cherry, e. g., Blue Note 4226), function in what is an essentially neobebop rhythmic framework. For completeness, I should add that inasmuch as my concern in this article is with saxophonists, I am omitting any effort to deal with the music of Cecil Taylor. Doubtless, however, his general ideas are no less crucial than those of Coleman for the development of the jazz revolution.

5. Album notes to *The New Wave in Jazz* (Impulse 90).

6. *Down Beat Record Reviews*, vol. VII, pp. 42-43.

As a further comment on the sad state of the critical art, note that one of the reviewers followed the album notes (by Nat Hentoff) in ascribing Coltrane's first solo on the track "Spiritual" to the soprano saxophone, but adding: "the soprano's timbre sounds much like his tenor's" (ibid., p. 41). Small wonder for the "resemblance" — Coltrane was actually playing the tenor! Does it come as any surprise, given this all too typical incident, that the critical profession is not held in higher esteem?

7. Recall that this was also the time of Leonard Feather's holy crusade in *Down Beat* against what he denigrated as "antijazz"; see, for instance, his column in *Down Beat*, February 15, 1962, p. 40. It was only subsequently that Feather underwent his conversion to the point of view that "critical infighting," as he terms it, is an unmitigated evil (*Down Beat*, December 16, 1965). Having inadvertently unleashed the contents of Pandora's Box, Feather now wistfully stands beside it, hoping in vain that he can somehow stuff the revolutionary furies inside again. His attention, as an Englishman, is properly directed to the legend of King Canute, whose enterprise Feather's resembles in its chances for success.

8. Since this "retreat" was not duplicated in Coltrane's personal appearances, my hunch is that the decision to make it came from Impulse rather than from Coltrane himself.

9. Actually, there is already a great deal of evidence that the more conventional jazz revolutionaries are deeply indebted to Coltrane — sometimes so much as to verge on plagiarism. Two instances come to mind. The first of these is Charles Lloyd's "composition," *How Can I Tell You?* (Columbia CL 2267), almost a note-for-note recapitulation of Coltrane's performance of *I Want to Talk About You* (observe the similarity even in titles) on *Soultrane* (Prestige 7142):

the second is John Handy's *If Only We Knew* (Columbia CL 2462), which is constructed on the same scale as, and which incorporates many identical phrases from, Coltrane's *Spiritual.* That neither of these two borrowings have ever been mentioned in print in any jazz magazine that I know of only underlines my earlier comments on the failure of the critics to appreciate the role of Coltrane's leadership on the younger jazz revolutionaries.

10. "His Name Is Albert Ayler," *Jazz,* December, 1965, p. 12

11. Even if one were denied the use of the recordings, it would be possible for a perceptive reader to infer the relationship between Ayler and Coltrane merely by observing the similarity of the complaints and the abusive language directed by the critics at each.

Incidentally, it is more than coincidental that, by virtue of also basing himself on *Chasin' the Trane,* Charles Lloyd's playing in *Ol' Five Spot* (Columbia CH 2267) takes on a decidedly Aylerish hue. Two men traversing the same road in the same direction are bound to wind up at the same destination.

Chapter 12

1. On *Coltrane "Live" at the Village Vanguard.*

Chapter 13

1. *The Autobiography of Malcolm X* (with the assistance of Alex Haley), Grove Press, New York, 1965, pp. 26-27.
2. Ibid., p. 68.
3. Ibid., pp. 242-243.
4. Ibid., p. 269.
5. Ibid., p. 404.
6. Ibid., p. 156.
7. Ibid., p. 157.
8. Ibid., p. 175.
9. Ibid., p. 173.
10. Ibid.
11. Ibid., p. 174.
12. Ibid.
13. See the *Autobiography,* p. 240.
14. Ibid., p. 294.
15. Ibid., p. 293.
16. Malcolm X, *Malcolm X Speaks* (edited by George Breitman), Merit Publishers, New York, 1965, p. 10.
17. Ibid., p. 9.
18. Ibid., p. 69.
19. Ibid., pp. 128-129.
20. Ibid., pp. 133-136.
21. Ibid., p. 137.
22. Ibid., p. 133.
23. Ibid., p. 232.
24. Ibid., p. 233.